WALL STREET ON SALE

WALL STREET ON SALE

How to Beat the Market as a Value Investor

The Techniques Used by Master Investor Warren Buffett and Others to Find Undervalued Stocks

Timothy P. Vick

Editor, *Today's Value Investor*

McGraw-Hill

New York   San Francisco   Washington, D.C.   Auckland   Bogotá
Caracas   Lisbon   London   Madrid   Mexico City   Milan
Montreal   New Delhi   San Juan   Singapore   Sydney
Tokyo   Toronto

McGraw-Hill

A Division of The McGraw·Hill Companies

Copyright © 1999 by Horizon Publishing Co., LLC. All rights reserved. Printed in the United States of America. Except as permitted under the United States Copyright Act of 1976, no part of this publication may be reproduced or distributed in any form or by any means, or stored in a data base or retrieval system, without the prior written permission of the publisher.

1 2 3 4 5 6 7 8 9 0 DOC/DOC 9 0 3 2 1 0 9 8

ISBN 0-07-134205-2

The sponsoring editor for this book was Jeffrey Krames, the editing supervisor was Donna Muscatello, and the production supervisor was Suzanne W. B. Rapcavage. It was set in Times New Roman by North Market Street Graphics.

Printed and bound by R. R. Donnelley & Sons Company.

This publication is designed to provide accurate and authoritative information in regard to the subject matter covered. It is sold with the understanding that neither the author nor the publisher is engaged in rendering legal, accounting, or other professional service. If legal advice or other expert assistance is required, the services of a competent professional person should be sought.

> *—From a Declaration of Principles jointly adopted by a Committee of the American Bar Association and a Committee of Publishers.*

McGraw-Hill books are available at special quantity discounts to use as premiums and sales promotions, or for use in corporate training programs. For more information, please write to the Director of Special Sales, McGraw-Hill, 11 West 19th Street, New York, NY 10011. Or contact your local bookstore.

Contents

Introduction

ONE HUNDRED AND FIFTY YEARS AGO, in his *Principles of Political Economy,* John Stuart Mill postulated that assets rise and fall in value based on the vagaries of human nature. When prices rise, the public perceives an opportunity for profit, bids up the value farther, and creates self-fulfilling prophecies. Falling prices spur a similar, though opposite reaction. "Disposition tends in itself to produce the effect which it looks forward to," Mill wrote.

Stocks rise and stocks fall, often for no reason other than that they are driven by fear, passion, and greed, our own understandable, albeit flawed, human emotions. This moody tug-and-pull on Wall Street offers tremendous opportunities to profit, especially when the public has mistakenly valued a company. Just a few years ago, people were afraid to pay 11 times earnings for Merck & Co. or Johnson & Johnson. Investors shunned Intel at 12 times earnings, backed away from Cisco Systems at $24, and wouldn't dare own bank stocks such as Wells Fargo at $75. Yet by 1998, investors were deemed foolhardy not to own these same stocks at a whopping four times the price and 30 times earnings! When you understand that Wall Street is little more than the personification—a mirror—of our very selves, you've taken the first step to achieving long-term success. The second step is to take charge.

My mission in this book is to show you how to take charge of Wall Street. You *can* own it using a method called *value investing.* Introduced in the mid-1930s, value investing has been practiced by many of the world's greatest market pros—Warren Buffett, Walter Schloss, Mario Gabelli, Michael Price, John Neff, John Templeton, and George Soros, to name a few. Their method of buying companies at a sale price has proven to be the most successful stock-picking tool ever devised.

With value investing, you can have your proverbial cake and eat it too. You can buy shares of the most popular companies on earth and enjoy the fruits of their growth. And because you refuse to pay outrageous prices, your returns will necessarily be greater, and you will expose yourself to far less risk of loss.

Yet to this day, value investing as a serious discipline is mostly ignored. The financial industry instead thrives off convincing you that investing is some kind of intangible, complex endeavor that you should never attempt yourself, much less understand. It turns investors into victims of their own emotions. Magazine headlines entice you toward "The 10 Best Stocks to Buy Now," while brokerages choreograph elaborate plans that have you switching stocks faster than dance partners. The industry has never appreciated the simplicity of buying $1 worth of assets for less than $1 and patiently holding onto your shares. In short, investing is not a fast waltz. Unfortunately, slow and steady success doesn't sell.

There is no better time to adopt value investing than now. Today, nearly half of all U.S. households participate in the stock market, yet the overwhelming majority of investors exhibit far less patience in planning their stock portfolios than they do their meals, vacations, or wardrobes. Fifteen years of bull markets have convinced investors that spending time on careful research is unnecessary and that no price is too high to pay, here, right now. Growth investing, buying stocks based on hoped-for future earnings gains, has supplanted prudent investing, just as it did in 1987, the early 1970s, and the Roaring '20s. For many investors, such unfortunate consequences, like all bad habits, will be repeated again and again.

The repeated findings of the past 20 years of research show that stocks rise slowly over time. Such findings are simple and incontrovertible, and so are these seven lessons they impart:

1. *Trading leads to inferior returns.*   You cannot beat the market by jumping in and out of stocks in a desperate search for quick gains. The more you turn over your portfolio, the more you will lag the market.

2. *The only proven way to beat the market is to link price to value.* Determine what a company is truly worth, buy below that price, and you will beat the returns of nearly every other investor.

3. *Most of the accepted principles of diversification should be ignored.* Cobbling together dozens of stocks to "protect yourself" necessarily

ensures inferior returns. So, too, does dollar-cost averaging, a trial-and-error approach that similarly leads to mediocre returns.

4. *Trading by technical indicators tends to hurt your returns more than help.* No one has ever devised a consistently successful formula for darting in and out of the market. There can be no substitute for evaluating a company before buying. To do otherwise—that is, to ignore value and a company's merits—is to invite risk of loss and reduce investing to gambling.

5. *Falling under the spell of "information" should be avoided at all costs.* To beat the industry at its game, you must ignore all of the cyclical forecasts about the economy, interest rates, earnings, and stocks.

6. *You can succeed in this business armed with little more than publicly available financial statements issued by companies.* Many active value investors rely on little more than annual reports, prospectuses, and proxy statements.

7. *Most of the information you need to evaluate a company can be obtained free via the Internet.* Individual investors now have at their disposal the same types of information that the legendary money managers have had.

The market's history has been fraught with gyrations. Investors must remember that to achieve $100 in gains, they must endure, on average, about $40 in setbacks. This two-steps-forward, one-step back process can be painful unless you are mindful of value. And, indeed, most investors are not. In spite of the lessons of research and obvious trends, most fail to prepare themselves for periodic losses. The long-term trend of stock prices is most certainly up. Continued growth in the economy and worker productivity should lead to steady growth in the intrinsic value of U.S. companies, which drives stock prices. Still, too many Americans stubbornly view investing as a virtual modern-day philosopher's stone, so convinced are they that the stocks they buy today will magically transform them into millionaires upon retirement. Right alongside them are the growth investors who champion the instant $100 killing, so oblivious to risk are they—the blind leading the blind. Value investors, on the other hand, look for ways to make $100 while avoiding those $40 losses.

This book synthesizes all of the major principles of value investing and explains many of the techniques that legendary investors like Warren Buffett have used to build their empires. I begin by summarizing the major themes of value investing and show how countless money managers have used the method to prosper. Later, I devote several chapters to teaching you how to evaluate a company for its investment merits. Finally, I illustrate how to assemble a portfolio of value stocks. In the appendix, I list my favorite websites for locating free information on companies and the stock market.

I am certain that this book will help to empower you so you can take control of your future and enhance your performance in the market through careful and wise investing. The principles herein are timeless and will assist you through good markets and poor, whether you decide to buy Internet stocks, shares of General Electric, Sony, Duke Power, or Bethlehem Steel.

Happy bargain hunting!

Timothy P. Vick
November 1998

Acknowledgments

THE EXTRAORDINARY TIME needed to complete a manuscript like this requires patience and diligence on the part of a lot of people. Of course, I must first thank my wife, Rebecca, for her continued support and copyediting, and my children, Calvin and Natalie, for their patience in putting up with dad's endless weekends and evenings on the computer. Special thanks to my editor, Jeffrey A. Krames, for guiding this project through to completion and wringing the most value out of the manuscript. Extended thanks as well to my colleague, Kenneth Pogach, a finance instructor at Purdue University, for helping me think through many of the critical valuation topics in this book. And thanks to Chris Vaughn at Horizon Publishing Co. for his assistance in preparing graphics and typesetting pages. Thanks to Warren Buffett, Walter Schloss, Charles Brandes, and the partners at Tweedy, Browne for giving me permission to reproduce valuable material in support of the book.

WHAT IS VALUE INVESTING?

"First of all, know value."

attributed to Charles Dow

W HEN BENJAMIN GRAHAM first laid out the principles of valuation in his groundbreaking 1934 treatise, *Security Analysis,* the concept of value investing did not exist. Graham himself would likely have objected to the phrase "value investing" and the way it has been twisted through the decades. Writing in the wake of the 1929–1933 bear market, the 40-year-old Graham wanted only to teach investors how to analyze financial statements and appraise a company's true value in the market-place. To him, buying a company without first analyzing its prospects was anathema—and insanely unwise.

The 700-page *Security Analysis*—esteemed today as the Bible of value investing—appeared in a time of utter recklessness. The financial markets in the first third of this century were generously manipulated—often by a single investor or banker looking to corner the price of a security or protect his profits. Before Congress passed strict disclosure laws in the 1930s, companies scarcely reported their financial results at all, and what they reported often couldn't be believed. Accounting rules were sparse, lenient, and not consistently applied across industries. Insider trading was not only rampant but permitted. Companies went public without supplying prospective investors with useful statistics on their operations. Information circulated slowly and unevenly, leaving the general public mostly in the dark about day-to-day trading and the shenanigans of lower Manhattan.

The landscape allowed rumors to run amok and drive stocks up and down with little regard for value or the plight of victims. Until Graham, no one had sat down and developed standard guidelines for analyzing a public company. A few academics had tinkered with the notion of intrinsic value. But their crude mathematical models found acceptance only in banking and academic circles. Middle America scarcely knew the difference between an investment-grade security and an outright sham.

In writing *Security Analysis,* Graham was not trying to concoct a get-rich-quick formula. Nor would he have appreciated being tagged "the father of value investing" or "the frugal investor." His contribution to the world was to impart objective sanity to a culture that saw the trading of paper certificates as an end, not a means. It made little sense to Graham that an investor would purchase an asset without first exploring its mechanics. He advocated kicking a company's tires and looking under the hood before telling the salesperson, "Buy me 100 at $50."

Kicking tires seems almost naive, but it forms the heart of value investing. When buying stocks, good research leads to good judgment. A consistent method leads to wise decisions. Paying a fair price leads to outstanding returns. "The fact that [value investing] is so simple makes people reluctant to teach it," billionaire value investor Warren Buffett once said. "If you've gone and gotten a Ph.D. and spent years learning how to do all kinds of tough things mathematically, to have to come back to this is—it's like studying for the priesthood and finding out that the Ten Commandments were all you needed."[1]

Today, many individuals confuse value investing with "cheap" investing. They see it as a strategy of buying unwanted companies, for those in dire straits or those whose stock trades below $10. Indeed, when I began publishing my investment newsletter, *Today's Value Investor,* in 1997, I was struck by the number of subscribers who believed—and hoped—I would recommend hot new growth companies priced at $2 a share. In the lexicon of a bull market, "value" had become associated with anything cheap in price.

To some extent, value and price join at the hip, as do value and growth. True value investors fixate on price; they never pay more for a share of stock than the company is worth. But they are just as concerned with

---

[1] L. J. Davis, *New York Times Magazine,* April, 1990.

growth as with price and value, for if a company cannot increase its earnings, net worth, and "intrinsic value" over time, there is no guarantee its stock will rise in value. By combining these three factors—buying growth at a value price—investors have enjoyed abnormal market-beating stock returns.

DEFINING "VALUE"

What do we mean by *value?* Everyone in the securities industry uses the term indiscriminately, often so loosely and frequently that it becomes a pat response for describing one's methodology. Millions of investors, including scores of fund managers, claim to be "value seekers." But as the evidence suggests, most of these people are no more seekers of value than traders who look for sudden rallies to spark their interest. To them, value becomes an asterisk applied in the absence of a rigid discipline. But the word *value,* in the financial and legal sense, has concrete, tangible meanings. Civil law recognizes several types of value:

Fair market value. This is the chief standard used in private asset appraisals, especially when assessing real estate or assets for tax purposes. In a nutshell, *fair market value,* or FMV, can be summed up as whatever someone will willingly pay for a similar asset. It is almost always defined in dollar terms since FMV reflects the amount of cash a buyer would be willing to put up and a seller willing to accept. The term assumes that both parties possess enough relevant information to appraise the asset being swapped. It also implies that neither the buyer nor seller actually sets the price; rather, the marketplace determines fair market value. You likely have participated in fair market valuations many times already. When buying or selling a home, you set the price based on local market conditions. If homes comparable to yours sell for between $200,000 and $220,000, the sale price of your home won't deviate much from that range. If it does, then a new standard of fair market value has been set for the neighborhood. Any time you buy a stock and willingly pay the going price, no questions asked, you accept the fair market value for the company.

Investment value. A company's *investment value* is unique to all potential buyers, because buyers possess their own rate-of-return requirements for an asset. For example, consider three investors who wish to buy shares of Procter & Gamble trading at $50. One investor wants safety of principal and will not accept price declines of more than 15 percent. The second wants—perhaps needs—20 percent annual returns on the stock and will tolerate higher share-price volatility to attain those goals. The third wants a dividend yield of at least 4 percent a year. Thus, each investor has established a different hurdle rate for the stock that can be satisfied only at certain prices. The first investor won't buy the stock if there's a chance it can drop below $42.50—15 percent below $50. The second won't buy Procter & Gamble unless it can climb to at least $60 in one year, or to $124 in five years. The third will buy P&G so long as the company's annual dividend stays above $2. Because each investor has established a unique minimum rate of return for the stock, it follows that they will place different values on the company. Each will buy or sell P&G only under strict and unique circumstances that are independent of the company's real value.

Book value. This standard of value measures the company's net worth on an accounting basis, that is, the per-share value of shareholders' equity. Many value investors rely heavily on this figure to find undervalued stocks. They reason, correctly, that a company cannot trade below its net worth for long. Either the stock should rise above book value or management should liquidate assets and return the proceeds to shareholders. I explore the significance of book value further in Chapter 12.

Liquidation value. This standard of value tests what an enterprise could fetch if all assets were sold, all receivables collected, and outstanding bills and debts paid. Liquidation value has little relevance to value investors since you should focus on going-concern companies, those expected to earn profits in the future and that stand little chance of going belly up. Liquidation value can come into play when the market severely oversells a stock (as it did with Chrysler in the early 1980s or Citicorp in 1991) and creates a bargain too tempting to overlook.

Intrinsic value. The notion of intrinsic value is not subjective but generic. It represents what an appraiser could conclude a business is worth after undertaking an analysis of the company's financial position. In the absolute sense, intrinsic value is the real worth of a company, the sale price investors could reasonably place on the company if they all possessed the same information and insight. In deriving intrinsic value, an investor attempts as much as possible to place a per-share price on (1) the company's assets, (2) the value of the company's expected future earnings or dividends, or (3) the company's sales or earnings growth rate.

Figure 1-1 depicts the relationship between standards of value. Here, I've superimposed four standards—market value, intrinsic value, book

FIGURE 1-1 The relationship between market value and other standards of value.

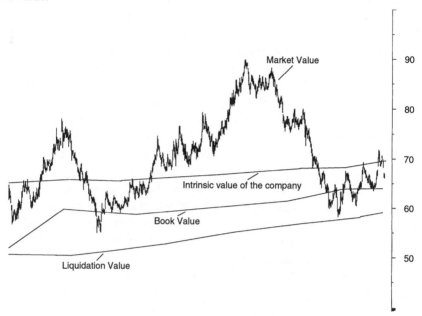

value, and liquidation value—for a hypothetical company to show how much these methods can differ. Market value is represented by stock price and is the most volatile. The up-and-down, daily fluctuations in market value reflect traders' continually shifting perceptions of the company's value. Practically speaking, the mercurial nature of market value makes it the least useful criterion for determining a company's true worth. In my hypothetical example, market value first rises from $60 to $80, falls below $60, rises to $90, and falls back into the $60s. Yet the underlying value of the company, whether measured by intrinsic value, book value, or liquidation value, does not change at nearly the same rate. The value of our hypothetical company, in fact, rises gradually, even during times when market value falls sharply.

A value investor looks for situations where market value falls below intrinsic value. The further below intrinsic value the stock falls, the greater the bargain and the greater your potential return. In this example, the stock twice fell below intrinsic value and temporarily fell below the company's book value. The stock reached its most attractive bargain price when it approached liquidation value and posed little risk of falling farther.

THE SEVEN PRINCIPLES OF VALUE INVESTING

There is nothing mysterious about value investing. Practicing it doesn't require computer algorithms or econometric formulas. You don't need an advanced business school education to master its tenets. A calculator and old-fashioned common sense will take you a lot farther. So will an uncluttered mind. Some of the most celebrated market pros force themselves to make errors by collecting and analyzing useless data, studying minute-by-minute movements in the market, and reacting to what statisticians call "noise"—events that have little relevance to the major trend. Individual investors do the same. They perceive Wall Street as a temple of knowledge, as if analysts and strategists are oracles gifted with the power to predict earnings, cash flow, and unemployment rates by waving a spreadsheet. In reality, Wall Street's eminent sages exist to sell you something and exploit your hunger to know the future. Their track record of predicting tomorrow's earnings or market movements is no better than the oracles on whom Greek farmers relied when planting crops.

The thousands of forecasting models Wall Street's pros have built and the millions of buy recommendations they have issued have proven to be no better medicine than a "chicken soup" approach to investing: Buy two stocks you like and call me in 20 years. Value investing, by contrast, can be practiced successfully by anyone. Its tenets and stupendous track record lay exposed to the world from all angles, like a Rodin sculpture or a trapeze act. Its underlying principles are elegantly simple—provided you possess the right temperament and mindset.

FIRST PRINCIPLE: BUY ASSETS ON SALE

The concept of buying goods on sale is as ingrained in the American psyche as watching primetime sitcoms. We take for granted the idea that any good—a bar of soap, a Pontiac Grand Am, or back-to-school clothing—is a better value when the price drops. When the local grocer advertises strip steaks on sale, your initial response might be to buy some. When your favorite fast-food restaurant runs a 99-cent sale on quarter-pounders, there's a tendency to forego a home-cooked meal and load up on a sack full of patties and fries. Why are Americans like this? Because we crave value. We make mental notes of what constitutes a fair price and often will wait until that price level is breached before we buy. We may scoff at a 24-pack of Pepsi priced at $5.99, but at $4.99 it's suddenly within our range of perceived value.

The financial markets may be the only institutions in the world that turn the basic doctrine of consumerism on its head. Investors are coached to believe that a stock is a better buy when the price rises, that it's "safer" to join the crowd in bidding the price up and "riskier" to buy a stock declining in price. Wall Street, you see, likes to implant a "fear of omission" in investors. We are led to believe that if we fail to buy a stock now, the price will only go higher and we will miss the rally.

The first principle of value investing is to buy securities on sale, just as you would toiletries or a new automobile. You should not differentiate consumer habits from investing habits. They are one and the same. Whether you buy a grocery store item, shares of Intel, a bar of silver, a Treasury bond, or preferred stock in your local utility, you should try to obtain it on sale, when possible, to maximize its value per dollar of investment. Of course, it's difficult to assess the value of consumer goods. No two shoppers, if queried, could calculate the true worth of a bottle of shampoo or a car. These goods possess intangible benefits; they provide utility to our lives in ways we cannot measure on a dollar scale. Common stocks, by contrast, can be valued very precisely. With the right tools, an investor can determine the true worth of the underlying company to within a few pennies per share. This gives investors a distinct advantage over consumers. Because prices in the stock market change instantaneously—often irrationally—investors can seize upon innumerable, recurring opportunities to buy shares in a company at a sale price.

The reason to buy low is simple: You increase your potential return. . . . Profits are predetermined when you buy shares, not when you sell them.

What constitutes a "sale" on Wall Street? Quite simply, when you are able to buy a dollar's worth of a company's assets or earnings for less than a dollar. The farther below $1 you purchase shares, the better your rate-of-return potential and the less risk of loss. Conversely, you never should pay more than $1 for $1 of underlying value. If a company is worth, say, $50 per share and the stock trades for $60, then walk away. You would not consider buying the company until the stock price fell below $50; the farther below $50 the better. As we show in later chapters, buying companies at bargain prices has historically produced market-beating returns, for the simple reason that undervalued situations, by definition, must end sometime. Sooner or later, the market realizes its mistake and bids up undervalued stocks at least to a fair value—often higher. The reason to buy low is simple: You increase your potential return. Buying General Electric at $40 will always provide a better return than buying it at $50. Profits are predetermined when you buy shares, not when you sell them. Selling only completes the transaction and confirms that your initial research proved correct.

SECOND PRINCIPLE: FORM A NOTION OF VALUE

The single most important task facing any investor is to appraise the assets on sale. Whether you wish to buy a condominium in Florida, a print by Erte, or a piece of Exxon, it is imperative that you form an opinion of the asset's worth. Most stock investors would confess to having no system for doing so. Having talked with hundreds of investors through the years, I dare say that few of them appraise a company's worth before buying shares. Some investors rely exclusively on charts and technical indicators when making trading decisions. Others tend to buy a stock because they read about it in the newspaper or heard an analyst promote it on television. Some jump on a stock simply because it announced a stock split, raised its dividend, or rose to a 52-week high. And a number of investors, quite frankly, buy stocks because they are unable to just say no to their broker.

Unfortunately, most investors probably spend more time planning their grocery list or garden than picking stocks that will make or break their financial security. Success in investing requires you to do homework. The great investors of the 20th century did not amass fortunes using trite charting methods or guesswork. They studied their targets and owed their success as much to analytical work as anything else. Before taking a position in a company, they learned all they could about the enterprise, the industry in which it operated, and its potential. Finally, they determined the maximum price they were willing to pay for the stock based on their appraisal of the enterprise. To do otherwise is to invite the element of chance into their trades. Any investor who commits money—be it $1000 or $50 million—without performing due diligence might as well be rolling dice. While you might reap big gains occasionally buying a stock recommended by a broker or a stock that just split, such gains are attributable only to random chance, not skill.

When business appraisers determine the value of a property, they must defend the value and methodology, sometimes in court. A poor appraisal undoubtedly will invite attacks by interested third parties—family members, shareholders, creditors, or lawyers for the target company. Individual investors are not beholden to such rigorous analysis. No one will ever challenge your decision to buy Caterpillar at $65, sell the shares when the company issues new bonds, or wait until the price drops to $50 before buying again. But you must be willing to justify an investing decision to yourself, to defend your methodology.

Valuing a company can be rigorous or relatively painless, depending on your circumstances. An analyst trying to evaluate an initial public offering for her firm must rigorously study every nuance of the company's operations. An investor looking for a good buy-and-hold company can suitably value the merits of an enterprise in only a few hours. Trust that you will know in short order whether the company meets your purchase criteria. It has been said that Warren Buffett knows within 20 minutes whether a company he is studying is worth buying. The methodology he uses (described in Chapter 15) is strict enough that he can reject 99 of every 100 companies very quickly. But once he targets a few potential investment opportunities, Buffett may spend days or weeks attempting to validate his initial instincts.

Buffett's approach is shared by most of the world's successful investors. They thoroughly evaluate a company and attach a value to the stock before buying it. The great investors do not invest blindly, nor do they approach investing using guesswork. Valuing a company before buying shares helps you in three ways:

It leads to consistent trading.   Very few investors set rigid buy and sell thresholds when they buy stock. As a result, their trading decisions are open-ended, which can lead to poor decision making and losses. When you buy without regard to value, you leave yourself vulnerable to many types of risk, including the risk that you paid too much for a company.

It helps you defend your strategy.   Psychologically, it is very important for investors to understand why they purchased shares. Those unable to justify a purchase to themselves will inevitably trade for irrational reasons. They are wont to sell a stock prematurely or ignore looming problems and hold a stock too long. Worse, they learn nothing from their mistakes and repeat them habitually when buying other companies.

It enables you to determine the rate-of-return criteria up front.   You should avoid purchasing a stock without first determining the return you expect from it. Don't buy shares simply because the stock might climb in value over the next few years. Buy it because it can increase 50 percent over two years or 100 percent over five years or 1000 percent over 15 years.

Once you set those types of goals, stick to them whenever possible. It is much easier to calculate a potential rate of return once you have determined a fair price for the company. If you determine, for example, that the stock is 50 percent overvalued, you should not hope for market-bearing returns over the next few years. Chances are good the stock will provide you a negative return.

Affixing value is not foolproof, and sometimes your valuation of the company proves erroneous. More often than not, however, this exercise will prevent you from chasing overvalued companies whose rate-of-return potential is reduced. Investors would be wise to remember a phrase from Robert Rubin, President Clinton's Treasury Secretary:

> In good times people tend not to very rigorous [when evaluating securities]. . . . Rigor is always appropriate when investing in markets, whatever the ultimate conclusions may be.[2]

THIRD PRINCIPLE: AVOID LOSSES WITH A "MARGIN OF SAFETY"

You cannot avoid periodic losses. But value investing allows you to minimize them significantly. As I show in Chapter 2, the ability to minimize losses leads to market-beating returns over long periods. In fact, various studies have shown that buying stocks at cheap prices relative to the market leads to outstanding returns over time. How cheap is cheap? There's no single answer. If you possess absolute confidence in your valuation methods, you can buy shares as soon as the price falls below what you deem to be a fair value. But to be safe, give yourself a price cushion, the bigger the better. Benjamin Graham, writing in 1949, dubbed this an investor's "margin of safety."

> In the old legend the wise men finally boiled down the history of mortal affairs into the single phrase, "This too will pass." Confronted with a like challenge to distill the secret of sound investing into three words, we venture the motto, MARGIN OF SAFETY. This is the thread that runs through all the preceding discussions of investment policy—often explicitly, sometimes in a less direct fashion.[3]

If you believe a company is worth $25 per share, you should nonetheless avoid pouncing upon shares as soon as they fall to $24. Such aggression works only if your valuation is on the mark. Leave yourself a wide enough margin of error to compensate for the possibility that your analysis was

---

[2] "Rubin Urges Rigor in Evaluating Market," *Wall Street Journal,* Section A2, May 6, 1998.

[3] Benjamin Graham, *The Intelligent Investor,* 4th ed., New York, Harper & Row, 1973, p. 277.

wrong or that later information will prove the company was worth less than you originally determined. It's possible the market has not finished distributing the stock. It may fall several more dollars after you buy it. The key to maximizing returns is to take full advantage of the public's disinterest in a company and wait until a stock falls far below its fair value to protect yourself. As Graham pointed out, investors can easily rationalize—after the fact—their decision to buy a stock, even when they paid too much. But these justifications tend to be subjective and reflect an unwillingness to acknowledge mistakes. The key is to leave ample elbow room for your mistakes.

> Probably most speculators believe they have the odds in their favor when they take their chances, and therefore they may lay claim to a safety margin in their proceedings. Each one has the feeling that the time is propitious for his purchase, or that his skill is superior to the crowd's, or that his adviser or system is trustworthy. But such claims are unconvincing. They rest on subjective judgment, unsupported by any body of favorable evidence or any conclusive line of reasoning. We greatly doubt whether the man who stakes his money on his view that the market is heading up or down can ever be said to be protected by a margin of safety in any useful sense of the phrase.
>
> By contrast, the investor's concept of the margin of safety . . . rests upon simple and definite arithmetical reasoning from statistical data.[4]

FOURTH PRINCIPLE: ADOPT A "FOR-SALE" PERSPECTIVE

Investing is intelligent, Graham said, when it is most businesslike, that is, when we treat it without passion and with strict regard to sound principles. I counsel investors and clients to view investing as a role-playing exercise, in which they assume the role of a business owner trying to decide whether a company is really worth the quoted price. Imagine that you are wealthy enough to purchase all of Coca-Cola, McDonald's, or Chase Manhattan Bank. How much would you pay for the entire company? What criteria would you use to evaluate these enterprises? Are their shares selling for an extraordinary price or an extraordinary value? We tend to fixate so much on the price of a single share that we lose sight of whether the market values the entire company properly. In July 1998, a share of General Electric sold for roughly $96. At the time, few investors quibbled over the selling price. Nearly every brokerage analyst covering GE had a buy recommen-

---

[4] Benjamin Graham, *The Intelligent Investor,* 4th ed. New York: Harper & Row, 1973, p. 283.

dation at that price based on their earnings projections. But their analysis missed a very important point. A single share of GE may have seemed reasonable at $96. But the market price for all of GE's common stock was $310 billion, the price you would pay to acquire the entire company. Was GE worth more than the annual economic output of 125 nations? By comparison, $310 billion could have bought you all the shares of the nation's six largest banks in 1998. Collectively, these banks earned twice GE's annual profits. If it seemed absurd to pay $310 billion for the entire company, then owning even 100 shares of GE should have been equally absurd. To quote Graham:

> It is an almost unbelievable fact that Wall Street never asks, "How much is the business selling for?" Yet this should be the first question in considering a stock purchase. If a business man were offered a 5% interest in some concern for $10,000, his first mental process would be to multiply the asked price of 20 and thus establish a proposed value of $200,000 for the entire undertaking. The rest of his calculation would turn about the question whether the business was a "good buy" at $200,000.[5]

Viewing a company in this manner helps you develop the proper perspective for analyzing its performance. If you own a company outright, you can claim all of the yearly after-tax earnings and cash flow generated by the enterprise. But that's all you are ever entitled to. Since there is no market for the stock of a private business, you must value the enterprise only on the earnings the company can generate on your behalf over time. You certainly would not value it based on the random, day-to-day fluctuations of your company's stock.

FIFTH PRINCIPLE: STICK TO IT

For more than a century, investment books have cautioned Americans against speculating on minute-by-minute movements in stock prices. They have counseled individuals that long-term buy-and-hold strategies work best. They have coached investors to ignore quarterly earnings and daily news headlines and focus on the big picture. Writers at the turn of the century warned investors not to chase overvalued banking stocks. No one listened. In the late 1920s, investors threw caution to the wind and bid up stock prices based on companies' hoped-for future earnings. The pattern repeated in 1968, 1973, and 1987.

---

[5] Benjamin Graham and David Dodd, *Security Analysis,* reprint of 1934 ed., New York, McGraw-Hill, 1997, p. 493.

In my years in the business, I've seen normally conservative investors throw money away on hot biotechnology stocks because a few fund managers were mesmerized by them. I've seen investors cast aside reason and buy stocks simply because the company announced a stock split—an everyday occurrence in 1997 and 1998—or met its earnings targets. I have seen elderly investors spend $100,000 or more of their retirement savings buying stocks of companies whose names they couldn't pronounce and whose products they barely understood. I have talked with factory workers who traded stocks based on daily volume patterns, or who wore quote machines around their belts lest they come in on the wrong side of a block trade.

The only "system" that has proven to work is the one that links share price to the company's performance.

They all shared an intoxicating drink—Wall Street's perpetual punch. One sip and reason all but disappears. The financial industry loves to serve up new methods, new "systems," and new justifications to compel you to join the fray. But the only "system" that has proven to work is the one that links share price to the company's performance. That's as it should be. In the short term, any blip of news can cause a stock to rise or fall in value. In the long run, stocks rise because the value of the company rises. Figure out what a company is really worth, buy below that price, and you will beat the market over time. Study after study has confirmed this. The beauty of a value-based method is its consistency. Buying companies below their true value has worked in times of high or low interest rates, a growing or contracting economy, and a strong or weak U.S. dollar. It has worked whether analysts, short-sellers, and arbitrageurs have liked the company or not. For as Roger Babson once said, time validates or repudiates every method:

> Plenty of schemes will work for a little while, and then they collapse. The only plan worthy of the name is one that can be relied upon permanently, whether business is good or bad and whether, in deference to one's vanity, the market is right or wrong.[6]

---

[6] Roger W. Babson, *Business Barometers and Investment,* 5th ed., New York, Harper & Brothers, 1951, p. 123.

If value investing has proven itself so successful, why doesn't everyone practice it? Perhaps because it is too simple. If Wall Street accepted the superiority of value stock picking, thousands of highly paid economists, analysts, strategists, fund managers, and brokers would be out of work. Their existence relies on buyers' obedience. The day that you wake up and decide you can invest for yourself and make more money doing it, their drink has lost its inebriating effect. On the other hand, we all should be grateful that value investing is not universally accepted. If it were, it would likely lose its usefulness as a relevant strategy. Once a successful method holds powerful sway on Wall Street and is adopted into the trading curriculum, it ceases to be useful. Over the years, many so-called can't-lose strategies have ceased to work because they became part of the public record. The Dow dividend strategy, the strategy of buying the highest-yielding Dow industrials stocks, began to fail in the mid-1990s after the media devoted unprecedented attention to it. Tens of thousands of investors and more than a few mutual funds fashioned their portfolios around this popular strategy. As a result, they bid high-yielding Dow stocks ever-higher and ultimately diluted their own potential returns. The creator of the strategy, Michael O'Higgins, later came to reject it, saying it no longer offered novel benefits because of its popularity.

SIXTH PRINCIPLE: BE A CONTRARIAN

Wall Street's great fortunes were not produced by passive buy-and-hold investors or by technical traders and chart watchers. The master investors—Warren Buffett, Mario Gabelli, John Templeton, George Soros, and others—took advantage of mispriced assets and held them until the rest of the world's investors recognized their mistake. They profited from the folly and foolish selling of others, snatching up prized securities trading at a fraction of their true worth. Buffett made a small fortune in the 1950s gobbling up and then selling unwanted stocks that he bought for three and four times earnings. Legendary fund manager John Neff took big stakes in Chrysler and Citicorp after Wall Street wrote them off. George Soros made almost $1 billion overnight in 1992 betting on the unthinkable, a sharp decline in the British pound. Peter Lynch rode the Magellan Fund into the history books buying unsexy consumer companies his peers had overlooked.

   To be a successful value investor, you must be able to defend your stance on a company and hold your ground, regardless of what the rest of the world believes. I once purchased shares of a small homebuilder, Continental Homes Holding Co., at a time when no one wanted the stock—literally. I bought 2000 shares one morning when the market opened and waited nearly two hours before the next trade, a 100-share lot, crossed the tape. Imagine the anxiety I must have felt. Of the six billion people on earth, I was the only one who wanted to invest in this company. A nervous investor might have sold the stock immediately, but I delighted in the lack of interest. The world's ignorance of Continental Homes meant I could scoop up more shares at any time—at a price I dictated. I did my homework and calculated that Continental was truly a steal; I valued the company at more than $30 a share, yet the stock sold for $16. Within six months, the stock raced to $36. The comic irony was that Wall Street didn't take much interest in the company until it rose above $30 and was overvalued again.

With a little digging you can find such opportunities, any day of the week. More than 2000 of the 10,000 publicly listed companies in America are overlooked by analysts. No earnings estimates exist, daily volume is light, and just a handful of mutual fund managers bother to examine a given company. The probability that these 2000 companies are mispriced from time to time is great. Larger companies occasionally become bargains, too, when they temporarily fall out of favor. Drug stocks such as Abbott Laboratories and Merck traded at just 12 times earnings in 1994, following months of manic selling by investors who focused too much on short-term news events and not enough on the fact that these companies were raking in profits. Callaway Golf traded at 11 times earnings in 1994, so fearful were investors that the golfing market was becoming saturated.

The unhappy consequences of following the crowd are carved like tombstone inscriptions on each day's financial pages. As James Goldsmith once said, "If you see a bandwagon, it's too late." Had you bought into the microbrewery craze of 1996, you would have sustained punishing capital losses for the next three years. Had you ignored the major retailers in 1995—as analysts preached, you would have missed one of the sector's greatest rallies in 1996 and 1997. Millions of crowd-following investors loaded up on Internet and semiconductor stocks in 1995 only to see their retirement dreams shattered within weeks. The best analysts on Wall Street led investors into oil-drilling companies in mid-1997, when most were already priced at 40 times earnings. Three months later, following the collapse of crude oil prices, nary an analyst would recommend these companies at the reduced price of 15 times earnings.

A contrarian investor doesn't automatically swim against the tide, however. Being an antagonist for the sake of being an antagonist is more dangerous than a strong undertow. The market makes just as many correct judgments of companies as incorrect ones. Hence, you should only fight the crowd when (1) the market's psychological reactions to events seem extreme and (2) financial data confirm the public's error. Never take the opposing side of the market without supporting evidence.

SEVENTH PRINCIPLE: IGNORE THE MARKET

It's a wonder investors don't trade 10 times a day given how the financial industry and the media bombard them with information. Most of the information they issue, however, is useless—unless you are in the business of day trading. Successful investors are patient. They concentrate on a company's longer-term potential, not on what can happen next month or next quarter. Tuning out brokers, economists, analysts, market strategists, and newscasters may be the best bit of advice this book can provide, for these "experts" will only cloud your judgment in making decisions. Once you see an undervalued situation in the market, pounce on it. Don't hesitate to buy because of current market conditions. You must learn to separate truly relevant information from the noise. Avoid dwelling on the U.S. dollar, interest rates, inflation, "breadth" in the market, the latest unemployment report, or the 200-day moving average of the Dow Jones industrial average. These events are irrelevant to whether a company offers a compelling value. The most telling factors when determining value lie in publicly available financial statements. A company's lengthy track record in the marketplace serves as a better guide than anything an economist or analyst can impart.

Likewise, the condition of the market is immaterial to what a company is truly worth. Value is determined solely by a company's performance, not by how the market wishes to price that performance. Whether the S&P 500 is poised to rally or is in the throes of a correction is inconsequential to your decision to buy or sell. Too many investors get lost in market timing and hesitate to buy good companies because the so-called market pros counsel against buying stocks. Worse, they make trading decisions based on day-to-day dips in price. They buy shares of a company for $20, then sell if the stock falls to $18. In their minds, they have made a mistake. Yet their only sin was that they happened to buy ahead of sellers—nothing more, nothing less. So long as the value of the company remains higher than your purchase price, you should ignore the actions of others.

I devote the remainder of the book to exploring these principles in depth.

C H A P T E R

2

THE HISTORICAL RECORD
OF VALUE INVESTING

> "We start with the assumption that the stock market is always wrong, so that if you copy everybody else on Wall Street, you're doomed to do poorly."
>
> *George Soros[1]*

GREAT MANY INVESTORS fall prey to the trappings of Wall Street. If they were even slightly aware of the misinformation fed them about stock picking and long-term returns, they would rise up and reject the trading methods they have used. One clear misperception that inhibits investors' returns is the "10-percent rule," the widely accepted notion that stocks perpetually rise an average of 10 percent a year. Statistically speaking, the theory would seem valid. After all, if data shows a consistent pattern over a 70 years, we can reasonably conclude that the next 70 years will bear the same results. Unfortunately, this is not the case; the stock market is neither reasonable nor logical. It doesn't obey set patterns or calendars and rarely behaves as predicted. In 1929, the public was misled by the same simplistic formulas. At a time when the market neared a historical high, Wall Street busily churned out data enticing people to invest for the long term. "Forget about valuation," these handbills exhorted, "keep holding on and your money will

---

[1] Robert Slater, *Soros, The Life, Times and Trading Secrets,* Irwin, Burr Ridge, IL, 1996, p. 83.

compound into a nice nest egg in 20 to 30 years." It took just about that long, incidentally, for the market to recover to its 1929 high. In the late 1970s, by contrast, when most investors were leery of buying anything, few were singing the praise of buy-and-hold investing. Fewer still were willing to commit their money for 20- and 30-year periods.

Indeed, what happens this year in the financial markets has little bearing on next year. What happened the past decade has no bearing on what will happen in the next. You cannot expect the market to march in lockstep to trite formulas. If you accept the fact that the future returns on stocks cannot be predicted with any accuracy, you will free yourself from mediocre returns, for it is by chasing misleading statistics, rather than focusing on companies, that investors condemn themselves to poor performance. Many investors intentionally craft portfolios with the explicit goal of obtaining an annual return of 10 percent. Why 10 percent? Because that's what market pundits say to expect. But the flawed assumptions behind the 10-percent goal will, over the long haul, unwittingly hurt these investors. In trying to attain these goals investors commit three cardinal mistakes: They diversify too much; they deemphasize the role of analysis and stock picking; and they fail to monitor their portfolios properly.

These three mistakes explain why most investors fail to achieve adequate returns. When you diversify beyond what is necessary, you lower your buying standards, and this increases risk. Investors with large portfolios tend to buy indiscriminately. They may create a portfolio of five quality stocks, then let it degenerate into 25 stocks of lower quality. For the sake of meeting their goals, they add stocks without regard to safety, risk, price, or potential returns. Such conspicuous buying naturally creates time pressures. By owning 25 or more stocks, investors create an unfortunate dilemma: Either they must devote hundreds of hours each year to watching those companies, or worse, they must ignore them out of expediency and neglect information that could have an adverse impact on those companies.

To lay the groundwork for successful investing, you must first lay to rest the 10-percent rule. The rule is a marketing gimmick, a mathematical fabrication concocted by the securities industry to keep money flowing through its doors. In good times, it is used to justify dollar-cost averaging and the unwarranted bidding of stock prices to unjustifiable highs. At its extreme, the 10-percent rule is exploited to coach investors to ignore price and value. Leading studies of the 1990s, for example, claimed investors would enjoy outstanding returns even if they invested once a year at the market's yearly peak. Of course, that claim can only be made in hindsight, after the market has rallied for several years. Only then could this strategy tempt a novice investor. Those who purchased stocks during the market peaks of 1929, 1968, or 1972 would have found themselves singing an entirely different tune.

It is wrong—and frequently risky—to link past returns to the future. Just because the S&P 500 index has risen at 10 percent annual rates does not mean it will return 10 percent over the next several decades. It may return 5 percent; it may return 18 percent. It may post negative returns for several consecutive years before resuming an upward course. The only evidence we have that stocks may rise 10 percent a year is the example of U.S. markets. Few of the world's stock markets, in fact, have existed long enough to allow any meaningful analysis of returns, so our conclusions about market returns are based on a data set of one—the U.S. experience of the 20th century. That's the same as assuming, as many credible and noncredible scientists have, that space aliens have heads, hearts, arms, and legs because humans do. Having only a single reference point distorts how we view the unknown. Furthermore, the 10-percent annual return presumes an investor bought the S&P 500 index, held every stock in that index for decades, reinvested all dividends in the same stocks, *and* constantly rebalanced the stock weightings within the portfolio to match the index. This is utterly impractical and renders all related studies meaningless. Most investors, in fact, obtain yearly returns that deviate greatly from the indexes, even when they attempt to create market-neutral portfolios, a point I raise in Chapter 14.

The good news is that once investors reject the 10-percent rule, they no longer are bound by limitations when setting goals. The purpose of this book is to convince you that it's possible to obtain returns far in excess of the market, whether the market rises 10 percent a year, 2 percent, or 20 percent.

If you can obtain even minor improvements over the market's return, you will generate staggering long-term results due to compounding.

The importance of beating the market cannot be downplayed. If you can obtain even minor improvements over the market's return, you will generate staggering long-term results due to compounding (see Figure 2-1). Assuming the market does rise 10 percent a year, an investor who begins with $10,000 and obtains 12 percent a year has 43 percent more earnings after 20 years than someone who ties the market. After 30 years, the investor has earned 72 percent more money. The results explode when an investor can attain returns above 12 percent. By earning 14 percent, you would have 192 percent more money in 30 years. If an investor can attain 16 percent, he earns 391 percent more money by year 30. Two forces create these astounding returns, time and the incremental rate of return. Beating the market consistently, even by a small amount, helps short-term returns. Over time, the results are magnified greatly. This has been a key element of Warren Buffett's success. Buffett, for example, set a goal 30 years ago to beat the Dow Jones industrial average by 10 percentage points a year. He has done so and in a way that has allowed his after-tax returns to skyrocket relative to the market.

Figure 2-1 also reveals the punishment for lagging the market. It is as substantial to the downside as the rewards were to the upside. After 30 years of 8 percent yearly returns, a portfolio lags the S&P 500 by 73 percent. Investors who have held significant amounts of bonds or income-producing stocks for the past 20 to 30 years find themselves in this category. While their yearly returns have more than offset inflation (an important consideration discussed in Chapter 5), they find themselves hopelessly behind the curve and without enough time to make up the difference.

FIGURE 2-1   The compounding advantages of beating the market (starting with a $10,000 investment).

Annual Gain

Year	8%	10%	12%	14%	16%
1	$10,800	$11,000	$11,200	$11,400	$11,600
5	$14,693	$16,105	$17,623	$19,254	$21,003
10	$21,589	$25,937	$31,058	$37,072	$44,114
15	$31,722	$41,772	$54,736	$71,379	$92,655
20	$46,610	$67,275	$96,463	$137,435	$194,608
25	$68,485	$108,347	$170,001	$264,619	$408,742
30	$100,627	$174,494	$299,599	$509,502	$858,499
35	$147,853	$281,024	$527,996	$981,002	$1,803,141

Market's assumed return

Indeed, only a few mistakes can keep your portfolio from attaining truly outstanding returns. Holding onto a few poor-performing companies for too long can set your returns back several years. So can selling a strong-performing company too early. A portfolio that is too large can prevent you from experiencing returns above 10 percent. A portfolio that is too small—five stocks or under—forces you to be nearly perfect in stock picking. One disastrous holding among those five could keep you behind the market for years.

THE STUDIES VALIDATING VALUE INVESTING

Fortunately, one method, and only one method, has been shown to provide the market-beating returns we seek—value investing. Let's consider some of the more credible evidence. Value investing has no standard definition. Thus its benefits have been hard to quantify. Value fund managers, for example, tend to rely on different combinations of financial data when evaluating a company. Research on the merits of value investing has focused on the benchmark ratios on which most managers rely: price-to-earnings (P/E), price-to-book value (P/B), price-to-sales (P/S), and dividend yield. Studies on these ratios have found significant and obvious benefits to using a value approach (see Chapter 9 for a discussion of dividends and Chapter 12 for an in-depth discussion of the remaining price ratios).

BENJAMIN GRAHAM'S NET CURRENT ASSET APPROACH

Benjamin Graham was among the first to study stock returns by analyzing companies displaying common characteristics. In the early 1930s, he developed what he called the *net current asset* approach of investing. This called for buying stocks priced less than 66 percent of the company's liquidity (working capital minus debt). For example, a company with current assets of $20 per share and current liabilities and debt of $15 per share has $5 per share in net current assets ($20 minus $15). Graham would buy the company if the stock sold for less than 66 percent of $5, or $3.33 per share. Graham employed this method consistently over the next 20 years managing money for private accounts. His studies showed that over a 30-year period, this method of buying stocks below their net current assets returned roughly 20 percent a year, far in excess of the market.

More than five decades later, in 1986, Henry Oppenheimer, an associate professor of finance at State University of New York, Binghamton, retested Graham's original theory and found it worked just as well in modern times. Oppenheimer found that the strategy of buying stocks priced at 66 percent of net current assets returned 29.4 percent a year from 1971 through 1983. By contrast, the NYSE-AMEX index of stocks rose 11.5 percent a year over the same period. Oppenheimer assumed the investor bought all stocks bearing this ratio each year and sold them a year later. Why would this magical relationship between stock price and balance sheet liquidity hold? In follow-up studies, the New York-based money management firm Tweedy, Browne Co. found that companies selling for such low ratios to their liquidity tended to be priced at "significant discounts to real-world estimates" of their sale or liquidation value. In other words, the market had driven the stock down to prices below what the company's assets could fetch in a fire sale, an unrealistic appraisal of an ongoing enterprise. Under such conditions, it was inevitable that the stock would rise.

THE TRINITY STUDIES OF 1995

Another leading value-oriented money management firm, Trinity Investment Management, has found that stocks bearing low P/E and P/B ratios or high dividend yields tend to beat the market average consistently and by a wide margin. In one study, it created a hypothetical portfolio containing the 30 percent of the S&P 500 companies with the lowest P/E ratios and tracked the performance for the 14-year period ending in December 1994. Each quarter, the portfolio was reshuffled; high P/E stocks were tossed out and replaced with a new group of low P/E stocks. This list returned an annual gain of 17.5 percent over the period versus 13.3 percent for the S&P 500. A $10,000 investment in the S&P 500 over those 14 years would have returned $57,441. A $10,000 investment in the low P/E portfolio would have returned $95,616.

The next study looked at the bottom 30 percent of S&P 500 stocks as classified by P/B ratios. The results were even better: an annual gain of 18.1 percent for 14 years versus 13.3 percent for the index.

Trinity then composed portfolios of the bottom 30 percent of the S&P 500 classified by dividend yield. In this case, it bought the 30 percent with the highest yield each quarter and tracked performance over 14 years. The results were stronger yet. The high-yield value portfolio gained 18.3 percent, five percentage points above the market. When Trinity combined all three factors, P/E, P/B, and yield, into one portfolio, that is, it utilized a combination of the three ratios when choosing S&P 500 stocks, the results improved further. S&P 500 stocks chosen based on those ratios rose an average of 20.1 percent between 1980 and 1994, beating the market by 6.8 percentage points a year (see Figure 2-2).

If such results are possible, why don't more fund managers buy stocks based on these ratios? Arguably, most fund managers would never admit

FIGURE 2-2   1980–1994 annual returns of the S&P 500 and subsets of the index.

Source: Association for Investment Management and Research.

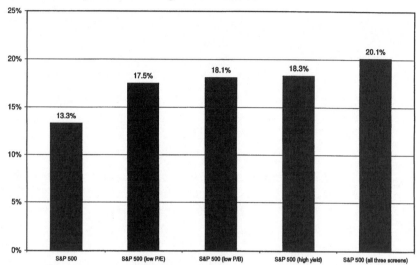

that stock picking could be reduced to such simple concepts. To do so is to acknowledge that their supposed "superior information" is, in fact, a commodity that may not hold any added value. Another reason may be that fund managers are under the gun to perform *now* and must therefore choose stocks capable of generating returns *today*. Value stock picking, by contrast, requires patience. While value investing has proven itself superior over long periods, it may yield unacceptably slow results in periods such as frothy bull markets when growth stocks garner all the attention. A third reason may be that stocks meeting the criteria Trinity Investment Management sought tend to be concentrated in a few industries. An investor who cobbled together a low-P/E, low-P/B, high-yield portfolio in 1996 or 1997, for example, would have been weighted down in insurance and bank stocks, oil and gas partnerships, real estate investment trusts, and electric utilities. Few fund managers could justify to their investors owning such a thinly diversified portfolio.

Trinity applied the same research to other subsets of the stock market—namely, small-cap, mid-cap, and other non-S&P 500 companies—and compared returns over 26-year holding periods. The results were the same: Value-oriented stocks consistently beat the returns of the market. I summarize their research in Figures 2-2 and 2-3.

FIGURE 2-3   Value versus growth stocks, by index (1969–1994).
Source: AIMR, 1995 Proceedings.

	S&P 500	Value Stocks	Growth Stocks	Difference
S&P 500	10.1%	11.4%	9.2%	2.2%
Index of 1000 Stocks	10.1%	11.4%	8.7%	2.7%
Large-Cap Stocks	10.1%	10.4%	8.8%	1.6%
Mid-Cap Stocks	10.1%	12.1%	8.4%	3.7%
Small-Cap Stocks	10.1%	13.3%	6.4%	6.9%

Trinity CEO Stanford Calderwood offered further explanations of this disparity. Over the past 70 years, dividends have constituted roughly half of investors' yearly returns. Since many value strategies emphasize dividends, value-oriented managers put less pressure on themselves to attain high returns from capital gains. Managers who wish to achieve high yearly returns without dividends must rely much more heavily on a good market and, I must add, clever stock picking. If the market rises 9 percent a year, value-focused managers who buy stocks yielding 4.5 percent need only a 4.5 percent average increase in share price to satisfy their goal. A fund manager who avoids dividend-paying stocks must obtain capital gains that on average double the value managers' returns. Furthermore, growth investors likely harm their returns by relying on estimates and forecasts, whereas value investors do not.

> Value managers place little dependence on what the future holds. In contrast, the information growth managers use is based primarily on forecasts—and history shows that these forecasts are not very reliable. . . . The value investment approach focuses on known fundamentals and seeks to identify not future rewards, but present value: below-market P/Bs and P/Es and above-market dividend yields. The driving determinants for value stocks are solid data with a history of being reasonably accurate. . . . Growth investors focus on favorable expectations—expected high short-term and long-term growth in earnings per share—and they are dependent on forecasting market and general market scenarios. . . . The academic literature is replete with studies showing the inaccuracy of earnings estimates.[2]

[2] Stanford Calderwood, "The Positive Bias for Value Investors in U.S. Equities," *Association for Investment Management and Research Proceedings*, 1995, pp. 4–13.

Others reckon that value investors do better than growth investors because of psychological factors, specifically, their lowered state of anxiety, and the tendency of stocks to "revert to the mean." Lewis Sanders, CEO of Sanford Bernstein, proposed this argument at a 1995 conference of the Association for Investment Management and Research. He outlined three psychological factors that work in favor of value-oriented investors.[3]

1. *Overvaluation of certainty*—Investors have "an overwhelming affection" for things that are certain. When they stumble across a financial security offering predictable rewards, they tend to consistently overbuy and overpay. Often, however, the rewards aren't certain; they are only perceived that way.

2. *Overreaction to big, but unlikely events*—In the same way people flock to state lotteries offering enormous, but miniscule probabilities of gains, investors pile into assets promising gains beyond what a reasonable person would know are being offered. The biotechnology crazes of 1991 and 1997, the Internet crazes of 1996 and 1998, and the microbrewery craze of 1996 were atrocious examples. Value investors avoided these types of situations—and the crashes that subsequently followed.

3. *Loss aversion*—Because the pain of loss tends to exceed the pleasure of gain, individuals often shun investments where a perception of loss exists. This explains why many individuals buy stocks only when they are rising, since rising prices validate their decision and make them feel part of the crowd. On the other hand, if a stock has a recent track record of providing losses for investors, the public tends to avoid the company for psychological reasons. Yet, the most profitable investments are usually outgrowths of public discouragement.

Sanders argues that this behavioral loop is closed by a process called *mean reversion,* which in financial terms describes the tendency of an asset's price to return to its underlying value. In simple terms, he wrote, "good things get worse; bad things get better." A stock that has suffered from public discouragement ultimately may turn into a strong vehicle for gains. Likewise, a stock or industry bid up to unsustainable levels is destined to crash to at least its mean value. Since value investors are likely to buy at the bottom and growth investors at the top, long-term returns should favor a value methodology.

[3] Lewis Sanders, "The Advantage to Value Investing," *Association for Investment Management and Research Proceedings,* 1995, pp. 28–34.

DAVID DREMAN: BUYING CHEAP WORKS WITHIN INDUSTRIES

In 1996, David Dreman, Chairman of Dreman Value Management and a noted market strategist for the past 20 years, took a different approach. He tested whether investors could obtain market-beating returns by buying the most undervalued stocks within individual industries. Previous studies tested performance across the entire market and found that you can beat the market buying stocks with the lowest financial ratios. Dreman discovered the same effect held for sectors of the market. If you bought, for example, retailers that bear the lowest P/E ratios, you significantly increased your returns over and above what you could have accomplished buying the highest-valued retailers. Dreman measured the performance of 1500 companies taken from 44 industries over a 25-year period (see Figure 2-4). The lowest 20 percent of P/Es within an industry tended to outperform companies bearing the highest P/Es by a wide margin, and beat the market. The 20 percent of companies bearing the lowest P/E ratios returned an annualized 17.7 percent over the 27-year period ending Dec. 31, 1996, versus the market's average of 15.3 percent. Had you, instead, purchased shares of the highest P/E companies within an industry, annualized returns would have been only 12.2 percent. The compounded difference between 17.7 percent and 12.2 percent is staggering. An investor starting with $10,000 would have accumulated roughly $572,000 in 27 years buying low P/E stocks. Buying high P/E stocks that compounded at 12.4 percent turned $10,000 into just $289,000.

Just as important, Dreman found, was the intrinsic merit of holding low P/E stocks in a poor market. The same lowest 20 percent of P/Es fell an average of 6.3 percent in down quarters. High P/E stocks, by contrast, fell an average of 8.6 percent, 37 percent more. The bottom line, according to Dreman:

FIGURE 2-4   Dreman's study of low P/E stocks (annualized returns 1970–1995).
Source: Forbes, *Sept. 23, 1996.*

	Within Industry	Entire Market	Quarterly Bear Market Return
Lowest P/E Quintile	18.0%	18.8%	−6.3%
Highest P/E Quintile	12.4%	12.5%	−8.6%
Market Average	15.1%	15.1%	−7.2%

We can use a low P/E strategy within industries as confidently as for the overall market. . . . Instead of simply buying the cheapest quintile in the market, you can get better diversification by buying the low P/Es across industries. You will get the same advantages in either case: The surprises will work for you rather than against you.[4]

Indeed, another indirect benefit to low P/E investing, Dreman pointed out, is that you can still diversify across industries, if that's your goal, and remain confident that you can beat the market.

Investors have an overwhelming affection for things that are certain. When they stumble across a financial security offering predictable rewards, they tend to consistently overbuy and overpay.

O'SHAUGHNESSY AND "WHAT WORKS"

If several decades of literature espousing value philosophies could not convince Wall Street, then a 1997 work by money manager James O'Shaughnessy should have. O'Shaughnessy painstakingly dissected the performance of hundreds of companies between 1950 and 1994 to find out which financial factors truly delivered consistent market-beating returns. By choosing 44 years of data, O'Shaughnessy eliminated potential bias in the study by bridging periods when growth and value stocks outperformed the market. Growth stocks performed exceptionally well in the 1960s and late 1980s, for example. Value stocks did so in the 1970s and early 1980s. O'Shaughnessy was not out to prove the superiority of one method over another, but what he stumbled upon was enormous in its implications. Like others before him, O'Shaughnessy found that buying stocks trading at low price-to-earnings (P/E), low price-to-book (P/B), and low price-to-sales (P/S) ratios (the three ratios most often used by value fund managers) produces market-beating returns. But he was the first to quantify this advantage over long periods.

The other potentially shattering effect of O'Shaughnessy's research was that it all but invalidated the concept of *efficient markets* (see Chapter

---

[4] David Dreman, "A New Approach to Low-P/E Investing," *Forbes,* Sept. 23, 1996, p. 241.

3), which argues that no individual or investing strategy can beat the market over time. To the contrary, wrote O'Shaughnessy:

> Far from following a random walk, the evidence reveals a purposeful stride. . . . The market clearly and consistently rewards certain attributes (e.g., stocks with low price-to-sales ratios) and clearly and consistently punishes others (e.g., stocks with high price-to-sales ratios).[5]

O'Shaughnessy first tested expected returns based on the P/E ratio at the time of purchase. He assumed that each year investors bought the 50 stocks sporting the highest and lowest P/E ratios and rotated their portfolios as valuations changed. He found almost no difference between the long-term performance of low P/E stocks and the entire universe of stocks. But low P/E ratios made a significant difference when buying large-cap companies. Between 1952 and 1994, large-cap stocks delivered annual returns of 12.6 percent. Low P/E large-cap stocks returned 15.5 percent. When compounded over 43 years, the 2.9 percentage point difference created a portfolio nearly three times as large. By contrast, buying the 50 large-cap companies sporting the highest P/E ratios provided annual returns of only 11.4 percent.

Buying companies based on their price-to-book value, price-to-cash flow, or price-to-sales ratios improved returns even farther. In all three cases, an investor beat the market by a significant margin—usually 2 percentage points or better—buying companies with the lowest ratios (see Figure 2-5). O'Shaughnessy found that the widest variance occurred when buying companies priced at low multiples to their sales. A portfolio of 50 companies with the lowest P/S ratios returned 18.9 percent a year over 43 years, versus 14.6 percent for all stocks regardless of P/S ratio. The advantages of buying companies bearing low P/S ratios are evident when we calculate how $10,000 compounds over 43 years (see Figure 2-6). O'Shaughnessy found significant differences like this across the board, whether studying P/S, P/B, P/E, or price-to-cash flow ratios. In general, lower ratios led to higher returns (see Figure 2-6). Buying at high ratios led to substandard returns.

THE 1994–1997 MARKET RALLY: GROWTH GARNERED THE ATTENTION, BUT VALUE WON

The question we must naturally pose is whether the returns found by Trinity Capital, Dreman, O'Shaughnessy, and others were unusual or perhaps a

---

[5] James P. O'Shaughnessy, *What Works on Wall Street,* New York, McGraw-Hill, 1997, p. 5.

FIGURE 2-5   How $10,000 compounds buying low price-to-sales stocks.

Year	All Stocks at 14.6%	Low P/S Stocks at 18.9%
1	$11,460	**$11,890**
5	$19,766	**$23,763**
10	$39,070	**$56,470**
15	$77,227	**$134,192**
20	$152,648	**$318,887**
25	$301,728	**$757,786**
30	$596,401	**$1,800,759**
35	$1,178,858	**$4,279,223**
40	$2,330,154	**$10,168,905**
41	$2,670,357	**$12,090,828**
42	$3,060,229	**$14,375,994**
43	$3,507,023	**$17,093,057**

FIGURE 2-6   The relationship between ratios and returns.
Source: What Works on Wall Street.

	Annual Return 1952–1994
All Stocks	14.6%
50 Stocks with Lowest Price/Book Ratios	**17.5%**
50 Stocks with Highest P/B	11.9%
50 Large Caps with Lowest P/B Ratios	**16.3%**
50 Large Caps with Highest P/B	12.3%
50 Stocks with Lowest Price/Cash Flow Ratios	**17.1%**
50 Stocks with Highest P/CF	10.8%
50 Large Caps with Lowest P/CF	**16.5%**
50 Large Caps with Highest P/CF	12.0%
50 Stocks with Lowest Price/Sales Ratios	**18.9%**
50 Stocks with Highest P/S	8.2%
50 Large Caps with Lowest P/S	**15.7%**
50 Large Caps with Highest P/S	11.0%

by-product of simpler market times. Despite overwhelming evidence to the contrary, many researchers still believe the market is unbeatable in the long term. To them, whatever inefficiencies existed in the past have since disappeared. With millions of investors watching the market, each capable of retrieving material information about a company within seconds via computer, surely it must be impossible to obtain abnormally good returns anymore. Yet I can say conclusively that the same relationships Dreman and O'Shaughnessy found continue to exist. To prove that the methodology remains valid, I tested the performance of stocks during one of the strongest market rallies in history—the November 1994 to mid-1997 rally—and found results strikingly similar to what O'Shaughnessy found has occurred since the early 1950s.

Hundreds of news articles during the mid-1990s foretold the death of value investing and championed the growth and momentum schools of investing. Yet the best-performing stocks during the late-1994 to mid-1997 period were stocks that traded at the lowest price-to-earnings, price-to-book value, and price-to-sales ratios (see Figure 2-7). I began by isolating S&P 500 stocks on Dec. 1, 1994, three weeks after Republicans won control of Congress and the stock market began a three-year rally. I tracked the performance of these companies to June 1, 1997, a 31-month period during which the index rose an astounding 85.3 percent. Over this period, the stock market best rewarded growth companies bought at a value, not at a big premium to earnings. The S&P 500 stocks that had the lowest P/E ratios in November 1994 outdistanced the returns of other stocks by a wide margin. Those stocks trading at a P/E ratio of under 7.0 gained an average of 228.3 percent over that period, compared to 85.3 percent for the entire index. Stocks sporting P/E ratios between 7 and 10 gained 100.4 percent on average. Returns fell sharply, however, when an investor bought stocks trading at higher P/E ratios. S&P 500 companies trading at P/E ratios above 30 on Dec. 1, 1994, returned an average of only 57.9 percent over the following 31 months. In normal markets, this return would have been exceptional, but from 1994 to 1997, it was mediocre, a situation investors brought upon themselves by overpaying for companies.

This relationship held when testing price-to-book value ratios for the same large-capitalization companies over the same period. S&P 500 companies that traded for less than their net worth (a P/B ratio under 1.00) on Dec. 1, 1994, returned an average of 152.1 percent by June 1, 1997, nearly double the index's return. Returns fell sharply as premiums to book value rose, with the exception of stocks that traded at P/B ratios between 2.00 and 2.49. This subset contained many technology companies, such as Intel and

FIGURE 2-7   Performance of S&P 500 stocks, Dec. 1994–June 1997 (return based on price/earnings ratio).

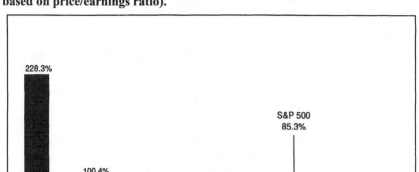

Cisco Systems, that were in the midst of explosive earnings growth, and a host of leading industrial companies that had artificially depressed their book values—and raised P/B ratios—by taking restructuring charges (see Chapter 11 for a more detailed interpretation of book value ratios).

The relationship between price-to-sales ratios and returns was not as strongly correlated during the 1994–1997 period. In fact, stocks trading at high P/S ratios tended to outperform the general index, a fact that can be explained only by the powerful rally in high-technology companies that tend to trade perpetually at high P/S ratios. Still, stocks sporting the lowest P/S ratios at the end of 1994 posted an average return of nearly 100 percent, beating the index by 14 percentage points.

Indeed, one conclusion we can draw from this experiment is the worthiness of buying growth at a discount. The best way to have ensured market-beating performance during the 1994–1997 period was to purchase companies at the lowest possible price relative to earnings, sales, and net worth. Detractors may point to a number of reasons why value-oriented stocks may have done better. Recall that in 1994, financial stocks hit a significant bottom and began an incredible rally as interest rates declined. Many of these companies, including Chase Manhattan Bank, J.P. Morgan, Merrill Lynch, Wells Fargo Bank, CIGNA, First Chicago, and dozens of regional banks, traded at P/E ratios below 10 in 1994. By mid-1997, their P/E ratios had more than doubled; for example, the average regional bank traded at 20 times earnings. Interest rates fell, bank earnings exploded, and investors rewarded these companies with higher and higher valuations. Many cyclical companies likewise traded at P/E ratios below 10 in 1994 amid recession fears that lingered, in some cases, well into 1997. Clearly these stocks suffered from forecasting bias.

Looking back at the types of stocks that rallied most, we can say without question that the market reinforced one of the core themes of value investing: to ignore forecasts and buy when the public has turned its back on good companies. Banks and cyclicals such as DuPont, Caterpillar, and Ford could not have rallied as much from 1995 through 1997 if the general public had not so diligently flogged them in 1994. Ford and other heavy industrial companies were sold during 1994 because of fears of a recession that never materialized. As the economy kept growing, the public came to realize it had wrongly disinvested in auto stocks and bid them to new highs. Bank stocks plunged in early 1994 owing to several interest rate hikes initiated by the Federal Reserve Board and widespread concerns over the federal budget deficit (which in the end shrank), rising inflation (which dissipated), and an economic slowdown (which never occurred).

YOU CAN'T IGNORE ANECDOTAL EVIDENCE

Finally, we have the track record of value investors themselves to validate the superiority of the method. It is no coincidence that many of the great money managers of the twentieth century and many of today's top-performing fund managers hail from the value camp. Nearly all of the money managers who have consistently beaten the market use variations of the blueprint created 65 years ago by Benjamin Graham.

In 1984, Warren Buffett was asked to speak at Columbia University on the fiftieth anniversary of the publication of Benjamin Graham's and David Dodd's *Security Analysis;* the topic: whether financial markets were efficient, as leading academics argued. For years, academics had placed Buffett and other value investors in the category of "six-sigma events," people who owe their fortune to random chance rather than intellectual prowess. To the academics who judged him, Buffett was merely the one person out of 10 million who happened to flip a nickel and drop 15 heads in a row. Buffett countered their attacks. If his success was due to chance, Buffett asked, how could they explain the fact that the most successful investors all studied Graham's value methods? Surely this was no statistical coincidence, Buffett suggested:

In this group of successful investors that I want to consider, there has been a common intellectual patriarch, Ben Graham. But the children who left the house of this intellectual patriarch have called their flips in very different ways. They have gone to different places and bought and sold different stocks and companies, yet they have had a combined record that simply can't be explained by random chance. . . . The common intellectual theme of the investors of Graham-and-Doddsville is this: they search for discrepancies between the value of a business and the price of small pieces of that business in the market. . . . Our Graham-and-Dodd investors, needless to say, do not discuss beta, the capital asset pricing model, or covariance in returns among securities. These are not subjects of any interest to them. In fact, most of them would have difficulty defining those terms. The investors simply focus on two variables: price and value.[6]

Indeed, what sets great investors apart from the crowd is their willingness to shun most of the accepted dogmas and theories Wall Street foists upon the public. Interestingly, many great value investors do not hail from New York City. Nor did they see a need to gravitate to Wall Street or another financial center. They came from midsized towns across America and conquered Wall Street, having learned their brand of patience hundreds of miles away.

MICHAEL PRICE'S AGGRESSIVE VALUE APPROACH

In 1974, after graduating from the University of Oklahoma, Michael Price took a modest-paying position working for Max Heine at Heine's Mutual Shares fund. The two developed an instinct for locating undervalued companies and scoring quick gains playing companies in liquidation. Through the years, Price's stock picking leaned more and more toward large-cap going concerns, but he remained fixed on grossly undervalued companies. Price's style is piranhalike. With several funds under his direction, he stakes big positions in individual companies, then forces management to make the changes he feels are needed to raise the stock price. His behind-the-scenes maneuvering in 1995 forced Chase Manhattan and Chemical Bank to merge. He would later take similarly hostile, but ultimately profitable, positions toward management at Sunbeam, whose stock soared after it replaced top management, and Dow Jones.

When his funds were smaller, Price focused more on small, undervalued companies and junk bonds. But as money poured into his Mutual series

[6] Benjamin Graham, *The Intelligent Investor,* 4th ed., New York, Harper Business, 1972, pp. 293–294.

FIGURE 2-8   Record of top value fund managers.

Source: Morningstar Inc.

	1990	1991	1992	1993	1994	1995	1996	1997
Michael Price	−9.8%	21.0%	21.3%	21.0%	4.6%	29.1%	20.8%	26.4%
Mario Gabelli	−5.8%	18.1%	14.9%	21.8%	−0.2%	24.9%	13.4%	38.1%
David Schafer	−10.1%	40.9%	18.7%	24.0%	−4.3%	34.2%	23.2%	29.3%
Ruane and Cuniff	−3.8%	40.0%	9.4%	10.8%	3.3%	41.4%	21.7%	42.3%
John Neff	−15.5%	28.6%	16.5%	19.4%	−0.1%	30.2%		
S&P 500	−3.1%	30.5%	7.6%	10.1%	1.3%	37.5%	23.0%	33.4%

of funds in the mid-1990s, he channeled more resources toward large-cap turnaround plays such as General Motors, Sunbeam, Philip Morris, Dow Jones, and McDonnell Douglas. His eight-year track record at his flagship Mutual Shares Z from 1990–1997 exceeded that of nearly all other equity fund managers (see Figure 2-8).

JOHN NEFF'S "WOEBEGONE" APPROACH

For 31 years, Neff piloted the Windsor fund, now part of the Vanguard family, and turned it into one of the strongest-performing funds before he retired in December 1995. Over those 31 years, the Windsor fund beat the S&P 500 twenty-one times and sported a compounded annual return of 13.7 percent, versus only 10.6 percent for the index. Neff's stodgy style reflected his Ohio roots and disdain for Wall Street's cutthroat sales bias. He staked money on what he called "dull and woebegone" companies that brokers shunned and the media held in disrepute, if they paid attention to the company at all. While a student at the University of Toledo, Neff studied and adopted Graham's methods and never strayed far from the master after that. Like Graham, Neff looked for certainty of returns and tended to buy companies with dividend yields much higher than the market average. The strategy reflected his conservatism and allowed Neff to rely less on bull markets and capital gains to obtain good returns. During Neff's tenure, dividends accounted for about 40 percent of the fund's total return. Neff also emphasized a company's balance sheet (debt levels, liquidity, and returns on equity), another holdover from Graham, and was reluctant to buy high P/E stocks regardless of market conditions or the company's growth rate. He fished the bottom on occasion, as when he placed big bets on down-and-out auto companies, airlines, and banks in the 1980s. Neff demonstrated great patience, often holding shares in a company for years if that's what it took for the market to appreciate the company's hidden value. Once the market bid up the company to a fair price, Neff sold.

MARIO GABELLI'S "BREAK-UP VALUE" APPROACH

The outspoken Gabelli, the founder of Gabelli Asset Management in Rye, New York, is among the most astute business appraisers in the industry, a signature crafted early in his career as an auto parts and broadcasting analyst. Broadcasting remains his specialty, and Gabelli is not averse to loading up his family of mutual funds with media, broadcasting, and niche telephone service companies. A Bronx native, Gabelli is at heart a bottoms-up analyst—he values businesses based on their expected cash flow, then determines whether the stock can rise appreciably over the next few years to at least its cash-flow value. His style combines several value approaches, and he places a great deal of emphasis on the quality of management and other intangible factors. Gabelli also has developed a specialty in break-up analysis. He appraises companies based on what their major divisions could sell for individually. Gabelli looks for a company capable of returning 50 percent within two years and is wont to hold a company at least that long to give the market time to reprice the company. But unlike Graham and the early value investors, who relied heavily on annual reports and avoided scuttlebutt, Gabelli is known for practicing due diligence and will amass as much information as he can on a company and its industry before investing.

DAVID SCHAFER'S "RELATIVE VALUE" APPROACH

Indiana-bred Schafer, founder of Schafer Capital Management and manager of the Strong Schafer Value fund, has built an enviable track record in the 1990s following a strict, disciplined strategy. Schafer tends to focus on large-cap companies and believes in keeping his portfolio rather small. Typically, his fund will hold no more than 30 to 35 large-cap stocks, each equally weighted. The secret to his success has been discipline, his focus on the most successful companies, and his ability to cherry pick large-cap companies with the best growth prospects. Schafer's basic strategy is to find companies whose earnings can grow faster than the S&P 500 but whose P/E ratios are below the index. If the index trades at a P/E of 20 and earnings for stocks within the index are growing at 10 percent rates, Schafer looks for stocks within that index with P/Es under 20 and earnings growth of at least 10 percent. This strategy, when successful, leads to returns that beat the index.

WILLIAM RUANE AND THE SEQUOIA FUND

Ruane, who has comanaged the Sequoia fund with Richard Cuniff since 1970, practices a form of value investing as similar to Warren Buffett's style as anyone in the business. They created the fund at the behest of Buffett, who had closed his investing partnership but wanted to recommend a fund for his clients. Ruane and Cuniff, in fact, load their fund with many of the same companies Buffett purchased for Berkshire Hathaway. The fund's results have validated their allegiance. For the 15-year period ending December 1997, Sequoia fund returned a compounded 19.5 percent a year, almost 2 percentage points ahead of the S&P 500. Ruane and Cuniff tend to hold the average stock four to five years to minimize tax effects and give their stocks time to appreciate fully. In a typical year, the fund may hold less than 20 securities—and likely will hold each for several years. The fund's largest holdings in 1997 were Berkshire Hathaway, Federal Home Loan Mortgage, Wells Fargo Bank, Walt Disney, Johnson & Johnson, Harley-Davidson, Fifth Third Bancorp, and Region's Financial Corp. One glance at this roster tells you that Ruane and Cuniff try to assemble large-cap companies with strong franchises. The fund's market-beating performance attracted so much attention and money that Ruane and Cuniff closed Sequoia to new investors in 1982, after accumulating $350 million in assets under management.

WALTER SCHLOSS'S SPARTAN APPROACH

New York-based money manager Walter Schloss combined Graham's puritan style of analysis with Buffett's spartan approach to fashion one of the most successful track records of any investor over the past four decades. From a small Manhattan office, the 81-year-old Schloss and his son, Edwin, have beaten the market since the mid-1950s using only the most basic tools of the trade: annual reports. They are living proof of the assertion that mom-and-pop investors can beat the market if they avoid risk and don't allow misleading information to cloud their decisions. Schloss has remained fiercely loyal to Graham's principles of buying companies priced below book value and holding them until the market recognizes its error. The key to successful investing, Schloss maintains, is to properly value a company's assets, since companies can easily manipulate earnings through accounting adjustments. Like Graham, Schloss puts little faith in earnings estimates or the guidance of management and avoids contacting companies before investing. His track record in the 1970s, during one of the most difficult market periods in history, cemented his place as one of the leading money managers of this century. Through 1997, Schloss earned a compounded 20 percent per year, versus 11 percent for the market. Operating as a limited partnership, Schloss charges a management fee of 25 percent of profits, but the father-and-son team refuses fees during losing years. The yearly results shown in Figure 2-9 below are net of fees.

TWEEDY, BROWNE'S OBEDIENCE TO GRAHAM

The partners at New York-based Tweedy Browne have practiced Graham's methods to the letter since 1958, when one of Graham's protégés, Tom Knapp, left his mentor and joined the Browne family's investing partnership. Tweedy, Browne continues to employ Graham's strict discipline of buying companies priced less than their net current assets or book value. The firm tends to focus on small, undervalued companies and prefers to buy them when insiders also are buying shares. Like Graham, the partners at Tweedy, Browne will not buy a company priced at high multiples to earnings, and they look for stocks whose earnings yields (the reciprocal of P/E

FIGURE 2-9   Walter & Edwin Schloss Ltd.
Source: Walter & Edwin Schloss Associates, L.P.

	Returns	S&P 500	Difference		Returns	S&P 500	Difference
1956	5.1%	6.6%	−1.5%	1977	25.8%	−7.2%	33.0%
1957	−4.7%	−10.8%	6.1%	1978	36.6%	6.6%	30.0%
1958	42.1%	43.4%	−1.3%	1979	29.8%	18.4%	11.4%
1959	17.5%	12.0%	5.5%	1980	23.3%	32.4%	−9.1%
1960	7.0%	0.5%	6.5%	1981	18.4%	−4.9%	23.3%
1961	21.6%	26.9%	−5.3%	1982	24.1%	21.4%	2.7%
1962	8.3%	−8.7%	17.0%	1983	38.4%	22.5%	15.9%
1963	15.1%	22.8%	−7.7%	1984	6.3%	6.3%	0.0%
1964	17.1%	16.5%	0.6%	1985	19.5%	32.2%	−12.7%
1965	26.8%	12.5%	14.4%	1986	11.9%	18.5%	−6.6%
1966	0.5%	−10.1%	10.6%	1987	20.2%	5.2%	15.0%
1967	25.8%	24.0%	1.8%	1988	29.8%	16.8%	13.0%
1968	26.6%	11.1%	15.5%	1989	2.2%	31.5%	−29.3%
1969	−9.0%	−8.5%	−0.5%	1990	−12.8%	−3.2%	−9.6%
1970	−8.2%	4.0%	−12.2%	1991	31.1%	30.4%	0.7%
1971	25.5%	14.3%	11.2%	1992	9.2%	7.7%	1.5%
1972	11.6%	19.0%	−7.4%	1993	20.2%	9.9%	10.3%
1973	−8.0%	−14.7%	6.7%	1994	11.4%	1.3%	10.1%
1974	−6.2%	−26.5%	20.3%	1995	21.2%	37.5%	−16.3%
1975	42.7%	37.2%	5.5%	1996	16.6%	23.0%	−6.4%
1976	29.4%	23.8%	5.6%	1997	22.6%	33.4%	−10.8%

FIGURE 2-10   Charles Brandes—Global Equity account.
Source: Brandes Investment Partners L.P.

	Returns	S&P 500	Difference
1980	34.3%	32.5%	1.8%
1981	13.6%	−4.9%	18.5%
1982	29.9%	21.5%	8.4%
1983	39.9%	22.7%	17.2%
1984	7.1%	6.3%	0.8%
1985	35.6%	31.8%	3.8%
1986	20.9%	18.7%	2.2%
1987	−2.5%	5.3%	−7.8%
1988	26.0%	16.6%	9.4%
1989	13.1%	31.7%	−18.7%
1990	−11.8%	−3.1%	−8.7%
1991	37.1%	30.5%	6.6%
1992	12.2%	7.6%	4.6%
1993	39.7%	10.1%	29.6%
1994	−0.2%	1.3%	−1.5%
1995	20.8%	37.5%	−16.7%
1996	22.4%	23.0%	−0.6%
1997	27.6%	33.4%	−5.8%

ratios) are competitive with corporate bond yields. Using this "margin of safety" approach, Tweedy, Browne has assembled a strong track record since the mid-1970s. A $10,000 investment in their equity portfolio in 1975 would have grown to $360,000 by 1995, versus $158,000 invested in the S&P 500. In December 1993, the partners created a publicly traded open-end mutual fund, Tweedy, Browne American Value. After its first five years, the fund established itself as one of the few that could keep pace with a frenzied market.

CHARLES BRANDES AND MODERN GRAHAM REVISITED
San Diego-based money manager Charles Brandes has posted an impressive track record of performance since 1974, remaining steadfastly faithful to Graham and Dodd's valuation principles. Brandes, also a noted author, preys upon companies that are priced in the market far below their intrinsic value. Like Graham, Brandes requires a wide margin of safety when

prospecting for companies and is willing to hold a stock three years or more to optimize its appreciation potential. He emphasizes stocks bearing low price-to-book value, price-to-sales, and price-to-earnings ratios and those with dividend yields that are competitive with corporate bond yields. Unlike other value-oriented managers, Brandes sets sell targets on his stocks when he buys them and believes in selling a company once its shares have risen back to the company's intrinsic value. Brandes had a difficult time keeping pace with the growth-oriented mid-1990s market, as have many other value-oriented managers. Still, a $10,000 investment in his Global Equity account in 1980 would have returned nearly $241,000 by the end of 1997, versus $173,000 for a similar investment in the S&P 500 index (see Figure 2-10).

WARREN BUFFETT'S "GROWTH AT A VALUE" APPROACH

At the top of mountain stands Nebraska native Warren Buffett, who worked for Graham in the 1950s, championed his value principles, and built the most impressive investing track record ever. A natural at valuing assets and identifying and exploiting mispriced stocks, Buffett opened a private investment partnership in 1957 with $100 of his own money, $105,000 scraped together from family friends, and the supreme confidence he could

FIGURE 2-11   Buffett Partnership, Ltd.
Source: Warren E. Buffett.

	Returns	DJIA	Difference
1957	10.4%	−8.4%	18.8%
1958	40.9%	38.5%	2.4%
1959	25.9%	20.0%	5.9%
1960	22.8%	−6.2%	29.0%
1961	45.9%	22.4%	23.5%
1962	13.9%	−7.6%	21.5%
1963	38.7%	20.6%	18.1%
1964	27.8%	18.7%	9.1%
1965	47.2%	14.2%	33.0%
1966	20.4%	−15.6%	36.0%
1967	35.9%	19.3%	16.6%
1968	58.8%	7.7%	51.1%
1969	6.8%	−11.6%	18.4%

beat the market by a wide margin. He folded the partnership in 1969, claiming he could no longer find enough undervalued stocks, and left a 13-year stock-picking legacy that may never be equaled. Buffett beat the major market indexes all 13 years, and by incredible margins. Buffett's stock-picking methods, detailed in Chapter 15, fuse value and growth styles. He built a $35 billion fortune buying strong undervalued growth companies capable of generating inflation-beating results over long periods. Early in his career, he sopped up shares in industrial companies selling at three and four times their earnings. Later, he bought controlling stakes in a number of companies and brought them under the umbrella of his holding company, Omaha-based Berkshire Hathaway. These acquisitions supplied the cash flow Buffett needed to further his investments. As Berkshire's holdings grew in value, Buffett adopted a buy-and-hold approach and concentrated on large companies such as American Express, Wells Fargo, Walt Disney, Gillette, and Coca-Cola. An investment of $10,000 in Buffett's original partnership in 1957 grew to roughly $289,000 by 1969. A similar investment in the Dow Jones industrial stocks would have returned just $25,000 (see Figure 2-11).

C H A P T E R

3

BEATING AN IRRATIONAL MARKET

"I'd be a bum on the street with a tin cup if the market were always efficient."

Warren Buffett[1]

N INVESTING, OPPORTUNITIES ARISE when you counter prevailing wisdom, no matter how deeply ingrained those opinions. Value investing, as a philosophy, occasionally relies on your ability to sell when the crowd wants to buy, to buy when they sell, or to cast a skeptical eye when events appear rosy. No task is more difficult, even for a seasoned investor. It's like telling you not to bet at a slot machine that has paid out 10 times in the last hour or to avoid a stock that has raced up 100 percent in two months.

Value investing, in essence, is as much a character trait as a methodology—a mentality shaped by experience, knowledge, and the desire to excel at investing. A pure value investor is a pure value seeker, a person unwilling to spend more than absolutely necessary on any good, be it a dinner, a bar of soap, a new car, a house, or a new blouse.

What's the difference between a value-oriented person and one who is not? The differences manifest themselves in everyday events:

- A value investor will rent a movie for $3 rather than race to the theater and pay $7.50 per person plus concessions.

[1] Warren Buffett, *Fortune,* April 3, 1995, p. 69.

- A value investor waits for Honda or Ford to offer rebates on a new car rather than pay $2000 more for the auto when everyone else wants one.
- A value investor buys a generic brand of cereal for $3.50 a box rather than a brand name, with identical ingredients, selling for $4.99.
- A value investor buys a winter suit in the spring at 50 percent off rather than paying top price when others rush to the stores.
- A value investor might pass up a Beenie Baby doll priced at $30 and buy a generic version of the toy that excites a child no less.

Do these examples of consumer behavior relate to investing? Absolutely. In each of the cases, the value-conscious consumer discovered a way to buy an asset at a reduced price or found an equivalent substitute selling for less. This type of behavior shouldn't be mistaken for being cheap. It reflects, instead, a desire to pay no more than a "fair price" for a good. Of course, the concept of fair price is elusive and highly subjective. To set a fair price, one must judge a good's worth before buying. In deciding to rent rather than buy a movie, the consumer must decide that $7.50 is too much to pay but that $3 is not. Likewise, the consumer scoffs at a $22,000 Taurus but finds a $20,000 sticker price two months later quite acceptable.

Indeed, all of these examples share a common theme: Buying a good for a lower price—or buying an identical substitute—is preferable to purchasing the same thing at a higher price.

THE STOCK MARKET: WHERE PEOPLE WANT HIGHER PRICES

The stock market is a peculiar institution, the only one in the world where participants feel more secure buying an expensively priced item than one reasonably valued. They seek confirmation from the actions of other traders and feel more confident buying a stock the public craves. They are taught to buy securities showing technical strength, those closing at a new high, exhibiting strong volume, or pushing through a moving average. And the industry induces them to measure a company's worth solely by its stock price. To most investors, a rising price indicates improvement in the company's intrinsic value, and a declining price represents the opposite.

The stock market acts as a conduit that shapes these misperceptions. Its primary function is to serve as a central marketplace where people around the world can shop for financial goods. Wall Street offers thousands of goods for sale each day at prices that constantly change. It's like a giant flea market for stocks, where demand is so exacerbated that no price holds for more than a few moments. One minute, a "good" called Hewlett-Packard sells for $60 a share; the next, $61. Come back in two days and someone may offer Hewlett-Packard to you at $65, or $64, or $54. Price is transitory in the stock market, and everyone, buyer and seller alike, has an opportunity to set the price at which he or she wishes to trade. There are no SKUs in this market, no checkout aisles, no seasonal markdowns that last through next Sunday. Goods trade at whatever prices the last person believed they were worth.

The stock market is a peculiar institution, the only one in the world where participants feel more secure buying an expensively priced item than one reasonably valued.

In older times, such "open outcry" markets flourished; we traded fish, spices, silks, and animals in great outdoor forums. To the extent that these markets brought together buyers and sellers in one location to exchange information and compare goods and prices, they were *efficient.* But these markets were never rational, nor could they ever be. Prices were arbitrary, subject to supply and demand and traders' *perceptions* of quality and risk. In addition, they suffered from what economists call *information asymmetry,* the fact that buyers and sellers do not possess the same information. A seller of Persian rugs may know that a glut of rugs exists and that great piles of them sit in a warehouse 50 miles away. An unwitting buyer may pay more for a rug than it is probably worth. Likewise, someone who sells a 1955 Mickey Mantle baseball card may be unaware of the card's rarity and may offer it for only $100, though an astute buyer might be willing to pay $5000. Similarly, buyers of corn may pay a premium for a bushel because they know of a torrential rain approaching that could destroy some of the region's planted crop.

There are many who believe the stock market—unlike the spice markets of yesterday—is rational, that prices are efficient, and that no bargains can ever exist. With so many millions of people worldwide studying the market, the theory goes, no stock can ever sell for more or less than its true worth, because if it did, other participants would quickly discover the price discrepancy and bid the shares to their rightful price. This argument was first put forth more than 50 years ago and has been many times since, but never as eloquently as by economist and Nobel Laureate Paul Samuelson:

If intelligent people are constantly shopping around for good value, selling those stocks they think will turn out to be overvalued and buying those they expect are now undervalued, the result of this action by intelligent investors will be to have existing stock prices already have discounted in them an allowance for their future prospects. Hence, to the passive investor, who does not himself search out for under- and overvalued situations, there will be presented a pattern of stock prices that makes one stock about as good or bad a buy as another. To that passive investor, chance alone would be as good a method of selection as anything else.[2]

Samuelson's contention, in a nutshell, is that investors cannot consistently benefit from timing the purchase and sale of stocks because no stock can stay mispriced for very long, if at all. Hence, all technical analysis—which uses price and volume data to time the purchase and sale of stocks—and all fundamental analysis is useless and provides the investor no benefit. Latter-day market strategists have taken Samuelson one step further and proclaim that the stock market is perfectly rational and efficient, that all stock prices are fair and reflect consensus opinions about a company's prospects. Since the consensus possesses all relevant information about a company, its conclusions cannot be wrong. Thus, stock prices reflect the intrinsic worth of the company at all times. Whether a stock such as IBM trades at 20 times earnings or 12 times earnings is irrelevant, according to this *efficient market theory,* or EMT. In both circumstances, IBM's price was rationally obtained from the interchange of buyers and sellers who were assumed to possess enough information to value IBM fairly.

This naturally begs the question: How can any company be fairly valued at 20 times earnings at one point in time and 12 times earnings at another? According to the EMT, such seemingly random price levels can be explained away by events that reduced or increased IBM's intrinsic value. Interest rates may have changed, the economy may have weakened, the computer sector may be experiencing an inventory imbalance, demand for PCs may be rising, IBM may have fired its CEO and replaced him, etc., etc., etc. Each new bit of information and its impact on IBM is absorbed immediately by market participants and the stock price adjusted. The sum total of all these events may mean that IBM's intrinsic worth declines drastically in just a few months. Therefore, it is only rational to assume that IBM's trading price falls to reflect the destruction of intrinsic value.

Parts of the EMT have merit. The stock market—the exchange itself—

---

[2] Burton G. Malkiel, *A Random Walk Down Wall Street,* 5th ed., New York, W. W. Norton & Co., 1990, p. 182.

is an efficient mechanism for conducting trades. Anyone who wants to participate can at any time pick up the phone and trade the stock of his choice at the price offered. It doesn't matter whether you're a $1 billion pension-fund manager, a schoolteacher, a retiree, or a PGA pro calling from a cellular phone on the ninth fairway. Anyone can participate.

But that's where efficiency stops. To accept that the market is rational is to turn over the reins to an invisible hand, to throw in the towel and acknowledge that you can't beat the system. It's like saying, "Don't strive for an A in biology because Mr. Higgenbothem has a reputation for never giving them." That's a patent recipe for mediocrity. The stock market, you must accept, is ruled as much by emotion as any other factor. Most of the time, it is neither ordinary, rational, nor fair. Rather, it reflects the random action of thousands of players making buy-and-sell decisions to attain unique goals. Each $\frac{1}{8}$-point change in a stock's price reflects what John Burr Williams, writing in 1938, deemed a *marginal opinion,* what one buyer and one seller agreed upon in one moment of time, nothing more. Williams argued that the market is really comprised of millions of fickle participants and cannot be viewed as a single entity whose output reflects a collective, consensus wisdom:

> Let us assume for a moment that the market contains only a single stock, and that none but investors buy and sell shares of this issue. Concerning its true worth, every man will cherish his own opinion; as to what price really is right, time only will tell. Time will not give its answer all at once, though, but only slowly, word by word, as the years go by. . . . The market can only be an expression of opinion, not a statement of fact. Today's opinion will make today's price; tomorrow's opinion, tomorrow's price; and seldom if ever will any price be exactly right as proven by the event.
>
> Both wise men and foolish men will trade in the market, but no one group by itself will set the price. Nor will it matter what the majority, however overwhelming, may think; for the last owner, and he alone, will set the price.[3]

Four years earlier, Benjamin Graham had hinted as much when he first presented the idea that market prices are set by the psychology of supply and demand:

> Evidently the processes by which the securities market arrives at its appraisals are frequently illogical and erroneous. These processes . . . are not automatic or mechanical, but psychological, for they go on in the

[3] John Burr Williams, *The Theory of Investment Value,* reprint of 1938 ed., Burlington, VT, Fraser Publishing Co., 1997, pp. 11–12.

minds of people who buy or sell. The mistakes of the market are thus mistakes of groups or masses of individuals. Most of them can be traced to one or more of three basic causes: exaggeration, oversimplification, or neglect.[4]

There's no disputing that stocks become mispriced owing to factors that textbooks can't explain. Consider how a typical stock—Exxon—might trade. An investor buys 100 shares of Exxon because he thinks the stock has dropped enough and is fairly priced. He is matched up against someone whose broker just convinced her to sell 100 shares. The next buyer of Exxon holds extra cash in her brokerage account and wants more dividends. She gets matched against a street-savvy technician whose computer just told him Exxon is overbought. The next trade is initiated by a father who needs to sell 500 shares of Exxon to help pay for his daughter's wedding. He's matched against a widow who just read a news article about Exxon and is impressed enough to place a 500-share buy order. The next trade, a buy order for 5000 shares, comes from a small business owner diversifying her employees' 401(k) plan. On the opposite side sits a mutual fund trying to dump a portion of its 60,000 shares of Exxon to lessen its exposure to energy stocks.

Demand is driven by psychological forces unique to each trader. Information becomes merely the excuse to place the order.

On and on it goes, a 6½-hour-a-day barter system initiated by investors whose interests, goals, limitations, access to news, and interpretation of events are as unique as fingerprints. Realistically, only 5 percent of the people buying and selling Exxon that day analyzed the company's prospects and placed a value on the company's shares. The remaining 95 percent used a tidbit of information as an excuse to act out a prevailing emotion or financial need. None of this suggests efficiency, but a system that holds stock prices hostage to the ebb and flow of emotion. Supply and demand truly drive prices on a day-to-day basis. Demand is driven by psychological forces unique to each trader. Information becomes merely the excuse to place the order.

[4] Benjamin Graham and David Dodd, *Security Analysis,* reprint of 1934 ed., New York, McGraw-Hill, 1997, p. 585.

At its worst, this outcry system results in organized chaos, panic, and true price inefficiency. Witness what happened in 1997 to Maverick Tube, the St. Louis-based maker of piping for oil wells. Amid a feeding frenzy for oil-drilling companies, Maverick's stock rose from $6 to $50 in nine months, then dropped again to $10 by mid-1998 (see Figure 3-1 below). Yet the company's earnings and net worth didn't rise ninefold. Nor was the subsequent collapse in price justified by fundamentals. Can such volatility be reasonable, or rational? Can one company be worth $6 a share in January, $50 by September, and $10 just seven months later? Absolutely not. We can say that in retrospect Maverick was fairly valued somewhere between those extremes and should not have fluctuated as much as it did. If the public had rationally priced Maverick, the stock might have risen slowly from $5 to $25 and remained at the price level for the next year. Instead, the stock was tugged up and down due to greed, fear, irrationality, and shifting perceptions of the company's prospects.

Was the market efficient in 1996 when Coca-Cola traded at 40 times earnings, even though the company's earnings were expected to grow at only 17 percent rates? If investors accepted Coke's valuation, then they should have questioned whether Microsoft was efficiently priced at *only* 40

FIGURE 3-1   Maverick Tube.

times earnings when earnings were growing at 35 percent rates. Was the pricing of Chase Manhattan efficient when the stock dropped to $12—five times earnings—in 1991 out of panic selling, only to rise above $100 in 1997? What was efficient about the 1993 feeding frenzy surrounding bankrupt LTV Steel, when investors piled in and bid a nearly worthless company up to $3 a share? The shares traded so far beyond the company's intrinsic worth that LTV officials had to issue public statements warning people the shares had no value.

Did General Electric's intrinsic worth increase 150 percent in 1995 and 1996? Judging from the stock price, it did. But was GE's price rational? Only to an EMT adherent. General Electric's earnings rose by only 32 percent during that time, and its shareholder's equity rose by only 38 percent. Yet the stock increased at four times the rate the company increased in value. The only plausible explanation for GE's rally was that its stock was grossly undervalued prior to the rally and merely caught up to GE's earnings trend. But to acknowledge that fact is to acknowledge that GE's stock was inefficiently priced before 1995.

The classic example, of course, occurred in 1987. Was the stock market efficiently priced before, or after, the Oct. 19 crash? Did the intrinsic value of U.S. companies really drop 22 percent in six hours as the stock market suggested? Not at all. Nothing changed in corporate America that tragic day. The economy plodded along as normal, consumers went on their merry ways shopping at retail stores, and assembly line workers kept up their normal pace of production. What changed that day were perceptions, perceptions that stocks had been unreasonably priced.

THE CYCLE OF IRRATIONALITY

We can create a general model of inefficiency from Figure 3-2. Here, I've presented the typical pattern of a company whose stock is alternatively bid above and below the company's intrinsic value. I've assumed that the company's intrinsic worth rises slowly and steadily over a period of years. As is evident from the chart, the stock rarely trades at exactly its intrinsic worth. Most of the time, it is either excessively overvalued or undervalued based on traders' perceptions of events. Such relationships, I pose, exist for nearly every stock that trades. We can break down these alternating price cycles into distinct stages, so numbered in the graphic:

> *Stage 1:* The stock trades at a level below its intrinsic worth owing to a number of factors, some relevant to the company, some not. At this stage, investors may fear that previous earnings disappoint-

FIGURE 3-2   The cycle of irrationality.

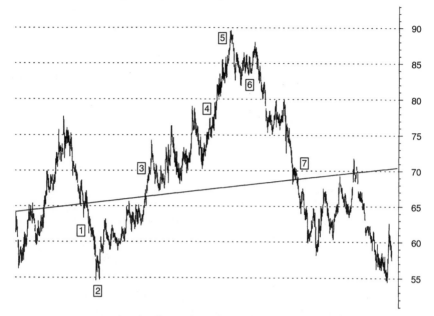

ments may be duplicated, or that a decline in general stock prices
may make investors reluctant to buy. Clearly, the stock price does
not reflect reality. At a price of $60, we can say that the stock
reflects the sum of the company's intrinsic value (approximately
$65) minus a discount ($5) that reflects investors' pessimism.

Stage 2: A state of maximum pessimism is reached, caused by factors
mostly unrelated to the company. While the company's intrinsic
value rises, the stock price declines sharply. At this point, the discount to intrinsic value is greatest; a period of maximum pessimism has been reached.

Stage 3: A general rally begins as traders' perceptions change. Note
that the company continues to increase its own value. But now,
the stock climbs at a rate faster than intrinsic value. At some
point, equilibrium is reached, but the stock rallies past its fair
value.

Stage 4: Following months of rallying and steadily improving perceptions, more and more traders pile onto the stock. Each day's rally
seems to confirm the decision to buy and daily volume is likely
strong. By this time, money managers, eager to flip a hot stock
for 20 percent or 30 percent profits, have jumped in. Buying

begets buying and the stock drifts farther away from its intrinsic value again. Price is now a function of two elements, the intrinsic value and a premium to account for traders' renewed enthusiasm. It's likely the stock's P/E ratio has outstripped its own growth rate, but that is of little consequence to buyers. Whereas months before few investors wanted this stock at, say, 8 times earnings, it is now deemed foolish not to own it at 20 times earnings.

Stage 5: The rally reaches a terminal phase. Daily price movements become more exaggerated and the stock trades so far above its intrinsic value that buyers and sellers must seek exogenous justification for their actions. Some believe the stock is worth this price because of lower interest rates; others seek a takeover premium. Wall Street's brokerages and analysts fuel the rally with buy recommendations based on overly optimistic earnings assumptions. By Stage 5, the past has become irrelevant. Traders bid up shares based on *hoped-for* future earnings.

Stage 6: With the shares priced so far above the company's intrinsic value, the stock is doomed to collapse. Indeed, a general decline begins, usually triggered by a single news event, but it lasts only temporarily, for in the initial stages of decline, many believe a mere correction is at hand and use the "dip" to prop up their positions. The analysts, meanwhile, are silent during the initial decline. They watch the shares tumble but reiterate their buy recommendations. A short-lived rally may follow.

Stage 7: The sell-off reaches torrid proportions. The rate of decline in the share price accelerates, and investors, one by one, turn pessimistic again. Still, they show no concern for intrinsic value, nor do they seem to care that the stock's price is becoming more attractive. They care only that their profits are sliding away and want to avoid the psychological trauma of having sold shares at a loss. At the bottom, the stock trades below its intrinsic value again.

I've seen this remarkable pattern develop hundreds of times through the years. Sometimes, such cycles take years to develop; on other occasions, just a few months. As these cycles progress, those who buy and hold their shares believe their stock purchases were rational and justifiable and that only the actions of others are foolish. What is most extraordinary is that participants never emerge the wiser. They will repeat the pattern another time with another stock. Coached to believe that prices are efficient, they are tempted to buy more shares as the price rises and avoid them as prices fall to a fair value. The wise course of action is to buy the shares only in stages 1, 2, or 3 and consider selling when the shares climb well above their fair value.

The most egregious examples of mispricing occur with cyclical stocks such as Citicorp, Caterpillar, Dow Chemical, and General Motors. These stocks tend to drop precipitously during weak economic times, almost always below their intrinsic values. Why? It's fear mostly. Traders sense the worse and fear being caught holding a stock that may decline indefinitely. But an investor with a knowledge of history knows that cyclical companies post erratic earnings depending on the economy. Dow Chemical's earnings may reach $8 per share in boom periods and $0.50 during recessions. That's a given. Why, then, do investors run from these types of stocks every few years knowing full well that earnings will bounce back? If true efficiency existed in the market, investors would overlook temporary sales setbacks and let Dow and Ford trade at prices that reflected their smoothed, long-term growth rates. But they don't. The same individuals who rush to buy Dow at 20 times earnings during an economic recovery balk at paying just 6 times earnings when the economy is beginning to slide. When a recession does come, you can be sure these same people wouldn't dare touch the Caterpillars of the world. Yet history has shown repeatedly that's precisely the time to buy cyclicals.

Having explored this topic in depth, we can say with utmost confidence that stock prices are not efficient. If they were, what could explain, for example, the *small-cap effect,* the fact that small-cap stocks tend to outperform large-caps over long periods? And what explains the fact that stocks bearing low P/E ratios have consistently outperformed higher P/E stocks, as we showed in Chapter 2? If price efficiency existed, P/E ratios would have no bearing on future price performance. But they do.

If financial markets were as efficient as some academics argue, we would expect that as many fund managers, trust officers, and institutional investors would beat the market as lag it. Since the market would serve as a benchmark to measure performance, then no pro would possess an advantage—50 percent should beat the average and 50 percent should lag it. Yet most pros lose ground to the S&P 500 over time. More than 90 percent of mutual fund managers, for example, lag the S&P 500 over multiyear periods. Obviously, much more is behind these figures than simple randomness. Back in the late 1970s, David Dreman, Chairman of Dreman Value Management, found the most probable answer. Studying the trading habits of the pros from as early as 1929, Dreman found that most institutional investors seemed to lag the market because of a "herd mentality." They tended to follow the market, not lead it, buying familiar stocks their peers bought without regard to price. They ignored stocks other fund managers ignored and jumped on those everyone purchased. Their herd buying was most intense near market tops, Dreman noted, which usually led them to suffer bigger losses than the average investor.

If these investors doom themselves to lag the market, as Dreman suggested, then the argument for efficiency is moot. Moreover, it follows that some investors can beat the market consistently.

A WORD ON INFORMATION ASYMMETRY

Information forms the lifeblood of investors. No matter how polished your analytical skills may be, you must possess timely, objective, and useful information to score successes in the market. The efficient market hypothesis assumes that every market participant has equal access to information and has the ability to screen it accurately and interpret it correctly. But if asymmetry exists, that is, if some investors possess more, or better, information than others, or if that information proves incorrect, then the concept of efficiency breaks down.

In outlining the case against efficient markets, we conclude by noting that most information comes to us in a highly tainted form and has a great bearing on the direction of stock prices. Since most information on which we trade contains some form of "spin," the possibility always exists that our reaction to that information proves erroneous. To advance my case, I offer three suppositions:

Information is not universally available.   The cost to obtain adequate sources of information handicaps most investors. Even today, when millions of investors have access via the Internet to what was once guarded information, they lack access to the types of information that can impact a stock in the near term. Investors cannot visit companies regularly, speak with trade associations, suppliers, distributors, or sit in on conference calls with management.

No two people interpret information identically.   We form our interpretations depending on our perspectives. As shown in the Exxon example earlier, investors trade based on their own financial needs, goals, limitations, access to news, and interpretation of events. Like the weather, we tend to view information in relative terms and from a current context. A 60-degree day in spring feels downright balmy after weeks of 30-degree days. The same 60-degree day in summer, on the heels of 80-degree days, would cause a chill in you. Likewise, a stock that rallies to $60 often seems a better buy than one that falls to $60, though an investor should be indifferent to both circumstances.

Information is usually spoon-fed to investors by people who want to influence the interpretation.   We cannot underestimate the role that Wall Street, the media, and newsmakers play in shaping our opinions and our decisions to invest. Any information that is filtered, and that includes about all that the financial industry generates, creates the potential for price inefficiency. Wall Street twists information innumerable ways: by issuing price targets on stocks, for example, estimating earnings in advance, leaking rumors of takeovers, or upgrading or downgrading companies for the flimsiest of reasons.

The media's desire to win subscribers leads reporters to generate news where none might exist, trumpet hot stocks after their best rallies have passed, or deluge you with articles like "The Top 10 Funds to Buy Now." The vast majority of investors attain their market information secondhand, usually through the media. Thus, they are exposed to the spins and biases already built into news stories. A reporter can severely distort information even with the tone she takes in composing an article. A misleading headline or a reporter's desire to sensationalize a trivial news occurrence can disrupt supply and demand for a stock. Consider the media frenzy created in 1995 when Intel discovered a minor flaw in its Pentium chips. The story first broke over the Internet when spreadsheet users complained to one another that some of their computer calculations were incorrect. Once a reporter discovered the controversy, the Pentium story quickly became the media's crisis of the week. Intel's stock fell sharply as the company devoted considerable time to fending off public criticism. No sooner had the story appeared than it disappeared from the front pages, but not before thousands of investors sold their shares and the market value of Intel's stock dropped by more than $6 billion. Here, investors' optimism over Intel's prospects suddenly turned to pessimism on the basis of trumped-up stories of little significance to Intel's long-term fundamental outlook. Intel quickly recalled the chips, took a quarterly charge against earnings, and put the issue behind it. The stock tripled in price over the next two years.

Investors who are wont to trade based on information are particularly vulnerable to interpretation bias. A favorite example of mine occurred on January 22, 1997, when major media outlets tried to interpret Federal Reserve Chairman Alan Greenspan's remarks before the Senate Budget

Committee. Depending on which news story you read the following day, inflation either was rising or holding steady; the economy either was growing nicely or in danger of overheating; and reporters either were trying to sway your viewpoint or didn't know what to say.

Consider just five of the headlines boiling down Greenspan's testimony that day:

- "Fed Chairman Sees a Pickup in Wages," reported *The Wall Street Journal*. The article said Greenspan hinted he would hike interest rates.
- "Greenspan Upbeat on Economy, Issues Wage Warning," read a headline by Reuters. According to the wire story, Greenspan was satisfied with the pace of economic growth and "gave little indication" the Fed was preparing to raise interest rates.
- "Greenspan Upbeat on Economy," ran *The New York Times*. "But he warns of pay gains," amended the story. "Testimony rallies market."
- "Greenspan Warns of Inflation," read the slug line to a story the Associated Press wired to member newspapers.
- "Fed Pleased but Puzzled," announced CNN's financial news network.

If you were unable to hear Greenspan's unfiltered testimony on cable television, your interpretation of his comments were formed based on what news service you happened on that day. If you picked up the newspaper one morning and the headline read, "Fed Chairman Hints of a Rate Hike," you might try to protect your rate-sensitive stocks by selling shares. But if the newspaper, recounting the same testimony, used the headline, "Fed Comfortable with Current Rates," you might feel relieved and compelled to do nothing.

Bear in mind that before the news of January 22, 1997, trickled down to you, it had been filtered no fewer than four times. First, the reporter would have interpreted Greenspan's remarks and condensed them to a few key points that made readable copy. Then, the reporter would have rendered her objective bias based on the interchange between Greenspan and senators that followed the testimony. If no senator questioned Greenspan on interest rates, the reporter might have concluded that the topic was of little news value and downplayed the story. Next, the reporter would have elicited reaction from experts. Because of deadline pressures, maybe she lacked the time to contact experts who believed rates would fall. Finally, the story would have been filtered at the copy desk, where a news editor and a night copy editor rearranged the article based on what they believed was important. One of them would have topped the story with a headline to summarize—probably in six words or less—what Greenspan said.

USE INEFFICIENCY TO YOUR ADVANTAGE

The information assembly line can severely alter our perceptions and cause us to take actions that lead to price inefficiency. But it's to your advantage that so many investors, including many "pros," believe in an efficient market, that a stock trading at 50 times earnings is fairly valued, and that the market can't be beaten. As long as value investors remain an insignificant minority, there will be ample opportunity to profit from such faulty logic. Your best profits will come from bucking conventional wisdom, carefully screening your information, and waiting for investors to misprice a company. To quote Benjamin Graham, "The market often goes far wrong, and sometimes an alert and courageous investor can take advantage of its patent errors."

BUYING WHAT IS KNOWN: THE USELESSNESS OF FORECASTS

"Forecasts are difficult to make—particularly those about the future."

attributed to Samuel Goldwyn

EACH YEAR, THE LEADING BUSINESS SCHOOLS graduate thousands of finance students taught the same arcane formulas, the same trading strategies, the same valuation principles, and the same forecasting models. It's no wonder that so few can see the broader context of their actions. No wonder, too, that so few beat the market over time; they futilely spend their days trying to beat each other. These graduates, who are today's market strategists, analysts, and fund managers, have become like Marshall McLuhan's fish that don't know they live in water. They swim in a tank separate from another fully functioning world, yet they believe the people on the outside of the glass need assistance. They, however, are the ones trapped.

Aristotle wrote that humans possess an innate desire to know the future. Perhaps no craving, he said, is exploited more. He could have been describing Wall Street. The financial industry exists officially to raise capital to help American industry prosper. But its *de facto* mission is to forecast, to exploit our craving to know what could happen tomorrow. If you understand this basic function of brokers, fund managers, analysts, investment bankers, the financial media, and economists, you will never fall prey to their game.

Legions of highly paid strategists, economists, and analysts spend their days picking tomorrow's winning stocks; predicting the direction of interest rates, the economy, or corporate earnings; or guessing the Federal Reserve's next interest rate move. Thousands more technicians plot stock price movements on computers, trying to predict tomorrow's chart breakout. Still others use sophisticated models to forecast which industries or economic sectors will perform best over the next 6 to 12 months. At the back end, tens of thousands of brokers package these pedantic predictions into sales pitches that entice you to buy. An equally large sales force pedals futuristic views of the market and compels companies and their employees to set up 401(k) plans, annuities, and college trusts, or to place all their available money in mutual funds.

In short, Wall Street exists to sell you something. All the financial information it issues, whether brokerage recommendations, price targets, market forecasts, earnings estimates, or performance figures, can be twisted to serve the purposes of whoever issues it. Wall Street generates reams of statistics for investors to digest, little of which has any relevance to your specific situation. In general, investors should be skeptical of almost all data offered them and never buy a stock based on future estimates other than those they themselves make. Philip Fisher said as much in 1958:

> I believe that the economics which deals with forecasting business trends may be considered to be about as far along as was the science of chemistry during the days of alchemy in the Middle Ages. In chemistry then, as in business forecasting now, basic principles were just beginning to emerge from a mysterious mass of mumbo-jumbo. . . . The amount of mental effort the financial community puts into this constant attempt to guess the economic future from a random and probably incomplete series of facts makes one wonder what might have been accomplished if only a fraction of such mental effort had been applied to something with a better chance of proving useful.[1]

Forecasting earnings or the direction of the economy and the stock market is as pointless as forecasting the weather. It can't be done with any cer-

---

[1] Philip A. Fisher, *Common Stocks and Uncommon Profits,* reprint of 1958 ed., New York, John Wiley & Sons, Inc., 1996, pp. 62–63.

tainty. Estimating tomorrow's temperature is relatively easy; use today's temperature as a guide. A 75-degree day, for example, is not likely to be followed by a 50-degree day or 100-degree weather. There is a high probability that tomorrow's temperature will be within a few degrees, up or down, of today's 75. The same holds true of a company's earnings. Next quarter's sales and earnings are likely to be close to this quarter's, barring seasonal factors. When you predict tomorrow's events, you can isolate and monitor only those variables likely to influence results. But when you extend your forecast outward, you allow more and more variables a chance to impart an influence on the outcome. You can predict tomorrow's weather with a high degree of certainty, but you can't predict next week's temperature or rainfall with the same certainty. You can't predict next *month's* weather at all. Systems such as weather and the stock market react to millions of variables that constantly change and impart an influence on one another.

I depict this in Figure 4-1 below, which demonstrates the range of outcomes one could expect predicting the future. The margin of error increases rapidly and parabolically the farther ahead one attempts to predict. Except

FIGURE 4-1   The impact of time on earnings forecasts.

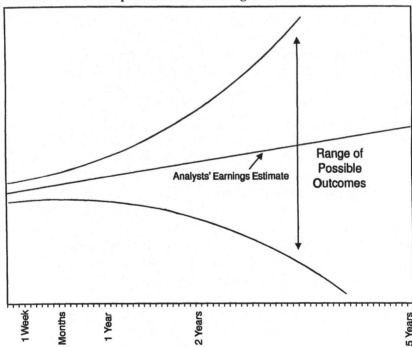

in rare instances, this relationship holds whether you are trying to predict a future stock price, earnings, sales, or the direction of the economy.

Predicting would be a viable vocation were it not open-ended. Time marches on and variables never cease changing, leaving most predictions without resolution. As soon as one quarter passes, analysts redress their models and try to predict next quarter's earnings. Their attempts to pin down "next period's earnings" or "five-year earnings growth rates" degenerate into futile efforts to hit moving targets. The few analysts who correctly predict a company's future earnings are plain lucky in many respects: lucky that a recession did not occur; lucky that interest rates didn't rise or fall; lucky that the CEO didn't die in a plane crash; lucky that the company didn't win—or lose—a major contract; lucky that federal regulators didn't impose a tariff on imports; lucky that the value of the U.S. dollar didn't fluctuate; lucky that the company didn't issue more stock, increase its long-term debt, or repurchase shares; lucky that the company didn't roll out a new product that doubled sales, or bombed; lucky that the company didn't use any of 100 accounting conventions to prop up earnings; and so on.

The track record of "expert" market forecasts is abysmal. Ninety percent of economists failed to predict the 1990 recession. Leading market strategists of 1929 failed to foresee the worst crash of this century, or the Depression it triggered. The largest investment houses forecast a bull market in Mexican stocks just before the government devalued the peso and sent stock prices reeling. Virtually no one predicted the seven-year decline in interest rates starting in 1991. Senior market analysts wrongly predicted the coming of a bear market numerous times between 1994 and 1998. Few foresaw the hyperinflation of the late 1970s. When Wall Street finally recognized the inflationary spiral trend, it expected more of the same, promising investors that gold could rise to $2000 an ounce and oil to $100 a barrel. At about the same time, most economists wrote off hopes for the sagging U.S. steel industry, which rebounded by the 1990s to become the world's most efficient and profitable again.

The opinions of analysts are perhaps the most suspect. Brokerages spend hundreds of millions of dollars a year researching companies and issuing earnings forecasts. But numerous studies have shown their forecasts to be—at worst—biased and flawed. At best, their predictions provide no added advantage to end users. In a painstaking 1996 study, David Dreman, the Chairman of Dreman Value Management, reviewed 94,251 earnings forecasts made between 1973 and 1996 and found that analysts had a 1-in-130 chance of guessing a company's quarterly earnings within 5 percent for four consecutive quarters. They had a 1-in-200,000 chance of correctly estimating earnings for 10 consecutive quarters. Other studies have found that analysts' recommendations tend to be overly optimistic. Analysts tend to ignore, or forgive, poor performance just to maintain a cozy relationship with companies. This is especially true for analysts whose firms help the company underwrite public offerings of shares. Their earnings forecasts tend to overshoot the mark and their stock picks tend to lag the market in the subsequent quarters.

In 1995, thousands of investors fell victim to one of the more botched forecasts this century—Micron Technology, the maker of random access memory chips used in computers. In 1994 and 1995, Micron was among the hottest stocks in America, rising from a low of $9 to $95. Driving this frenzy were seasoned analysts whose wildly optimistic earnings estimates later proved horribly wrong. Starting in 1993, Micron's earnings began accelerating when sales increased 60 percent. Per-share earnings rose from $0.03 in 1992 to $0.52 in 1993 and $1.92 in 1994. Earnings hit a record $3.95 in 1995 when sales doubled in less than a year.

Then analysts made a typical, fatal mistake: They extrapolated recent growth rates into the future. Analysts kept increasing their earnings forecasts and maintained buy recommendations on Micron even as it approached $90 a share. A few even projected Micron would earn $17 a share within a year or two! Unfortunately, the bottom dropped out within months. Korean and Taiwanese chipmakers, envious of the incredible profit margins Micron and others enjoyed, boosted capacity and glutted the chip market. Prices for random access chips fell 75 percent in 1996 and another 40 percent in 1997. Though Micron's sales kept rising, net income dropped like a rock. By early 1997, the same analysts who led investors into Micron based on galactic forecasts had lowered their earnings estimates to $2 per share or below. The stock later bottomed at $17.

Examples of overly optimistic forecasts get downright comical when viewed in their proper context. Back in the mid-1960s, analysts enthusiastically recommended IBM on the premise that earnings could grow 16 percent a year—perpetually. These inflated assumptions pushed the investing public into Big Blue and subsequently caused the stock to reach generous levels. Evidently, no one bothered to check the analysts' math. IBM recorded $5.345 billion in sales in 1967 and $651 million in net income. Had IBM grown at the rate analysts projected, IBM's 1997 sales would have been $458.9 billion, or 6 percent of total U.S. economic output, and it would have earned $55.9 billion, 16 times Microsoft's 1997 profits. Somewhere over that 30-year stretch, IBM's earnings wandered off their predicted pathway. The company's 1997 sales and earnings were just 17 percent and 10 percent, respectively, of what had been expected 30 years earlier.

Another example of atrocious advice concerned Oracle, the $6 billion database software maker, whose 30 percent yearly earnings growth in the 1990s made it a darling among technology analysts. Plugged as a "can't miss" buy-and-hold company, Oracle rose in price from a split-adjusted $5 in 1992 to $42 by August 1997. At its peak it traded at nearly 45 times earnings on the belief that earnings growth would be strong—and perpetual. Wall Street was in for a shock on December 8, 1997, when Oracle announced that earnings growth for the quarter would slow to just 4 percent. The stock lost 29 percent that day. Three days before Oracle announced poor earnings, analysts were still upgrading their views of the company. One of them concluded that Oracle's earnings could grow at 30 percent rates for at least five more years.

Part of the blame for Oracle lay squarely on the shoulders of analysts. Fault also lay with the legions of money managers and investors who relied on analysts for guidance. A few weeks prior to Oracle's sharp decline, Merrill Lynch released a telling study that asked institutional investors—mutual and pension fund managers—to list the most important criteria they use in buying or selling a stock. More than half said they traded based on an earnings surprise. If a company missed analysts' earnings target, they sold. When the company exceeded the target, they bought. Not surprisingly, 48 percent of institutional managers said they rely on analysts' estimates to make trading decisions.

Merrill Lynch's study, in essence, described the life and death story of many stocks. Analysts, under pressure to issue recommendations favorable to companies, often fail to spot signs of trouble and keep investors buying at fundamentally unsound prices. Few investors realize that analysts are grossly overworked, follow more companies than they can monitor properly, and are compensated mostly for their ability to woo companies and win underwriting business. Making accurate predictions is not part of their job description.

At the back end, hundreds of fund managers—themselves under pressure to report the best quarterly results—take their cues from analysts' biased earnings estimates and dance in and out of stocks for quick profits or losses. They, too, are beset with daily pressures of which investors are not aware. The average fund manager owns too many stocks to monitor and is forced to buy favorite stocks at higher and higher prices because investors keep sending in monthly 401(k) checks. The pressure to report continually strong quarterly results forces them to trade first and evaluate later. What often starts as a reasoned buy-and-hold strategy for hundreds of fund managers degrades into tape watching, bets on short-term earnings, and basis-point chasing. The alternative is to be caught lagging their peers or a market index. What results is a herd mentality and the rapid, irrational movement in and out of stocks based on actual and rumored quarterly earnings. In the end, decisions are made on the basis of outright guesswork by analysts who are, for the most part, relying on companies for guidance. The companies themselves, having mastered this ritual and fearful of upsetting Wall Street, resort to any measure of accounting trickery to maintain the semblance of earnings predictability. The companies that participate in this process willingly sacrifice long-term strategic success for the rewards of maintaining good relations with the brokerages and fund families. This critical path of information runs full circle, adding folly upon folly at each level. CEOs resort to guessing their earnings months in advance to feed hungry analysts who steer the multibillion dollar bets of fund managers. One faulty forecast begets another and another.

When investing is buoyed by short-term earnings—which, in turn, swims on the current of predictions—it ceases to be investing, and becomes gambling.

That analysts' estimates are wrong more than 80 percent of the time is inconsequential to the parties playing this game. No one wants to be caught dead holding a stock their peers are dumping. No one wants to miss a rally expected of a company that beats its earnings estimates. It's a great self-affirming, promotion-oriented network, provided that details, like fundamentals, don't gum up the works. The 1929 stock crash arose from similar activity. As stock prices climbed higher, traders turned increasingly myopic, buying when earnings expectations rose and selling when companies missed their quarterly targets. Prices climbed so high that fundamental justifications for buying stock could no longer be offered with a straight face.

Investors must avoid flowing with these currents, for they lead to whirlpools. When investing is buoyed by short-term earnings, which, in turn, swim on the current of predictions, it ceases to be investing and becomes gambling. When earnings targets become ends unto themselves, investors lose sight of price and value and are prepared to pay anything for a company.

It's one thing to estimate earnings; Wall Street does this constantly. It's quite another to estimate what a company is truly worth or how much a company's value changes when information changes. Wall Street almost never does this. When a company announces a merger, for example, investors often jump into the stock without examining whether the deal will increase the value of the company. Instead, they rely on analysts' back-of-the-envelope appraisals of the deal or management's optimistic projections of synergy. Absent any meaningful direction from analysts, speculators and momentum traders take matters into their own hands. They interpret information as they see fit and unload or buy hundreds of thousands of shares within a few hours. The unsuspecting public likely sees the sharp movement in the stock price, assumes the market has correctly interpreted the results, and swims with the tide. Roger Babson, writing in 1951, probably summed up this futile exercise best:

> Success comes not so much by forecasting as by doing the right thing at the right time and always being willing to keep one's course prudently protected. Much more money is made by directing one's business and investments with a stability of purpose to benefit from good times while avoiding the losses of panics than by trying only to forecast prosperity or panics and then pursuing a policy based wholly on the belief that said forecast must prove true.[2]

AVOID RELYING ON COMPANIES;
THEY CAN PREDICT EVENTS NO BETTER

Companies are by no means innocent bystanders. They have learned how to play the game as well as anyone. They use accounting rules to their advantage and manipulate their revenues and costs to ensure that quarterly results meet Wall Street's expectations. Or they take restructuring charges to reduce their reported costs and improve profit margins. Companies in danger of reporting a weak quarter sometimes take restructuring charges to obscure their poor performance and give Wall Street the impression that it's cleaning house. Some intentionally coax analysts into lowering their earnings estimates ahead of reported results. Then they surprise Wall Street with strong earnings that push the stock price up several dollars. This sort of chicanery occurs daily and is one of the reasons investors cannot fixate on short-term results.

On occasion, companies shoot themselves in the foot by wrongly forecasting demand. NIKE, the $9 billion-a-year maker of athletic footwear

---

[2] Roger W. Babson, *Business Barometers and Investment,* 5th ed., New York, Harper & Brothers, 1951, pp. ix–x.

and apparel, saddled itself with more than $500 million in unwanted shoe inventories in late 1997 when Asian economies plunged into a recession. Just before the collapse, Asian markets were on fire for NIKE's products; sales in Japan alone were growing at 75 percent to 90 percent annual rates. When Asian currencies declined in value in the autumn of 1997, the price of imported products skyrocketed and Asian consumers experienced a drop in the purchasing power of their money. Overnight, NIKE's shoes were being priced 25 to 30 percent higher to people whose real incomes had fallen. NIKE not only failed to anticipate the currency situation, it increased production to flood Japan with even more shoes, just when the bottom dropped out. As NIKE's CEO, Philip Knight, explained in a conference call, "In a perfect world, we might have done less business in Japan. In retrospect, there were some warning signals when sales [in Japan] were rising 80 percent. But we foresaw 5 percent to 10 percent [additional] growth in consumer demand and we ordered 60 percent more [shoes] from a year before. The [order] cancellations were massive."

This begs the question: If a company cannot anticipate its revenues and earnings with any accuracy, despite having hundreds of sales, marketing, and distribution personnel throughout the world gathering intelligence, how can one analyst sitting behind a desk in New York, Boston, or Chicago do any better? One cannot totally fault NIKE for a slide in sales because of an unexpected economic problem. But NIKE set the stage for its own downfall by relying on optimistic sales forecasts. Times were good in Asia and NIKE's marketing staff and economists predicted more of the same.

Fluor, an $8 billion-a-year construction company, experienced a similar fate in 1997 when its ambitious worldwide expansion was tripped up by sluggish overseas economies. By 1997, Fluor had projects underway in nearly 50 countries. The company had construction contracts for everything from petrochemical plants and copper mines to new sports stadiums and corporate headquarters. By its own admission, Fluor overcommitted to Asian nations at the wrong time. First, two of its power generation projects experienced huge cost overruns, and the company was forced to take write-downs against earnings, causing the stock to plunge. Next, Asian currencies plummeted and formerly cash-rich nations found themselves without enough hard currency to complete infrastructure projects. Fluor's quarterly earnings plunged and the company was forced to respond by closing down foreign field offices, laying off employees, and taking restructuring charges against earnings. IBM experienced the opposite problem in 1995 when it severely underestimated consumer demand for personal computers and failed to deliver enough PCs through its sales channels for the Christmas holiday. IBM reportedly left upwards of $1 billion on the table through faulty forecasting.

Financial writers have filled volumes with examples of forecasts that blew up in the faces of normally prudent companies. Homebuilders turn so eager and confident in the economy that they buy huge tracts of marginal land and build "spec" homes just as the economy slows. Vineyard owners in Napa Valley plow their hillsides and increase their acreage just in time to see wine demand drop. Semiconductor companies spend two years and $1.5 billion constructing new manufacturing plants that come online right as the industry peaks. Oil companies ramp up drilling activity and pipeline construction just as crude oil prices begin to fall. Retailers and restaurant chains accelerate the pace of store expansions and use up precious cash just when the public begins to tire of its wares or concept. Like second-rate politicians who believe their chances of winning are great up until election day, when they lose as badly as polls forecast, many companies cannot bring themselves to accept the reality of the marketplace. Nor are they especially equipped to adapt to the market's ever-shifting demands and wants. Their flaws are human—they project what is happening now into the future—but costly nonetheless to investors.

The purpose here is not to berate management for their mistakes, but to expand the premise that accurate business forecasting is next to impossible, even for those in the know, and should not be made the keystone of valuation. As fund manager Mario Gabelli once bluntly said, "Buy what is, not what will be."[3] Markets are not dependable, short-term or long-term, because they are random-acting. All markets, whether for athletic shoes, computers, cars, Barbie dolls, luggage, medical care, stocks, or bonds, are driven by the predictability of unpredictability. Daily fluctuations in these markets reflect the sum total of all participants—buyers and sellers— behaving individually and acting out prevailing personal needs and wants. If enough people crave a piece of Jordache luggage or a Jeep Cherokee one quarter, for whatever reason, sales will be strong. The next quarter may be a totally different story.

To rely on the future or the unpredictable means gambling on events outside your realm of control. Nothing adds more risk to otherwise judicious investing.

[3] Charles Whitfield, "Wisdom from the Mount: Gabelli Speaks to a Packed House," *The Bottom Line,* from the website of Gabelli Asset Management, April 17, 1997.

UNDERSTANDING THE BOND-STOCK RELATIONSHIP AND EARNINGS YIELDS

"The worst way to combat inflation is to buy something as a supposed 'hedge' at an inflated price."

Gerald Loeb[1]

BY **1997, FULLY 43 PERCENT** of American households had invested directly or indirectly in the stock market, according to pollster Peter Hart. Most of those households participated in the market indirectly by having their money invested for them through mutual funds, 401(k) plans, or individual retirement accounts. A minority bought stocks directly to maintain control of their own destinies. Presumably, Americans have acquired a sense of urgency in the 1990s, for just five years earlier, less than 20 percent of households invested in stocks. No single reason explains why Americans have flocked to Wall Street in the 1990s. To many, stock investing is and always will be a sophisticated game—like Baccarat or Keno—that offers mentally

---

[1] Gerald M. Loeb, *The Battle for Stock Market Profits,* New York, Simon & Schuster, 1971, p. 138.

challenging fun. Others see investing like deer hunting, where the goal is to emerge with the biggest trophy at the end—in this case, a pile of assets. Millions more look to the stock market as their financial savior, a highway for building up enough wealth to retire. Others pile in to earn seemingly easy gains.

Sociologists might argue that investing has no valid purpose except to prove one's mettle in a competitive, survival-of-the-fittest social structure. Indeed, there's no debating that many people buy and sell stocks for the pleasure of building an empire, in the same way that people amass a fleet of antique automobiles they will never drive or sell. Like Scrooge McDuck, Walt Disney's miserly aristocrat, hoarding wealth with no end purpose is a goal in itself.

To economists, investing is a vital component of any flourishing nation. Societies invest to advance their lot, to fund research and development projects that ultimately improve productivity and spread wealth to the greatest number of people within that society. The benefits of investing, theoretically at least, come full circle. When we deposit $1000 in the local bank, the bank might lend $1000 to an entrepreneur who wants to expand a manufacturing facility. The $1000 loan might pay for a new piece of equipment that allows the entrepreneur to lower prices and increase sales by 50 percent. The increase in sales enables the company to open a second sales office and hire six new workers. Those workers, in turn, earn a paycheck they deposit in their local bank, and so on. The more money invested in an economy, the more it produces, the more efficient it becomes, and the more money that is eventually recycled for future expansion. There is no zero-sum game in investing; all participants benefit when money circulates freely and is used for productive purposes.

Individuals, of course, need not stew over their role in this great economic circle. You must strive for self-preservation. *You must preserve what you own and allow your assets to compound at a rate that compensates you for the natural depreciation of those assets.* Whatever rate of return you earn on your assets must beat the yearly rate at which your assets depreciate in value. Keeping your returns above the rate of depreciation allows you to maintain or increase your standard of living over time. If your assets provide a 5 percent yearly return, and your assets naturally depreciate in value by 4 percent a year, you will improve your net worth and standard of living by 1 percent a year. Obviously, you must pick the right mix of assets to stay ahead of depreciation. If all of your investable assets were tied up in automobiles, you would see a decline in your net worth because an automobile might lose 10 percent to 20 percent of its value each year and offer no appreciation potential. If your money is in real estate, you will do considerably better. Home prices tend to rise 1 percent to 5 percent a year, which generally is sufficient to keep pace with inflation.

Assets such as automobiles, homes, stocks, and bonds depreciate because of *inflation,* which reduces the value of what you hold year after year. If the annual return on your investments cannot beat the rate of inflation, you lose net worth—permanently. Even if your assets rise in value, your standard of living can drop if the assets do not rise enough to offset general price increases. Thus, the first axiom in the bond-stock relationship: *The principal reason we invest is to preserve the value of our assets from the effects of inflation.*

Inflation truly is the most potent scourge an investor confronts. It is a hidden tax on your wealth, and one you cannot control. For example, you have no control over the rate at which the Federal Reserve Board increases the money supply or the amount of borrowing the federal government does. You have no say in the spending and monetary policies of foreign governments. But you feel the effects when nations devalue their currencies, keep wages artificially low, or encourage foreign investment inside their borders.

> Inflation truly is the most potent scourge an investor confronts. It is a hidden tax on your wealth, and one you cannot control.

Inflation's effects on investment are not to be taken lightly. Rising prices can wreak devastating consequences on your portfolio if your rate of return does not keep pace. For example, if prices rise 4 percent and your money sits in a bank savings account earning 3.5 percent, you are losing purchasing power. It's as if government taxed your profits at a 163 percent rate. Think about that for a moment! There's no difference between earning 3.5 percent with no inflation and losing 163 percent to taxation and earning 3.5 percent with 4 percent inflation and losing 28 percent to taxes. Your after-tax proceeds are identical. When inflation exists, it's as if the government simply raised your tax rate. The higher the rate of inflation, the more hidden taxes you must pay.

Market strategists once assumed that inflation helped investors because

FIGURE 5-1   Inflation-adjusted 10-year returns—S&P 500.

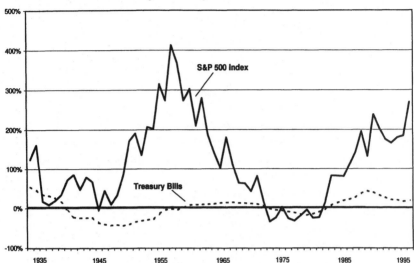

it allowed companies to raise prices at will and report better sales and earnings. That thinking has been abandoned. Today, more investors see inflation for what it truly represents, a competitive force that can push smart investors out of stocks and into securities that compensate them for rising prices—namely bonds. If you are not diligent in picking the right stocks and fail to recognize the relationship between stocks and bonds, you can suffer extraordinary losses of purchasing power. Many investors who began buying stocks in the mid-1960s, for example, experienced yearly market returns that failed to keep up with inflation. (see Figure 5-1). Someone who bought S&P 500 stocks in 1965 experienced no inflation-adjusted gains until 1983—18 years later! During that period, they would have been much better off buying 90-day Treasury bills and rolling them over continuously. This phenomenon occurred because of rising inflation in the 1970s and the fact that stocks could not keep pace.

Because of the constant risk of inflation, stocks necessarily compete with bonds. This becomes apparent when studying great multiyear movements in the stock market. When inflation rises over an extended period, and bond yields rise, price-to-earnings ratios of stocks tend to drop. When inflation falls, bond yields fall and stocks rise. Yet over long periods, stocks have proven to be the best inflation hedge. They have beaten yearly rates of inflation by wide margins. As such, they have provided much better inflation-adjusted returns than bonds, real estate, savings accounts, and automobiles. Jeremy Siegel, professor of finance at the Wharton School of the University of Pennsylvania, has set forth a persuasive argument in favor of stock investing. Siegel painstakingly charted inflation and the returns on stocks and bonds from 1802 to 1992 and found a startling relationship: stocks consistently beat inflation by about 6.7 percentage points a year over the long term. This remarkable correlation has held up despite major shifts in our economy and fundamental changes in the ways we use money and labor. Thus, if investors want to ensure that the real-dollar value of their investments is preserved, they must invest in stocks. No other asset class, Siegel wrote, offers a long-term return nearly as compelling or inflation-beating as common stocks:

> The fact that stock returns have compensated for inflation should come as no surprise. Since stocks are claims on the earnings of real assets—assets whose value is intrinsically related to labor and capital—it is reasonable to expect that their return will not be influenced by inflation. This is particularly true since . . . in the long run, the rate of inflation is caused by monetary expansion, which influences input and output prices equally.[2]

THE BOND-STOCK RELATIONSHIP

The correlation between stocks, inflation, and bonds that Siegel studied is not as remote as might seem. In fact, all three forces tend to interact and influence one another. When inflation rises, interest rates rise and bond prices fall. When inflation falls, the opposite occurs. Stocks tend to react similarly to the rise and fall of bond yields and interest rates. Over long periods, in fact, stock and bond prices tend to react similarly to the same information. Financial markets cannot contradict one another; they react to the same news in the same way. The bond market cannot anticipate inflation at the same time stock investors anticipate deflation.

The true relationship between stocks and bonds lies in their *coupons,* the amount of yearly returns you can expect to take out of each investment. A bond's coupon is straightforward. It is the amount the corporation pledges to pay you each year as a percentage of the bond's par value. If a company issues a bond with a $1000 par value and a coupon yield of 6.5 percent, the company has pledged to pay bond owners $65 a year (6.5 percent of $1000) until the bond matures. No matter how many times or at what price the bond changes hands in subsequent years, the $65 yearly coupon remains fixed. If General Electric issues a 6.5 percent, 10-year

---

[2] Jeremy Siegel, *Stocks for the Long Run,* New York, McGraw-Hill, 1994, p. 157.

bond that matures in 2008, any buyer who desires to hold the bond for one year will get $65 in payment from GE.

Because the yearly coupon payment never fluctuates, the price an investor would willingly pay for the GE bond depends on three factors: (1) the expected rate of inflation over the remaining life of the bond; (2) the prevailing yield on government bonds maturing at the same time; and (3) the *risk premium* bondholders expect based on their perceptions of GE's financial stability. The first two factors go hand in hand. The expected rate of inflation is assumed to be priced into government bonds. If bond traders expect inflation to rise, say, 4 percent a year over the next 10 years, a 10-year government bond should yield at least 4 percent. In all likelihood, it might be priced to yield closer to 6 percent to take into account any unforeseen risks. The yield on a 10-year General Electric bond will reflect both the yield on a riskless 10-year government bond (in this case, 6 percent) plus a premium for the risk that GE defaults on the debt. Thus, a GE bond might yield the 6.5 percent we assumed above.

An investor who buys the bond pays $1000 up front to get $65 a year in coupon interest. At the end of the tenth year, that same investor will sell the bond back to GE for the full $1000 in par value. The investor's earnings stream will look like this:

	Yearly Coupon	Cumulative Return
1999	$65	6.5%
2000	$65	13.0%
2001	$65	18.5%
2002	$65	26.0%
2003	$65	32.5%
2004	$65	39.0%
2005	$65	45.5%
2006	$65	52.0%
2007	$65	58.5%
2008	$65	65.0%

The price of GE's bond would not fluctuate if interest rates remained the same. Why? Because the yearly coupon return of $65 stays constant and because there is no added or lessened risk of inflation eating away the returns. This bond, then, provides full inflation protection—*as long as interest rates do not rise during the bond's 10-year life.* When rates rise, new investors must be compensated for the loss of purchasing power. They demand that the bond sell below its $1000 par value. If the price drops to $975, a new investor not only gets a $65 yearly coupon but the chance to sell the bond back to GE in 2008 for $25 profit. The bond's annualized yield to maturity will now rise above 6.5 percent. Similarly, a decline in interest rates will cause the bond's price to rise above $1000. Investors will seize the opportunity to hold a bond yielding more than the rate of inflation and bid up the price until the bond's yield to maturity falls below 6.5 percent.

Common stocks offer their own form of coupon yield: the yearly earnings generated by the company. Whatever profits the company generates each year must be reimbursed to you at some point. Thus, yearly earnings function as a coupon. The key difference is that earnings are paid later rather than today. Just as a bond possesses a yield to maturity, a stock has an *earnings yield* that allows you to compare it to bonds, interest rates, and inflation. As such, the same relationship used to determine the attractiveness of bonds applies to stocks. Your goal is to find companies whose yearly earnings coupons can beat inflation. Your secondary goal is to latch onto an earnings stream that can beat the prevailing yield on government bonds. If you cannot find companies capable of generating bond-beating returns, prudence demands that you invest your money in bonds until the time comes when stocks trade at attractive yields again.

> Just as a bond possesses a yield to maturity,
> a stock has an *earnings yield* that
> allows you to compare it to bonds,
> interest rates, and inflation.

We can see this relationship at work in the real world when we study companies showing little or no earnings growth. If a company's earnings did not fluctuate year in and year out and the market expected zero future growth, the company would be valued based on just two factors: (1) the prevailing rate of return on government bonds, and (2) a premium that accounts for any risk inherent in the company. For example, if a company generates $1 per share a year in earnings and does so perpetually, its stock functions as a bond. In pricing this stock, the investor merely needs to know what a long-term government bond currently yields. Then the investor must factor in the probability, or *risk,* that the company may not earn $1 per share. The higher the risk, the more the stock must yield, and the lower the shares will trade. If a 30-year Treasury bond yields 7 percent, the stock needs to trade for $14.28 per share to yield the same 7 percent. Presuming the company possesses some risk, the market may wish to value the company at less than $14.28 per share. At a price of $13, the $1 in earnings would represent a 7.69 percent yield. At $14, the earnings yield is 7.14 percent. If interest rates never fluctuated and the company continued to earn $1 per share, we would expect the stock's price to remain frozen.

This direct relationship between earnings, government bond yields, and stock price should hold *in perpetuity,* so long as the company can generate $1 per share on shareholders' behalf each year. What happens, however, if yields on government bonds rise or fall? The stock should behave like a government bond would. It should fall in price if rates rise and rise in price if rates fall. If interest rates on 30-year bonds rise to 8 percent, then our hypothetical stock must fall in price to $12.50 per share for its yearly earnings to yield 8 percent ($1 divided by $12.50 is 0.08). If interest rates fall to 6 percent, we would expect this stock to rise to $16.67 per share ($1 divided by $16.67 is 0.06).

Why does this relationship occur? Because in our example, we chose a company whose earnings were so predictable they were, in essence, a coupon payment that shareholders could count on. If the company returns the entire $1 per share as a dividend each year, then its shares are nothing more than a bond dressed in stock's clothing. Consider a real-life example—the common stock of Pittsburgh & West Virginia Railroad. This company operates as a real estate investment trust and owns 112 miles of track in Ohio, West Virginia, and Pennsylvania that it leases to Norfolk & Western. The lease runs 99 years at fixed yearly payments. Because it holds the same assets year in and year out and charges a flat fee for use of the assets, Pittsburgh & West Virginia's yearly revenues have been identical, just under $1 million dollars. Net income has been approximately $800,000 per year, and it consistently earns $0.55 per share. The company has returned substantially all of its yearly earnings as dividends. As a result, there has been little increase in the company's net worth, which was $6 per share at the end of 1997. An investor who buys the stock at $7 and sells the shares after 10 years can expect the following returns:

Year	Price	EPS	Book Value	Dividends	Cumulative Return	Return on a $7 Purchase
1998	$7	$0.55	$6	$0.55	$0.55	7.9%
1999		$0.55	$6	$0.55	$1.10	15.7%
2000		$0.55	$6	$0.55	$1.65	23.6%
2001		$0.55	$6	$0.55	$2.20	31.4%
2002		$0.55	$6	$0.55	$2.75	39.3%
2003		$0.55	$6	$0.55	$3.30	47.1%
2004		$0.55	$6	$0.55	$3.85	55.0%
2005		$0.55	$6	$0.55	$4.40	62.9%
2006		$0.55	$6	$0.55	$4.95	70.7%
2007		$0.55	$6	$0.55	$5.50	78.6%
2007	$7 sale				$12.50	178.6%

If you were to buy a 10-year, $7 bond with a 7.9 percent yearly coupon, you should expect nearly the same returns. Not surprisingly, Pittsburgh & West Virginia's stock has shown little upward or downward movement for several years, owing to two facts. The earnings have been fixed, and the company's net worth has not increased. By paying out all of its earnings as dividends, Pittsburgh & West Virginia has reinvested no money in the business to raise the value of shareholders' equity. The stock has fluctuated solely because of the up-and-down movements in interest rates. Rates fell steadily between 1991 and late 1993, during which time the stock climbed nearly 48 percent. In 1994, the stock fell as rates climbed. Over the following three years, the stock gyrated as Treasury bond yields moved up and down between 6 percent and 8 percent. In late 1997, Pittsburgh & West Virginia began to rally as rates broke below 6 percent.

The share-price movements of Pittsburgh & West Virginia help reiterate a central theme of investing: *Stocks are merely bonds with less predictable coupons.*

ELECTRIC UTILITIES AS PROXIES FOR BONDS

The electric utility industry offers a wonderful case study of the relationship between stocks and bonds. Traditionally, utilities return most of their earnings as dividends, and their growth rates have been virtually flat. Thus utility stocks have shown many of the same characteristics as a bond. They have provided a steam of predictable earnings that are returned, not retained, by management. In recent years, prices for utility stocks have moved counter to changes in interest rates and will likely continue to do so. When interest rates rise, utility stock prices fall. This relationship has held over long periods—one year or more—and shorter periods of days or weeks as well. Researchers isolating the daily price movements of electric utility stocks have found that interest rates tend to be the biggest cause of price fluctuations. Figure 5-2 below shows this relationship at work from 1990–1998. The strong correlation between utility prices and interest rates exists because of the bond-stock relationship. If utilities were like any other sector whose earnings were less predictable, prices of utility stocks would fluctuate far more randomly because the yearly coupon would be less predictable.

THE EARNINGS YIELD AXIOM

We started this chapter by noting that stocks are essentially bond substitutes. To extend this argument, let's now look at how earnings relate to yields. A key tenet of successful investing is to improve the rate of return on your original investment. You can do that by buying shares in a com-

FIGURE 5-2   Electric utilities vs. 30-year Treasury Bonds.

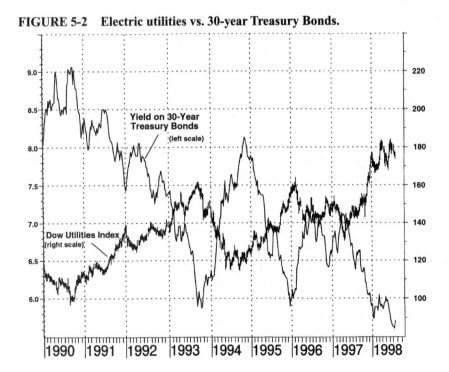

pany whose *earnings yield* can grow over time. A company's earnings yield is merely the company's earnings divided by the current share price. If a company earns $2 per share and trades for $40, its yield is 5 percent. That is, the yearly earnings generated on your behalf constitute 5 percent of your original investment. Seasoned investors would recognize immediately that an earnings yield is merely the inverse of the familiar price-to-earnings (P/E) ratio. It holds the same relevance. When investing, you should try to buy stocks trading at the highest possible earnings yield, or the lowest possible P/E ratio. Doing so better ensures that your future returns can beat inflation.

When a company's earnings increase, the rate of your return on your original investment (the earnings yield) grows as well. It also follows that the share price will eventually catch up to that earnings growth. A predictable, growing earnings stream leads to share price increases that correlate highly with the growth in earnings. For example, consider a company that earns $1 per share for investors, trades at $20, and whose earnings grow at 25 percent annual rates. Substituting yearly earnings as the "coupon," we can evaluate this stock just as we did the General Electric bond above:

	EPS	Coupon Return on $20 Price
1998	$1.00	5.0%
1999	$1.25	6.3%
2000	$1.56	7.8%
2001	$1.95	9.8%
2002	$2.44	12.2%
2003	$3.05	15.3%
2004	$3.81	19.1%
2005	$4.77	23.9%
2006	$5.96	29.8%
2007	$7.45	37.3%
2008	$9.31	46.6%

By 2008, the company's yearly earnings constitute a 46.6 percent return on your original investment. That coupon return is far in excess of any presumed inflation that could occur and is especially alluring when compared to the returns of a bond. Had you bought a bond paying a 5 percent coupon in 1998, it would still return 5 percent in 2008. If the stock continues to trade at an average of 20 times earnings as it did in 1998—a reasonable assumption, the shares would sell for $186.20 in 2008, an 831 percent return on your original $20 investment. The yearly earnings also would grow by 831 percent over the same period.

Consider another real-life situation—steelmaker Nucor—whose stock fell below $40 in mid-1998 and offered an attractive earnings yield. Nucor has posted unquestionably the best track record of profitability in the steel industry. Sales and earnings have grown at compounded rates of 17 percent since the mid-1960s. Since concentrating its operations on steel joists in 1966, Nucor has never lost money, an astounding record for a company in such a capital-intensive, cyclical industry. This 30-year uninterrupted growth streak lays an invaluable foundation for valuing Nucor, for it allows you to make reasonable assumptions about future earnings. We can, for example, assume with some confidence that Nucor can continue increasing its earnings at 17 percent rates. We can say with greater certainty that Nucor should increase earnings by at least 10 percent a year. And there is an almost 100 percent chance Nucor can increase earnings by at least 5 percent rates.

Assume that Nucor continued to grow at 12 percent annual rates. This is how the company's earnings stream would compare to a $40 initial investment:

	EPS	Return on $40 Price
1997	$3.35	8.4%
1998	$3.75	9.4%
1999	$4.20	10.5%
2000	$4.71	11.8%
2001	$5.27	13.2%
2002	$5.90	14.8%
2003	$6.61	16.5%
2004	$7.41	18.5%
2005	$8.29	20.7%
2006	$9.29	23.2%
2007	$10.40	26.0%

It should be evident why Nucor was so attractive. When Nucor fell to $40, long-term Treasury bonds yielded only 5.7 percent. Thus, Nucor's earnings offered an immediate premium of 2.7 percentage points over a government bond. While that premium may not have seemed enticing to investors desiring high, immediate returns, the table shows that Nucor's coupon return would continue to increase, while a government bond's coupon would remain fixed. The real value of owning Nucor lay not in its then mediocre return but in the continually higher coupon returns Nucor offered as its earnings grew. In the first year, Nucor would deliver $3.35 per share in earnings, an 8.4 percent return on your money. The following year, Nucor's anticipated earnings of $3.75 per share represents a 9.4 percent earnings yield. If interest rates remain at 5.7 percent, Nucor's yield would beat Treasury bonds by 3.7 percentage points. By 2007, Nucor's earnings would provide a 26 percent annual return on your original $40 investment.

As impressive as this earnings stream sounds, investors could enhance their returns further if either of two events occurred.

1. *Nucor's growth rate sped up beyond 12 percent.*   If earnings grew at 15 percent annual rates, Nucor would earn $3.85 per share in 1998, an earnings yield of 9.6 percent on a $40 investment. Already, Nucor's earnings would be beating a Treasury bond by 390 basis points, a spread that would continue to grow. By 2007, Nucor would earn $13.56 per share, an earnings yield of 33.9 percent on the original investment. What are the odds that bonds would yield close to 33 percent in 10 years?

2. *Investors were offered the company at less than $40.*   If traders subsequently bid Nucor down to, say, $35, the company's earnings yield would be so attractive relative to bonds that it would behoove long-term investors to pick up some shares. Even presuming 12 percent growth, the coupon stream would improve dramatically. Nucor's long-term returns would beat inflation by a wide margin in the first year and all subsequent years, unless the U.S. economy experienced a prolonged period of financial distress. This fact potentially made Nucor one of the best "bond-stocks" you could buy in 1998.

Of course, earnings growth alone doesn't guarantee bond-beating returns. What made Nucor so attractive was its relatively cheap price—$40, or 11 times 1997 earnings. If an investor had paid 20 times earnings for Nucor, or $67, then the yearly earnings yield, assuming 12 percent growth, would have been far less attractive:

	EPS	Return on $67 Price
1997	$3.35	5.0%
1998	$3.75	5.6%
1999	$4.20	6.3%
2000	$4.71	7.0%
2001	$5.27	7.9%
2002	$5.90	8.8%
2003	$6.61	9.9%
2004	$7.41	11.1%
2005	$8.29	12.4%
2006	$9.29	13.9%
2007	$10.40	15.5%

Who would dare pay 20 times earnings for Nucor? Plenty of investors did in late 1997, when the stock rallied briefly above $60. But within months, these momentum chasers had lost 33 percent of their investment. In retrospect, what they bought at $60 was a riskier coupon yield, their punishment for paying a high premium for Nucor's present earnings. As is evident by the table, Nucor's earnings in 2007 likely would beat inflation but not enough to provide you comfort. Keep in mind that you *assumed* a 12 percent growth rate in earnings and placed your faith in Nucor's ability to deliver that rate of return. It's entirely possible that Nucor's growth rate never again will reach 12 percent, although it's unlikely given Nucor's stable 30-year track record. Because you relied on an assumption that could later prove wrong, you might pay dearly for Nucor's earnings and leave yourself with a smaller margin of error, as buyers at $60 did. In addition, interest rates could rise over the next several years, a fact that would not only undercut Nucor's stock price but reduce the spread between Nucor's earnings yield and the yield on government bonds. If both events occurred, a slower growth rate coupled with higher interest rates, Nucor's yield could drop below those of government bonds. In such circumstances, it would be more prudent for an investor to buy bonds, since they already are priced to take inflation into account.

SIX RULES FOR COMPARING STOCKS TO BONDS
Let's summarize these major points again:

1.   *Your overriding goal as a stock investor is to find companies whose returns can beat inflation.* Two hundred years of market history

have proven that stocks offer a nearly guaranteed means of beating inflation.

2. *Your secondary goal is to beat the risk-free returns of government bonds, which are already priced to anticipate inflation.* If the stocks you select cannot beat a bond's return, you are better off putting your money into bonds.

3. *The proper way of comparing a stock's potential return to a bond's return is to compare their respective coupons, the money that can be generated on your behalf each year.* When evaluating a bond, the relevant return is the yearly coupon. When evaluating a stock, the relevant return is the earnings you predict the company can produce each year going forward.

4. *When possible, you should try to buy a stock whose current earnings yield, current earnings divided by price, is near or above yields on a long-term bond.* If interest rates are 6 percent, you need an earnings yield close to 6 percent; that is, the company's P/E ratio should be at or under 17. If rates are 8 percent, you should look for companies priced at 12.5 times earnings or less.

5. *The only time you should accept earnings yields that are lower than bond yields is when the company is growing and is expected to generate an earnings yield that would soon surpass bond yields.* A high growth rate compensates for a low earnings yield. But the company's coupon yield should still compare favorably to a bond within a few years. If you must wait five years or more for earnings to catch up to bond yields, you are likely overpaying for the company.

6. *Buying growth companies at the cheapest possible price is the best way to ensure that you can beat bond yields by a wide margin.* You should try to take advantage of the compounding effect of earnings growth, which provides a higher and higher rate of return on your initial investment.

Buying growth companies at the cheapest possible price is the best way to ensure that you can beat bond yields by a wide margin.

It is this compounding phenomenon that makes owning growth companies so rewarding. Continuous growth in earnings leads to continuous growth in the return on your investment, which should lead to higher and higher share prices over time. Consider how someone who bought Philip Morris in 1988 (at a split-adjusted price of $7) fared over a 10-year period:

	EPS	Return on $7 Price
1988	$0.74	10.6%
1989	$1.01	14.4%
1990	$1.28	18.3%
1991	$1.51	21.6%
1992	$1.82	26.0%
1993	$1.35	19.3%
1994	$1.82	26.0%
1995	$2.17	31.0%
1996	$2.56	36.6%
1997	$3.00	42.9%

What gave Philip Morris such a high yearly coupon return, of course, was its relatively low valuation of $7, or 9.5 times earnings. If an investor had made the mistake of buying Philip Morris at $14, the coupon returns would have been half that.

It's no coincidence that Warren Buffett's Berkshire Hathaway portfolio includes so many growth companies from the consumer industry. Many writers and analysts have speculated that Buffett performs detailed financial statement analysis to find all his winners. But from all appearances, what Buffett covets most is a stable, growing earnings stream with coupons that beat bond yields. Take, for example, the earnings stream of newspaper publisher Gannett Co., in which Buffett bought a minority stake in 1994. Buffett paid approximately $24 (split adjusted), or 16 times earnings, for 4.9 percent of Gannett's shares. At the time, 30-year bonds yielded 7.8 percent. Buffett's returns, compared to a 30-year government bond, have been exceptional (see Figure 5-3). Buffett, in fact, was willing to pay a premium for Gannett, based on the fact that Gannett's earnings yield would quickly surpass the yield on bonds. Going forward, analysts were projecting that Gannett's earnings would grow at nearly 13 percent annual rates. Thus, Gannett offered Buffett a compelling earnings stream, especially after bond yields fell to around 6 percent in late 1997.

Not surprisingly, Gannett's stock rose by more than 150 percent in the three years subsequent to Buffett's purchase. By early 1998, newspaper properties such as Gannett had been bid up to between 20 and 25 times

FIGURE 5-3   Gannett's actual and expected earnings yields, 1994–2002.

	EPS	Return on $24	30-Year Yield	Spread
1994	$1.62	6.8%	7.8%	−1.0%
1995	$1.71	7.1%	6.9%	0.2%
1996	$1.96	8.2%	6.5%	1.7%
1997	$2.48	10.3%	6.5%	3.8%
1998	$2.78	11.6%	6.0%	5.6%
1999	$3.14	13.1%	6.0%	7.1%
2000	$3.54	14.8%	6.0%	8.8%
2001	$3.99	16.6%	6.0%	10.6%
2002	$4.50	18.8%	6.0%	12.8%

earnings. Buffett profited from the improvement in Gannett's earnings—which could have been predicted studying the company's historical earnings record—and from the market's willingness to pay ever-higher premiums for those earnings.

WHEN BONDS BECOME ALTERNATIVES TO STOCKS

Using the methods shown above, an investor can determine whether a stock offers a better or worse potential return than a bond. *Generally speaking, stocks are more attractive when they offer earnings yields equal to or greater than bond yields.* By contrast, bonds are most attractive when their yields far surpass the average earnings yields of stocks. By mid-1998, for example, a 30-year government bond yielded around 5.7 percent. But the average S&P 500 company traded at 30 times earnings, a yield of 3.3 percent. Given that the rate of growth of corporate earnings was falling in early 1998, bonds looked far more attractive than stocks. At the rate corporate earnings were growing, it would take several years before earnings yields would catch and surpass bond yields. Thus, the prudent course for investors was to avoid most common stocks and buy only those possessing exceptional yields.

Another way of viewing this relationship is to compare a company's likely earnings over the next several years with what a 3-month Treasury bill, the least-risk investment available, could provide over the same time. This exercise allows you to determine whether valuation levels and presumed growth rates for a company are realistic or simply rely on optimistic assumptions coming to fruition.

For this example, let's focus on two stocks, Microsoft and drugstore retailer Walgreen, both of which traded at huge premiums to their earnings throughout 1997 and into 1998. In July 1998, Microsoft traded at 71 times earnings, though earnings were expected to grow at only 22 percent annual rates. Likewise, Walgreen traded at 46 times earnings, a price that represented three-and-a-half times its earnings growth rate of 13 percent. In buying companies so generously priced, an investor must make sure the companies can guarantee returns that beat a Treasury bond. But that was not possible with Microsoft or Walgreen in 1998, not without help from a fickle market. Both stocks were pushed up to such extremes that buyers had to *hope* that enough investors piled into the stock after them to push the price up. Otherwise, these companies' earnings streams could not possibly return one's investment in a suitably short period.

Let's assume you had the choice of buying a $117 share of Microsoft—the split-adjusted price in July 1998—or a $117 Treasury bill that rolled over each year at a 5.25 percent rate. Let's also assume you could hold either investment five years. At the end of the fifth year, you would collect $34.11 in interest on the T-bill, making the total proceeds from the sale $151.11. For Microsoft's stock to beat the returns of a T-bill, it would have to trade higher than $151.11 at the end of the fifth year. That may seem like an easy target to hit until you consider Microsoft's earnings stream. If Microsoft's earnings grew at the rate analysts expected, its earnings yield would remain far below bond yields, even after holding the stock five years.

Microsoft's Earnings Yields

	EPS	Return on $117
1998	$1.61	1.4%
1999	$1.96	1.7%
2000	$2.39	2.0%
2001	$2.92	2.5%
2002	$3.56	3.0%

Another way to view this tradeoff is to determine the P/E ratio at which Microsoft must trade to beat a T-bill. To do this, compare the proceeds of the T-bill—in this case, $151.11—to Microsoft's presumed earnings at the end of the fifth year, $3.56 per share. Microsoft's stock returns will beat a T-bill only if it trades above $151.11 at the end of the fifth year. Given that earnings are projected to be $3.56 in the fifth year, Microsoft must trade at 42 times earnings in 2002 to beat the bond's return. More to the point, *it must trade at inflated premiums to its earnings over a five-year period to guarantee you a bond-beating return.* What are the chances this will occur? Should an investor rely on traders to keep the share price pumped up for five more years? Not at all. Yet that was the underlying logic that resulted in investors paying so dearly for Microsoft's earnings. Investors should never pin their hopes, and returns, on the chances that other investors will bid the stock to fundamentally dangerous levels.

In this case, Microsoft should not have been purchased at $117, since Microsoft's earnings could not have surpassed 1998 bond yields for several years. For the stock to beat a T-bill, analysts' earnings projections would have to prove true, a predicting trap you want to avoid when possible. In defense of the company, Microsoft has provided a long history of high growth, which makes the company an attractive buying target from time to time. But because the stock was priced so high relative to the company's growth rate, an investor took the risk that exogenous factors would spoil the future earnings stream.

Walgreen's valuation, in retrospect, was just as extreme. Between mid-1994 and July 1998, the stock more than quadrupled while annual earnings growth averaged only 13 percent. In fact, Walgreen has provided one of the most stable growth records in the retail sector. Earnings have grown at rates between 11 percent and 14 percent for several years. The market kept rewarding steady-growth companies and pushed this stock higher and higher. In early 1994, investors shunned this company at 12 times earnings. Four years later, they were in a frenzy to buy Walgreen at 46 times earnings. Those who were buying at the top—$48—inherited the following coupon yields:

Walgreen's Earnings Yields

	EPS	Return on $48
1998	$1.00	2.1%
1999	$1.13	2.4%
2000	$1.28	2.7%
2001	$1.44	3.0%
2002	$1.63	3.4%
2003	$1.84	3.8%

Presuming Walgreen's earnings grew at 13 percent annual rates, an investor would have to wait nine years—until 2006—before the company's *predicted* earnings would match bond yields prevailing in 1998. Only then would Walgreen begin to offer a bond-beating return. Of course, any number of factors, including a bear market, could occur within those five years to upset our assumptions. A bear market could drive down Walgreen's stock to 13 times earnings, its historical average, which might put the earnings stream in jeopardy and would decrease the chances that the stock's performance could beat a bond.

Using the same analysis we showed in the Microsoft example, Walgreen would have to remain overvalued for a period of years to guarantee investors any chance of beating a bond. Assume you could buy a $48 share in Walgreen or a $48 Treasury bill that rolled over at 5.25 percent a year. After five years, the value of the T-bill would grow to $62. For Walgreen's stock to beat the T-bill, it must rally to at least $62 by the end of the fifth year, 2003. By that time, as we showed above, Walgreen would earn an expected $1.63 per share. This means that Walgreen's stock would have to trade for at least 38 times earnings in the fifth year to beat a T-bill. In other words, it must remain overvalued for the next five years. The likelihood of this happening is slim and might hinge on circumstances—an ongoing bull market—on which you don't want to rely.

THE RELATIONSHIP BETWEEN BOND YIELDS AND STOCK PRICES

To this point, I have stressed the need to compare earnings yields to prevailing bond yields. In general, stocks are attractive when their earnings yields rise near or above bond yields. They are most attractive when the earnings yield exceeds bond yields and the company's growth rate ensures bond-beating returns in the future. This leads to the summary question: How much should an investor pay for a common stock given prevailing bond yields? That will depend largely on the company's growth rate. For as I stated above, a company with an outstanding growth rate can be purchased at a very low earnings yield provided that earnings yields quickly surpass bond yields. To be safe, an investor should look for an earnings stream that can beat bond yields within 2 to 3 years. I have summarized these principles in Figure 5-4, which lists the maximum P/E ratio (the inverse of earnings yield) you should pay given the following bond yields and growth rates. When possible, try to obtain a stock at a P/E ratio below these suggested ratios.

FIGURE 5-4 **Maximum P/E ratio for buying.**

Company's Sustainable Growth Rate

Bond Yields	Flat	10%	20%	30%
4.50%	22.2	26.9	32.0	45.4
4.75%	21.1	25.5	30.3	43.1
5.00%	20.0	24.2	28.8	40.9
5.25%	19.0	23.0	27.4	39.0
5.50%	18.2	22.0	26.2	37.2
5.75%	17.4	21.0	25.0	35.6
6.00%	16.7	20.2	24.0	34.1
6.25%	16.0	19.4	23.0	32.7
6.50%	15.4	18.6	22.2	31.5
6.75%	14.8	17.9	21.3	30.3
7.00%	14.3	17.3	20.6	29.2
7.25%	13.8	16.7	19.9	28.2
7.50%	13.3	16.1	19.2	27.3
7.75%	12.9	15.6	18.6	26.4
8.00%	12.5	15.1	18.0	25.6
8.25%	12.1	14.7	17.5	24.8
8.50%	11.8	14.2	16.9	24.1
8.75%	11.4	13.8	16.5	23.4
9.00%	11.1	13.4	16.0	22.7
9.25%	10.8	13.1	15.6	22.1
9.50%	10.5	12.7	15.2	21.5
9.75%	10.3	12.4	14.8	21.0
10.00%	10.0	12.1	14.4	20.5
10.25%	9.8	11.8	14.0	20.0
10.50%	9.5	11.5	13.7	19.5
10.75%	9.3	11.3	13.4	19.0
11.00%	9.1	11.0	13.1	18.6
11.25%	8.9	10.8	12.8	18.2
11.50%	8.7	10.5	12.5	17.8
11.75%	8.5	10.3	12.3	17.4
12.00%	8.3	10.1	12.0	17.0
12.25%	8.2	9.9	11.8	16.7
12.50%	8.0	9.7	11.5	16.4
12.75%	7.8	9.5	11.3	16.0
13.00%	7.7	9.3	11.1	15.7
13.25%	7.5	9.1	10.9	15.4
13.50%	7.4	9.0	10.7	15.1
13.75%	7.3	8.8	10.5	14.9
14.00%	7.1	8.6	10.3	14.6
14.25%	7.0	8.5	10.1	14.4
14.50%	6.9	8.3	9.9	14.1

IMPROVING RETURNS WITH A BUY-AND-HOLD APPROACH

"When the capital development of a country becomes a byproduct of a casino, the job is likely to be ill done."

John Maynard Keynes

Successful value investing requires that you never allow exogenous factors to enter into your trading decisions. The two general rules for buying and selling are (1) *do not trade stocks frequently* and (2) *hold stocks for a period sufficient to allow the shares to reach their true value.*

How long is long enough? There's no single answer. The great value investors differ widely on this question and have formed their own rules for holding a stock. Figure 6-1 shows the average holding periods of several value fund managers during the 1990s. Mario Gabelli, for example, looks for a 50 percent return within two years before he contemplates selling. Turnover at his Gabelli Asset fund has averaged about 18 percent in recent years, meaning he holds the average stock about five-and-a-half years. Michael Price of Mutual Shares Z has been more aggressive than Gabelli. This decade he has held stocks an average of 21 months. Like Gabelli, Price prefers to hold stocks at least two years, regardless of returns, to optimize their appreciation potential.

Warren Buffett, by contrast, would scoff at such impatience. As the king of buy-and-holders, he is wont to hold stocks "forever." Buffett plans to own his core holdings, what he calls "inevitables" (Coca-Cola, Gillette, etc.), until he dies, at which point the shares will revert to a trust. But Buffett's approach is relatively unique and wouldn't apply to most investors. Buffett has the luxury of owning companies outright, which puts him in a position to control their actions and financial policies. He can collect earnings and dividends from these companies and not worry about stock market vagaries.

But Buffett has not always been a buy-and-hold investor, a point I make in Chapter 15. His methodology has evolved to suit his personal circumstances. With more than $30 billion in net worth, Buffett can no longer flip small, undervalued companies for a profit as he did in the 1950s and 1960s. Those companies' contribution to Berkshire Hathaway's bottom line would be insignificant today, so Buffett must pass over many choice small caps. He compensates for this handicap by purchasing and holding large-cap stocks with strong franchise values. By focusing on large-cap companies too large to buy outright, Buffett places his portfolio at the mercy of the market and must stomach endless twists and turns in share price. But the types of stocks he now owns are more likely than other companies to provide stable returns well into the next century. Over time, he stands an excellent chance of meeting his financial goals.

Whether owning small or large companies, Buffett, Gabelli, Price, and the others have operated from a straightforward game plan—to own companies until they no longer provide a satisfactory return on their investment. There are many reasons, both intuitive and rational, why holding stocks for longer time periods is the best course of action. Perhaps the most compelling reason for holding is that investors sabotage their returns by trading too frequently. Many investors fail to realize that when they *trade* stocks, rather than invest for the long term, their stock-picking and stock-timing skills must be impeccable. If they cannot successfully time tops and bottoms or at least earn a profit on a higher percentage of their trades, they *will* fail to beat the market. Moreover, their returns are likely to lag those of a buy-and-hold investor.

Most bond, options, futures, and commodities traders *lose* money over time because they trade so frequently. They strive so hard to compete at these zero-sum games that they unwittingly create a natural escape velocity for their money. Over time, their winning trades likely equal their losing trades, but they will continually lose a fraction of their money to commissions and dealer spreads. Just as the moon lost its atmosphere molecule by

FIGURE 6-1 Asset turnover ratios at selected value funds.
Source: Morningstar, Inc.

Fund	Manager	1991	1992	1993	1994	1995	1996	1997	Avg. Holding Period (yrs.)
Babson Value	Nick Whitridge	31%	17%	26%	14%	6%	11%	17%	5.7
Gabelli Asset	Mario Gabelli	20%	14%	16%	19%	26%	15%	22%	5.3
Heartland Value	William Nasgovitz	79%	76%	51%	35%	31%	31%	55%	2.0
Legg Mason Value Trust	William Miller III	39%	39%	22%	26%	20%	20%	11%	4.0
Mutual Shares Z	Michael Price	48%	41%	49%	67%	79%	58%	50%	1.8
Oakmark	Robert Sanborn		34%	18%	29%	18%	24%	NA	4.1
Sequoia	William Ruane	36%	28%	24%	32%	15%	23%	8%	4.2
Strong Schafer Value	David Schafer	55%	53%	33%	28%	33%	18%	23%	2.9
Yacktman	Donald Yacktman			61%	49%	55%	59%	69%	1.7

molecule, their portfolios would eventually whittle to nothing if they kept playing the game. It's akin to a roulette table. A gambler could break even perpetually were it not for "0" and "00" on the wheel. As it stands, the casino will, over time, slowly siphon your cash, a few percentage points at a time.

Like roulette, investing is a game—a "loser's game," to borrow a phrase coined by analyst Charles Ellis. In a 1975 article published in the *Financial Analysts Journal,* Ellis equated investing to a cutthroat tournament where tens of thousands of individuals claw past one another to find the few "undiscovered" stocks that can generate market-beating returns. Any game that competitive, Ellis said, causes players to make unforced errors, just as in golf or tennis. The most successful investors, he concluded, are not the most savvy people or those with the best resources or those who make the best killing on a single stock. Rather, they are the ones who make the fewest mistakes during their careers.

> Most institutional investment managers continue to believe, or at least say they believe, that they can and soon will again "outperform the market." They won't and they can't. . . . The belief that active managers can beat the market is based on two assumptions: (1) liquidity offered in the stock market is an advantage and (2) institutional investing is a Winner's Game. [My] unhappy thesis can be briefly stated: Owing to important changes in the past 10 years, these basic assumptions are no longer true. On the contrary, market liquidity is a liability rather than an asset, and institutional investors will, over the long term, underperform the market because money management has become a Loser's Game.[1]

In a loser's game, such as golf, the actions of the loser determine the outcome. If Nick Faldo wins the British Open, he owes most of his success to the fact that his competitors made more mistakes than he during the four-day tournament. Not to take anything away from Faldo's game, but if he wins a tournament shooting 10 under par, he should walk away feeling fortunate that no other golfer *happened* to shoot 11 under par that week. Likewise, in the investing world, there might have been many Warren Buffetts by now. But Buffett sits on top because he has made the fewest mistakes over his 40-year career. Those he made were "sins of omission," in which he failed to buy a stock that rallied or sold a stock too soon. The loser's game scenario is similar to what Donald Trump once said about real estate investing: "Protect the downside and the upside will take care of itself."[2]

---

[1] Charles Ellis, "The Loser's Game," *Financial Analysts Journal,* July/August 1975, p. 95.

[2] Donald Trump, *The Art of the Deal,* New York, Warner Books, 1987, p. 48.

Ellis helped prove Trump's dictum by showing that frequent trading (high turnover) and the desire to win necessarily lead a money manager to experience substandard returns. He captured his thoughts in a wonderfully simple formula:

$$\text{Required return} = \frac{(\text{turnover rate} \cdot 2x) + y + (z \cdot \text{market's return})}{\text{market's return}}$$

where x = the average commission costs including dealer spreads,
         y = the fund's management and custody fees, and
         z = the fund manager's desired rate of return goal

A simple example will show what a powerful formula Ellis discovered. Assume that a fund manager's goal is to beat the S&P 500 by 5 percentage points a year and that the market is expected to rise 10 percent. To attempt this, the fund manager trades stocks an average of every six months (a turnover rate of 200 percent). Applying a 3 percent average commission rate and 0.20 percent management fees, you have:

$$\text{Required return} \ = \frac{[2.0*(2*.03)] + 0.002 + (1.05*.10)}{0.10}$$

$$= \frac{0.12 + 0.002 + 0.105}{0.10}$$

Required return $= 2.27$

Simply stated, if the manager wants to beat the market by 5 percent, he or she would have to deliver gross returns (before transaction costs) 2.27 times, or 127 percent, better than the market. By trading so often, the manager would keep increasing transaction costs and unwittingly raise the hurdle rate. And what a hurdle rate it is! For every one percent gain in the market, the manager's stocks must rise by 2.27 percent to beat the market, net of transaction fees.

What if the manager simply wished to mimic the S&P 500's returns? We'll substitute 1.00 in the numerator instead of 1.05. According to Ellis's formula, the average trade would have to beat the market by

$$\text{Required return} \ = \frac{[2.0*(2*.03)] + 0.002 + (1.0*.10)}{0.10}$$

$$= \frac{0.12 + 0.002 + 0.10}{0.10}$$

Required return $= 2.22$

As you can see, by lowering his or her expectations, the manager didn't lower the hurdle rate by much but still must deliver gross returns 2.22 times, or 122 percent, better than the market. The main driver of Ellis's formula, it turns out, is the turnover rate. The lower the turnover rate, the lower the required return on each trade. Let's assume that the manager turned over the portfolio only once a year (a turnover rate of 100 percent). Trades now must beat the market by an average of 62 percent to net the same returns.

$$\text{Required return} = \frac{[1.0*(2*.03)] + 0.002 + (1.0*0.1)}{0.1}$$

$$= \frac{0.06 + 0.002 + 0.1}{0.1}$$

$$\text{Required return} = 1.62$$

Needless to say, when I first read Ellis's article and reflected on its implications, it woke me up like a cold shower. It had the effect that St. Paul's Epistle to the Romans must have had on Martin Luther in 1508, when he discovered that what he had been taught went contrary to his own reasoning. Ellis's formula cast doubt on every article, thesis, and commentary made on the benefits of trading and thrust the fields of market timing and technical analysis into a dark light. To this day, Ellis's research begs a difficult question: If trading is potentially a punishing, losing exercise, why do so many in the field still attempt to time the short-term movement of stocks? The explanations lie outside the realm of this book, but we can conclude that it has more to do with crowd psychology, greed, and emotion than with reason.

The notion of fair value is revealed in company-prepared statements; it cannot be deduced from a gyrating stock price.

While we're on the subject, however, we must dispel the notion that technical analysis, the interpretation of price movements and chart patterns, can play a role in value investing. *It cannot.* As a value investor and part owner of a company, you should never let chart patterns, short-term market movements, or price and volume patterns form the basis of your trading. Your role is to comb through financial information to determine a "fair value" for the company. The notion of fair value is revealed in company-prepared statements; it cannot be deduced from a gyrating stock price. Indeed, to follow the rigid mathematical games of technical analysis is to place your faith in efficient markets, which we repudiated in Chapter 3.

Follow-up research has proven what Ellis stated 24 years ago. A monumental 1998 study by University of California, Davis, finance professors Terrance Odean and Brad Barber confirmed that frequent trading leads to inferior returns. Odean and Barber studied the trading activity of 78,000 households over a six-year period ending December 1996. Surprisingly, they found that the average investor's stock picks kept pace with the market. During the six-year period, the average household earned 17.7 percent a year, which was slightly ahead of the market's six-year return of 17.1 percent. However, the *net return,* subtracting commission and bid-ask spreads, was 15.6 percent a year. Yearly returns fell the more often households traded. The 20 percent of households that traded the most—as measured by portfolio turnover—earned an average yearly net return of just 10 percent. Households trading the least obtained an average net return of 17.5 percent. In other words, the average investor would have done just fine if he or she didn't trade in and out of stocks desiring better gains. Indeed, success goes to investors' heads and they force themselves to make errors that cost them dearly. The difference between a 10 percent yearly return and a 17 percent return is astounding when you compound results over a decade or two. Their conclusion:

> Our most dramatic empirical evidence supports the view that overconfidence leads to excessive trading . . . It is the cost of trading and frequency of trading, not portfolio selection, that explain the poor investment performance of households during our sample period.[3]

By the late-1990s, the results of such overconfidence had become apparent. In 1997, the average stock had been held in portfolios about 17 months, according to New York Stock Exchange figures. Six years earlier, investors held stocks an average of 26 months, or 50 percent longer. Seen in this context, the results obtained by Odean and Barber were hardly surprising. By 1998, investors were brimming with such confidence they seemed to attribute success mostly to their own stock-picking abilities, not the bull market. They increasingly believed they could dart in and out of stocks, perfectly time, tops and bottoms, repurchase their favorite issues at a later

---

[3] Terrance Odean and Brad Barber, "The Common Stock Investment Performance of Individual Investors," working paper presented at the Graduate School of Management, University of California, Davis, 1998, p. 2.

date, and still make a profit. But instead, they doomed themselves to mediocre returns.

RULES FOR HOLDING A STOCK
To further this discussion on holding period, let's set forth three principles:

1. *Your holding period must be sufficient for the market to reevaluate the stock.*   Thus, you should never set unrealistic time schedules on your holdings. To expect any stock to rise substantially in a short period is absurd. The more you expect the stock to rise, the more undervalued it must be relative to the company's intrinsic value. Additionally, you can never trust other investors to perceive the same undervalued conditions you perceived. If they did, the stock no longer would be of value, and value investing as a methodology would disappear. The fact that you may be recognizing a stock's potential first necessitates patience on your part.

    Successful stock picking, like science, is a form of discovery. It may take time before the market's momentum crowd latches onto your idea. Just how long you must wait depends on circumstances unique to each company. Harley-Davidson declined from $49 to $33, a nearly 33 percent drop, starting in mid-1996, but it didn't remain at such bargain prices for long. Its undervalued state was recognized almost immediately. Harley-Davidson reversed course in April 1997 and rallied to a new high within three months. At its first peak, the stock traded for 25 times earnings. When it bottomed, the stock sold for 17 times earnings. By contrast, Superior Industries languished in the low $20s—at 13 times earnings—for nearly two years before investors finally realized the company's inherent value and began bidding the shares up.

> The fact that you may be recognizing a stock's potential first necessitates patience on your part. Successful stock picking, like science, is a form of discovery.

No matter how long you must wait, however, it's imperative that the company continues to reward you by generating earnings on your behalf. For as I show in later chapters, you own the company's earnings and are entitled to a share of them. Theoretically, the shares should climb at least by the amount of per-share profits earned and retained by the company over your holding period. That's why investors should preference profitable companies.

2. *You should hold a stock as long as it continues to meet or exceed your expected returns.*   Value investing can be open-ended. As long as a company remains undervalued, its stock should be held— unless another, more suitable undervalued company can be found. But once the stock begins to rally, value investors often are faced with a difficult decision: Do you sell as soon as the shares become fairly valued or let profits ride? And if so, for how long? In this respect, investors best serve themselves by not attaching fail-safe price levels. Letting profits ride is the natural and prudent course. Selling should be considered only when (a) the stock has risen to extremely overvalued levels, (b) other, more attractive investments become apparent, or (c) the company has fully delivered its expected earnings to you and can no longer maintain its present pace of growth.

3. *At minimum, assume that you will hold the stock at least two years, the time often necessary to lift the stock to its fair value.*

WHY LONGER HOLDING PERIODS ARE PREFERRED

If the stock market rose or fell consistently or at least moved in tandem with sales or earnings growth, there would be no need for market timing. We would not need to perform technical analysis, nor would we need the thousands of analysts, market strategists, and fund managers trained to sift through financial information and predict the course of events. We could simply pick the stocks likely to show the best earnings stream over the next several years and hold on for the ride.

But the market never behaves as expected—and never will. It may be the most random acting institution on Earth. It weaves and cuts in erratic patterns that resemble the Alaskan coastline more than an efficient pricing mechanism. These price undulations—the short-term reversals of trend— are the source of the market-timing school of investing. The fact that these fluctuations can create big profits is the reason so many people attempt to time a market or stock. Look at Figure 6-2 and you'll see why. I've picked two hypothetical stocks that rise from $10 to $25. One rises erratically, the other consistently rises to $4, then falls back $2. On paper, someone who

FIGURE 6-2   The pitfalls of short-term timing.

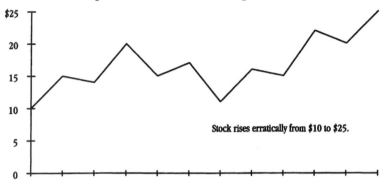

Stock rises erratically from $10 to $25.

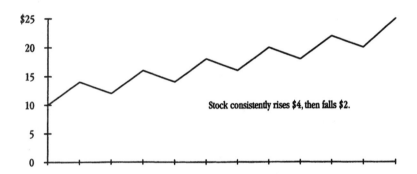

Stock consistently rises $4, then falls $2.

Erratically Rising Stock

Strategy	Trades	Commissions	After-Tax Gains	After-Tax Returns
Buy and hold—100 shares	**2**	**$24.75**	**$1,008**	**102%**
Exactly Timed Tops, Bottoms	12	155.99	2,780	281
Missed Tops, Bottoms by 5%	12	117.41	1,529	154
Missed Tops, Bottoms by 7.5%	12	102.52	1,075	109

Consistently Rising Stock

Strategy	Trades	Commissions	After-Tax Gains	After-Tax Returns
Exactly Timed Tops, Bottoms	2	$125.41	$1,782	180%
Missed Tops, Bottoms by 2.5%	12	109.42	1,282	130
Missed Tops, Bottoms by 5%	12	95.88	877	89

buys either stock at $10 and holds it to $25 picks up $15 in gains for a return of 150 percent.

THE "WINNING POINTS" METHOD

But because the two stocks fluctuated, they create the potential for much better gains than $15. In fact, the more a stock fluctuates, the more opportunities exist to beat its end-to-end return. I call these opportunities winning points, and define them as the maximum possible gains for a stock based on its volatility. In my example, though the two stocks rise a total of 15 points from beginning to end, the top one creates potentially 30 winning points of gain for someone who times buy and sell decisions exactly at the extremes. Winning points are simply the sum of all the rallies. The stock on the bottom of Figure 6-2 creates 23 winning points (five 4-point rallies and a final 3-point rally). Thus, on a $10 investment, it is possible to reap $23 in gains playing the stock's rally to $25. Had these two stocks fluctuated more than shown, there likely would have been still more winning points. In actuality, it's possible to attain infinite returns on your investment if the stock fluctuates enough over a long period. Consider General Motors, which hovered between $30 and $65 between 1988 and mid-1997. A buy-and-hold investor would have earned $35 in profits from beginning to end, for a compounded annual return of about 9 percent. But GM fluctuated so much over that period that traders could have more than quadrupled their money playing the shorter-term rallies to their fullest, then bailing out. On 10 separate occasions, GM rallied $10 or more in a few short months, then fell back again (see Figure 6-3). During one stretch, GM gained more than $30, then nearly lost it all. Traders able to time the stock successfully on a *day-to-day basis* could have made at least eight times as much money on GM as a buy-and-hold investor.

ON TIMING PEAKS AND TROUGHS

So why don't more people time the market successfully? Because they can't. Market timers try to make careers from these short-term opportunities. They also make huge mistakes if they can't take full advantage of those opportunities. The tables in Figure 6-2 above show what happens to someone who tries to trade the hypothetical stocks at their peaks and troughs but fails to time those extremes precisely. As you can see, the investor does not have to err too much to cut into returns and strip away all the advantages of timing. Recall from the earlier example that the person who buys 100 shares at $10 and times the stock exactly attains a net gain of $2780, or 281

FIGURE 6-3   General Motors.

percent (assuming 1 percent commissions on purchases and sales), easily beating the buy-and-hold investor.

But look at what happens if traders can't time their trades precisely. The gains are reduced by nearly one-half when they miss the tops and bottoms by 5 percent. When they miss by 7.5 percent, their net gains fall below those of the buy-and-hold investor. A 7.5 percent spread is not all that large. On a $15 stock, that represents only $1.13. If the stock peaks at $15 but you fail to sell until it reaches about $14.25, factoring in commissions and dealer spreads, a buy-and-hold investor would beat your returns. Indeed, on a small-cap, low-priced stock, you can miss the peaks by that much just by accepting the bid-ask spreads.

Notice, too, that to earn the $2780 profit, *traders must reinvest all the proceeds from the previous sale.* Thus, they constantly buy in at higher and higher prices, which raises their break-even point, increases their downside risk, and may even give them fewer shares in the end. That's an important point to remember. Taking partial profits in the market or reinvesting only a portion of your past proceeds could lower your overall dollar gains and make it less likely that you can beat a buy-and-hold position.

A REAL-LIFE EXAMPLE: THE DOW INDUSTRIALS 1988–1996

Assume for a moment that you bought the Dow Industrials index on January 1, 1988, and held it through August 1996. You would have bought the index at 1938.83 and held it up to 4640.84, for a before-tax return of 139.4 percent. After-tax returns would have been 94.5 percent. Could you have beaten those returns by timing the market? In theory, yes, because the Dow Industrials experienced enough volatility—deep enough price reversals—to create sufficient winning points. Looking at only the intermediate-term trends of the market—and not daily fluctuations, the DJIA created 4830 winning points over that seven-year period, about 78 percent more than the market's absolute rise. The reversals created 2128 losing points. Had you exactly timed the tops and bottoms, you would have seen after-tax gains, commissions included, of 186 percent, versus 94.5 percent for a buy-and-hold investor (see Figure 6-4).

But as the chart shows, it wasn't that easy. If you mistimed your buy and sell decisions by 5 percent, that is, bought 5 percent off the bottom and

FIGURE 6-4   Timing the Dow Industrials, Jan. 1988–Aug. 1996 ($1,000 invested in the DJIA; assumes 1% commissions & 31% tax rate).

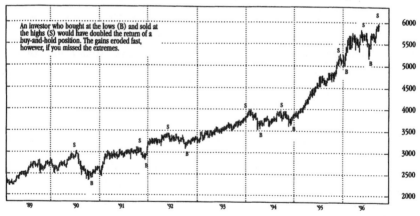

Strategy	Trades	After-Tax Gains	After-Tax Returns
Buy and Hold	2	$2,495	130.0%
Exactly Timed Tops, Bottoms	16	5,056	263.4
Missed Tops, Bottoms by 2.5%	16	3,418	178.1
Missed Tops, Bottoms by 5%	16	2,179	113.5

sold 5 percent off the top, your gains would have been just 92 percent, and a buy-and-hold investor would have beaten your returns. I know of no investor capable of picking peaks and troughs with 5 percent precision. Looking back, in fact, an investor could have easily missed a peak or trough by 5 percent. In most cases, they would have missed a market top or bottom by just a week or so. Investors would have needed to react quickly to market movements and then crossed their fingers.

Why did poor timing erode the gains so quickly? It's because of psychology and momentum. Stocks tend to show their fastest percentage advances and declines near their extremes. A great example was the 96-point sell-off of February 4, 1994, the day the Federal Reserve announced its first of several interest-rate increases. The market had peaked four days earlier but provided no strong signs that a sell-off loomed. The 2.5 percent drop blindsided timers who did not get out fast enough. Another example was the market's rapid reversal in April 1997, when the Dow Industrials lost nearly 10 percent, suddenly changed direction, and rallied 20 percent within two months. Such reversals are typical. Rallies get their fuel from quick spurts and die when momentum builds too fast. Market timers tend to miss these occasions because they cannot consistently trade at exact tops and bottoms.

As I said earlier, it was possible to generate 4830 winning points for yourself by perfectly timing the Dow Industrials between 1988 and August 1996. But how would you have known when to trade? Which indicator(s) would you have used? I have tested dozens of commonly used price and volume indicators in years past and found that none could have exactly called the peaks and troughs of that seven-year period. Some indicators weren't even close and would have had to be used with other indicators to enhance returns. Among the mistakes these technical indicators made:

- Most of the methods tested would have flashed sell signals in 1995 and again in 1996 at index levels averaging around 4350. Thus, you would have missed the market's next 4000 points of gains.
- Most price-volume indicators would have caused you to trade excessively in 1990 and again in 1992, a period of low volatility when the market gave off several false buy and sell signals.
- Anyone who traded based on dividend yields (sold when the S&P 500 stocks yielded less than 3 percent) missed at least three years of subsequent rallying and gains of more than 100 percent.
- Even value investors who tried to time markets based on rigid trading criteria (low price/book, price/earnings, and dividend/price ratios)

would likely have stayed out of the market and missed the strong mid-1990s rallies.

Compare the results of money managers and the point becomes more clear. Upwards of 80 percent of stock fund managers, many of whom rely on various timing models, fail to beat the S&P 500 each year, despite multimillion-dollar research budgets and access to up-to-the-minute information. And some of the industry's most respected fundamental and technical analysts have advocated high cash positions since 1991. Their clients have missed one of the great rallies this century.

The best way to rebuff market-timing philosophies is to reduce them to absurdity. I've created seven "commandments" to guide an investor through the timing process. Hopefully, as you apply these principles to your stock holdings, you will conclude that it's best to let the company's actions dictate value, not the market.

THE SEVEN COMMANDMENTS OF MARKET TIMING

1. *Define first how long you are willing to stay invested in the market.*
   Your holding period will determine whether it makes more sense to hold or trade. The longer your presumed holding period, the more sense a buy-and-hold strategy makes.

2. *The expected volatility of the market over that time period must be pronounced enough to give you a chance at beating a buy-and-hold strategy.*   Otherwise, it is best to hold.

3. *The more volatile the market is, the more "winning points" are created.*   Thus, the more chances exist to make a profit and to beat the buy-and-hold returns. When volatility is low, the opportunities to successfully time the market dry up. In these environments, it's best to keep your money invested.

4. *The less volatile the market or stock, the more losing trades you will have.*   Your timing model will be generating too many buy and sell signals that are close together. You'll also pay commissions on each trade.

5. *In order to trade a stock successfully, it has to be able to generate many more winning points than losing ones.*   A ratio of at least 2:1 is preferred. The general trend must be upward and expected to stay that way.

6. *Your chances of beating a buy-and-hold position will depend mainly on how close to the peaks and troughs you trade.*   Mistiming mar-

ket extremes by just a few percentage points can wipe out most of the advantages of timing.

7. *No technical indicator has ever been devised to predict the exact peaks and troughs of a stock or market.*   And none ever will. The factors that cause the market to gyrate change constantly and are too numerous to quantify successfully. Even if these factors could be quantified, most individual investors lack the resources and access to enough information to create such models.

C H A P T E R 7

INVESTING FOR RAPID PAYBACK

> "It's a real tragedy when you buy a stock that's overpriced, the
> company is a big success, and still you don't make any money."
>
> *Peter Lynch[1]*

I N ALMOST EVERY ENDEAVOR that involves money, we are taught to
think in terms of return. When you open a savings account at the
local bank or thrift, the first question you ask probably relates to the
interest rate on the account. *Rate of return* becomes the defining
parameter since nearly all other factors are equal: Savings accounts
are insured, they pay interest with the same frequency, and banks charge
nearly equivalent account maintenance fees. Given a chance to evaluate
several savings accounts, you probably will opt for the one paying the highest interest rate. Why? Because you understand that higher returns equate
to faster payback.

When you gamble, whether on horses, roulette, or state lotteries, your
mind works through similar exercises. You try to assess which game, horse,
or combination of numbers, coins, or bars will return your original investment most quickly.

The concept of payback is universally known and practiced by businesses too, small and large alike. It forms the foundation of every capital-
spending decision by management. When developers purchase tracts of

---

[1] Peter Lynch, *One Up on Wall Street,* New York, Penguin Books, 1989, p. 244.

land and price the parcels for sale to builders, they calculate how quickly their investments in new streets, sewers, and utility hookups will pay off. The sooner their start-up investment is returned, the sooner they can deploy the proceeds into another development. When an oil company considers whether to expand a refinery, it projects sales and profits years in advance to determine the yearly rate of return and payback period.

Similarly, when Cracker Barrel executives sit down and decide whether to build new restaurants, they look first at *return on investment,* or the payback period. Building a new Cracker Barrel restaurant requires upwards of $3.5 million to buy land, erect a building, equip it with kitchen fixtures and tables and chairs, stock the kitchen with food and the store with novelty items, and buy advertising time or space in local media. Management's financial goal, then, is to earn $3.5 million in bottom-line profits on that restaurant as soon as possible. The longer it takes to earn $3.5 million, the longer Cracker Barrel's money is tied up and can't be recycled to open other restaurants. Fortunately, Cracker Barrel has one of the fastest payback periods in the restaurant business, which is the reason it is so profitable. Its stores earn upwards of $1 million in profits a year, a 25 to 30 percent return on the company's original investment. This allows the corporation to earn its money back in roughly three years.

WHAT CONSTITUTES ADEQUATE PAYBACK?

How long should an investor wait to get back his or her money? As a rule, when buying a *private* business, the enterprise should generate enough profits—or cash flow—to return your original investment *within five to seven years.* If you spent $200,000 building a car wash, for example, you want a minimum average annual return of $28,000 to $40,000. If it takes longer than seven years to recoup your money, you should seriously consider walking away from the venture. With each additional year, the chances increase that uncontrollable factors—a slowdown in the economy, inflation, new competition, the loss of key contracts or employees, etc.— will cause an unexpected slowdown in sales and prolong the payback period. When the payback period reaches 10 years or more, investors are literally tossing their money away. Not only are they subject to those unexpected factors mentioned above, but the yearly returns are undercut too much by inflation.

Let's say Home Depot builds a new store in Dallas at a cost of $15 million. In making this decision, the company believes the store can generate an average of $20 million a year in sales and $3 million a year in after-tax profits. If all goes according to plan, payback on the original $15 million investment would occur at the end of the fifth year, a suitable return of 20 percent a year. But what happens if Menards, Lowe's, and Hechinger's all open stores in Dallas within two miles of Home Depot's? It's doubtful that Dallas residents could patronize all four stores frequently enough to make them profitable. More likely, Home Depot could not attain its $20 million annual sales targets. It could respond by increasing advertising expenses or cutting prices, but at the risk of lower profit margins and bottom-line earnings. If annual profits ultimately drop to $2 million, Home Depot's payback rises to seven-and-a-half years. At profits of $1.5 million, payback climbs to an abysmal 10 years.

Of course, inflation also can erode the value of profits from the Dallas store. With annual inflation at 3 percent, the company's inflation-adjusted return on a $1.5 million profit in the 10th year is only $1.12 million. Home Depot would not recoup its $15 million original investment until the beginning of the 13th year. If inflation averaged 5 percent, full payback would not occur until the first quarter of year 15.

By now, it should be apparent why a business prefers rapid payback. Any number of events could occur in those later years to upset Home Depot's predicted profitability. Dallas might suffer a housing market recession and building material sales could slump. Sales and property tax rates might double for the store. The city council might approve a retail strip center a mile away that takes away all the store's business. Or the council might create an enterprise zone giving Home Depot's competitors a tax break, thus allowing them to lower prices.

PAYBACK INVOLVES CHOICES

While it sounds avaricious to expect payback within seven years, consider that you have tens of thousands of public and private investment opportunities worldwide from which to choose. Those offering the fastest paybacks given an acceptable amount of risk should be chosen first. Why wait for a 10-year payback on a car wash when the laundromat down the street offers to pay you back in half the time? If both bear the same risks, all of your resources should be directed toward the laundromat.

Indeed, two concepts are critical to and implied in payback analysis: (1) the idea of *opportunity costs* and (2) the axiom that *returns must be measured in tangible terms.*

Measuring Opportunity Costs

In classical finance, payback is a competitive concept. Since the goal of an enterprise is to maximize the total return on investment, every dollar spent by a business on a capital project must generate the highest possible return. Thus, every project must be justified on the basis that it represents the best use of cash, for the enterprise can and should sink its money into a project that is returning more.

Obviously, rates of return vary by project and will be determined by a host of factors, not the least of which are pricing and the industry's competitive situation. A new golf course built in a city with no other golf courses may generate a 30 percent annual return on investment, but only a 10 percent return if four other courses exist nearby. A newspaper with a monopoly in its hometown will generate a much higher return than yet another tabloid opened in New York City. Rate of return varies by industry too. A new $500 million auto assembly plant may generate only a 7 percent return for Chrysler or Ford, while a microprocessor plant may generate a 25 percent return for Advanced Micro Devices or Intel. A new McDonald's or Wendy's restaurant in Canada may generate an 18 percent annual return on the company's investment.

Theoretically, an enterprise willing and able to build either an auto plant or a golf course should build the golf course. But that's not always practical. General Motors is in the business of making cars, where its core competencies lie, not in manicuring fairways. When faced with the choice of constructing a golf course or a plant, GM must always opt for the plant, even though it generates lower annual returns. Similarly, golf course designer Pete Dye should never try to oversee a Buick assembly line.

But GM always has other options at its disposal. Rather than build a new plant, it can modernize a poorly performing existing plant and perhaps boost rates of return above 7 percent. It may choose to buy a supplier that is earning more than 7 percent on its invested capital. GM may close a money-losing plant and boost corporatewide rates of return as a result. It may sell a plant and use the money to pay off 8 percent loans. Or GM may simply invest the $500 million in government bonds and try to obtain returns higher than 7 percent. If any of these alternatives can generate a better return than the *projected* return on the new plant, GM should undertake that project first.

As an investor, GM must look at all spending decisions as opportunities won or lost. Every dollar spent on one project is a dollar unavailable for other projects. Never mind that GM may be expanding its output or adding workers with that one dollar. It's not enough that GM plows its money back into the company. That dollar must provide a suitable return as measured against what GM could have earned on that dollar somewhere else.

We look at our investments in similar ways. Because the market tempts us with thousands of potential investments each day, we have learned to screen all investment choices until we find just a few that meet our risk/return characteristics. Likewise, we've learned to measure returns against a benchmark of performance, usually a stock index. If your broker said that your portfolio increased 12 percent in value last year, you'd probably be elated, that is, until she told you that the stock market rose 18 percent. Once you learn that competing investments can outperform your own, you must adapt your thinking and look at opportunity costs. In this case, the opportunity cost of your money is great. You lost the chance at an extra six percentage points because you chose your investments poorly.

Returns Must Be Tangible

The second critical concept in understanding payback is that it must be measured in tangible terms. There must be a standard unit of performance allowing you to measure whether project A is better than project B, whether the golf course is superior to the auto plant, or whether Home Depot's Dallas store is better than no store at all. That unit of performance is *cash flow*—or its proxy, *net income.*

Most investors mistakenly measure payback in terms of stock performance, but they delude themselves. Stocks represent a perception of value, not actual value. This should be painfully obvious to investors who have watched their shares fall drastically when a company reports good earnings, or who have witnessed abrupt up-and-down movements in a stock though no material change in the company's profitability has taken place. The stock market is not an arbiter of exact value but a forum for individuals to exchange their judgments of value.

> The stock market is not an arbiter of exact value but a forum for individuals to exchange their judgments of value.

The proper measure of stock returns must be net income because net income is tangible. It is not fleeting, like share price. It can't evaporate like a bull market. When a company earns $1 million of profit in a year, the company's net worth should increase by $1 million. The profits are added to the balance sheet as *retained earnings,* which increases shareholders' equity and the value of the enterprise. The company, of course, can return the entire $1 million as dividends—which shareholders are entitled to. Or it can "retain" all of that $1 million and plow it back into the company, hopefully to generate future earnings. Alternatively, it can return some to shareholders and retain the rest, the most commonly strategy.

Either way, as a shareholder you have a claim on that $1 million. If you own 1 percent of the stock, you are owed $10,000. If you own one one-millionth of the company, you are entitled to claim $1. The company can pay the entire claim to you now, pay some and retain some, or retain it all for now.

When you buy a stock, you own a claim on all the company's future earnings. That's why you bought shares in the first place, to take part in the company's success, whether for one quarter, one year, or a decade. That's the only real return you are guaranteed. No guarantee exists that the stock will increase in value. The price of the stock, in fact, may never change over your holding period. That's because nothing compels the shares to rise except public demand, which is fickle. A war could break out, the nation could plunge into a recession, a bear market could begin, or mutual fund managers may simply tire of owning your stock. Any of these factors could cause a prolonged decline in the share price. Procter & Gamble's stock declined for seven consecutive years between 1973 and 1979, a period in which sales tripled and net income doubled. Wal-Mart's stock peaked in 1993 and didn't rally to a new high for nearly four years, over which time earnings continued to rise and sales doubled to more than $100 billion.

How do you measure payback with earnings? Very simply, you total up a company's earnings and compare them against your original investment. If you spent $50 on DuPont's stock, you are paid back fully when DuPont generates $50 in per-share net income starting from the time you bought it. If DuPont consistently earns $2 per share a year, the payback period is 25 years. If DuPont earns $2 per share the first year, you have garnered only a 4 percent return on your money. *The performance of DuPont's stock during that first year is irrelevant!* It may have rallied 30 percent; it may have dropped 20 percent; but it has no bearing on measuring performance. While you may delight in seeing DuPont's stock rally 30 percent, you must take solace in the fact that the rally was undeserved. Certainly it was unjustified by the meager 4 percent return on your $50. The stock might reverse course the next year and drop precipitously. Likewise, a 20 percent decline in DuPont's stock would be just as irrational, since the intrinsic value of the company rose.

Stock price movements cannot serve as a measuring stick for payback. Stocks fluctuate in random, nonsensical patterns, sometimes reflecting the true value of the company, oftentimes not. They are like the broken clock, correct twice a day and far off the mark most of the time. Net income, by contrast, is tangible and fixed in time. It is backed by hard dollars management earned on your behalf that increased the net worth of the company. Stock prices are backed only by the faith buyers have in them—at that moment. Measuring payback by stock price swings is like trying to measure the value of a thoroughbred horse by the odds bettors placed on his winning. It is ludicrous.

Admittedly, few investors would hold DuPont long enough for the company to earn $50 per share after tax. Nor would they hold most other stocks that long. Likely, they would hold it two years or less, a common holding period for the average investor. Yet the same analysis applies. No matter your holding period, you should expect the company to generate earnings that are either returned to you or retained to enhance the company's intrinsic value.

If you held DuPont's stock two years, over which time the company generated $5 in per-share earnings, you should expect a combination of $5 in dividends and retained earnings. If all $5 is returned as dividends, you should expect no movement in the share price, since DuPont has not increased its per-share net worth. If it retained all $5, it is reasonable to expect the stock to climb at least $5 over that two-year period. If management put that $5 to good use building more efficient plants, paying off debt, or expanding into new foreign markets, DuPont's net worth should rise more than $5 per share, which should result in at least a $5 increase in share price.

Over longer periods the same relationship should hold. If DuPont generated $25 in per share earnings over the next 10 years, you should expect, at minimum, a $25 increase in share price. On a $50 initial investment, that's a total return of 50 percent and an annual return of 4 percent. You may be dissuaded by a measly 4 percent annual earnings return, but for most of the market's history that has been the norm. Until recently, stocks had a tendency to rise in tandem with the increase in companies' net worth. Recent high-flying returns, with stocks rising two and three times as fast as earnings, are abnormal and must eventually revert to the mean.

Between 1928 and 1997, the Dow Industrials index rose an average of only 4.9 percent a year, not 10 to 15 percent as is commonly believed. Earnings for the Dow Jones Industrial companies grew at 4.7 percent annual rates during that 69-year period. Book values for the Dow Industrials companies grew at about 4.3 percent annual rates (see Figure 7-1). So there has been a close correlation between share-price growth, growth in earnings, and growth in shareholders' equity.

FIGURE 7-1   Book values and prices for the Dow Industrials 1929–1997.

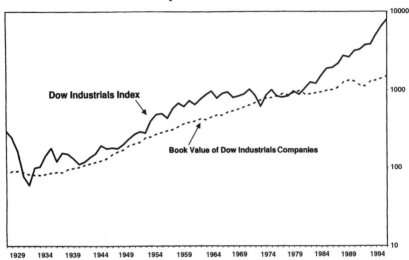

USING P/E TO LINK NET INCOME TO PAYBACK

How does net income relate to payback? It's through our expectations, which are best reflected in the price-to-earnings (P/E) ratio assigned to a stock. The P/E ratio reflects the premium that investors willingly pay for a share of the company's present and future earnings. If the P/E is 20, investors pay $20 for every $1 of earnings the company currently generates on their behalf, which is the same as getting a 1/20th yearly return on their investment. If the P/E is 50, they receive a 1/50th return on their original investment, or an *earnings yield* of only 2 percent. If the P/E is 8, the earnings yield is 12.5 percent.

Why, then, do investors chase high P/E stocks knowing that the company's payback period will be longer? Because of the company's earnings growth rate, which is the final yardstick for measuring payback. The faster a company's earnings grow, the quicker the company generates the earnings needed to return your investment. If DuPont's earnings start at a base of $2 a year and grow at 10 percent annual rates, your $50 investment will come back to you much faster than if DuPont's earnings grow only 5 percent a year. The expectations of DuPont's future performance are captured, theoretically, in the P/E ratio. If investors believe DuPont's earnings can rise 10 percent each year, they might be willing to pay 20 times earnings for the stock. If their expectations are that DuPont's earnings will grow only 2 percent, the stock's P/E might be 10.

There's no magic formula dictating how a P/E ratio should relate to growth. Investors will tolerate a different relationship based on how they interpret information. Theoretically, a company growing at 15 percent a year ought to trade at an average P/E ratio of 15. If earnings grew at 35 percent rates, you would expect an average P/E of 35. In practice, such pleasant states of price/earnings equilibrium rarely exist. Because investors are quick to react to new inputs, such as a change in interest rates, poor near-term earnings, or a weak economy, their *perceptions* of growth will constantly change, as will the P/E ratio. A software company may trade at a P/E of 46 one month, 52 the next, and just 35 the next. All the while, earnings may be growing at a constant rate. A start-up biotechnology company may trade at a P/E of 20 one year, 100 the following year, and 15 the next.

This suggests a trial-and-error process in which investors are constantly adjusting their growth estimates. It's a game value investors should ignore, for in nearly all cases, investors will harm their returns making bets on stock movements and reacting to short-lived trends.

THE PAYBACK TABLE

There is, however, a formula—far from magic, but beautifully simplistic—that lets you put P/E, net income, and payback in perspective and ensures that you never overpay for your share of a company's earnings. It's summed up in my payback table (see Figure 7-2). Using this table, you can gauge quickly whether a company can return your money within a short period. For example, assume that Philip Morris trades at $45 and generated $3 per share in earnings over the past year. Its earnings have grown at 15 percent annual rates. With the stock at $45 and earnings at $3, we can easily calculate the P/E ratio to be 15. In order to own a claim on Philip Morris's $3 of earnings, you would have to pay $45. Is that a fair price? You cannot draw any conclusions until you compare the $45 sale price to Philip Morris's growth rate. If Philip Morris showed no growth, it will perpetually earn $3 per year, meaning it would take the company 15 years to generate $45 in earnings and pay you back fully. Obviously, that's too long for any investor to wait.

But if earnings grew 15 percent a year, Philip Morris would generate $45 in earnings much quicker. How much quicker? Glance at the chart. When a stock trades at a P/E of 15 and earnings grow at 15 percent rates, payback occurs in about eight years. You can easily verify this relationship mathematically. Starting with a $3 earnings base, Philip Morris's future earnings would be $3.45, $3.97, $4.56, $5.25, $6.03, $6.94, $7.98, $9.18, and so on. By the eighth year, Philip Morris's combined earnings would finally equal and then surpass $45.

FIGURE 7-2 **Payback periods on stocks (length of time (in years) it takes a company to generate enough earnings to return your investment).**

P/E Ratio

EPS Growth	5	10	15	20	25	30	35	40	45	50	55
2%	4	9	13	16	20	23	26	29	32	34	37
4%	4	8	11	14	17	20	22	24	26	27	29
6%	4	8	10	13	15	17	19	20	22	23	24
8%	4	7	10	12	14	15	17	18	19	20	21
10%	4	7	9	11	13	14	15	16	17	18	19
12%	3	6	9	10	12	13	14	15	16	17	17
14%	3	6	8	10	11	12	13	14	15	15	16
16%	3	6	8	9	10	11	12	14	14	14	15
18%	3	6	7	9	10	11	12	12	13	13	14
20%	3	6	7	8	9	10	11	12	12	13	14
22%	3	5	7	8	9	10	10	11	12	12	12
24%	3	5	7	8	9	9	10	10	11	11	12
26%	3	5	6	7	8	9	10	10	10	11	11
28%	3	5	6	7	8	9	9	10	10	10	11
30%	3	5	6	7	8	9	9	9	10	10	10
32%	3	5	6	7	7	8	9	9	9	10	10
34%	3	5	6	7	7	8	8	9	9	9	10
36%	3	4	6	6	7	8	8	8	9	9	9
38%	3	4	5	6	7	7	8	8	8	9	9
40%	3	4	5	6	7	7	8	8	8	9	9

■ Attractive/Undervalued Zone
▨ Neutral Zone
☐ Unattractive/Speculative Zone

What if Philip Morris's earnings grew only 8 percent a year? According to the table, payback would occur in 10 years. If earnings grew at 30 percent annual rates, payback comes in only 6 years. Unquestionably, a 6-year payback is more desirable than 8 years, or 10. Just as shorter payback was desirable when evaluating private businesses—as discussed earlier—it is paramount when buying the stock of a public business, which leads to three important summary points:

1. *Earnings payback is the only true measure of expected investment performance.* You cannot use expected stock price movements when predicting returns.

2. *A stock offering a lower payback is superior to a stock with a higher payback, holding other factors equal.* If given a choice between two roughly similar stocks—Eli Lilly and Merck, for example—the

stock offering the fastest payback not only is the most undervalued, it offers more upside stock potential.

3.   *A stock's payback period constantly shifts according to the market's transitory perceptions.* But you should not alter your perceptions to join the crowd. You should wait until a stock reaches a reasonably low payback price before buying.

If possible, wait until a stock reaches the attractive *payback zone,* highlighted in darker-shaded gray in the table. Stocks with payback periods below seven years are considered well undervalued relative to their growth rates. Novellus Systems, a maker of semiconductor equipment, was an excellent example in 1996. The stock plunged to $32 during the summer, or just six times earnings. Yet earnings were growing at 28 percent annual rates. According to the payback chart, Novellus offered a payback period of just four years. The stock turned on a dime and rallied over the next 16 months, hitting $130 by October 1997.

The beauty of the payback method is that you don't have to change your parameters to fit the times. It is useful in any market, regardless of economic conditions, interest rates, or the company you are evaluating. It is useful in bull markets, when most investors are willing to pay higher and higher prices for companies, and in the throes of a bear market.

PAYBACK AND GROWTH, A SECOND PRACTICAL METHOD

A second, equally simple approach to analyzing payback is to chart a stock's progress against its change in earnings. Theoretically, a company whose earnings grow at 15 percent annual rates should see its stock climb an *average* of 15 percent a year, assuming the market continues to attach the same multiple (P/E ratio) to the stream of earnings. Note, I used the word *average* to describe predicted price movements. Over long periods, we can expect a stock's earnings growth rate to match exactly its stock price growth rate. In the short term, it rarely happens. Take, for example, drugstore chain Walgreen, whose earnings have tended to rise about 13 percent a year. Though earnings are consistent, investors nevertheless must expect random, short-term stock price movements. Let's assume that Walgreen's stock experienced yearly changes of 15 percent, 25 percent, minus 20 percent, 40 percent, and 14 percent. These yearly changes are highly erratic, yet over time they will even out. The stock will eventually trade at a P/E ratio close to its growth rate. In this example, Walgreen trades at a P/E of 13 at the end of the fifth year, just what we might have expected.

	EPS	Price	% Increase	P/E
1998	1.00	$13.00		13.0
1999	1.13	$14.95	15	13.2
2000	1.28	$18.69	25	14.6
2001	1.44	$14.95	−20	10.3
2002	1.63	$20.93	40	12.8
2003	1.84	$23.86	14	13.0

If we were to project Walgreen's earnings and share price over longer periods of time, we would expect the same trends to hold true. As long as earnings growth averaged 13 percent, the share price would grow at the same average rate. Thus, by the year 2008, we would expect earnings to reach $3.39 per share. We also would expect the stock to trade around $44 by the end of 2008. Of course, any number of factors could cause the stock to trade far above or below $44 in 2008. In a bear market, investors may choose to value Walgreen at just 8 times earnings, or $27. Conversely, pharmaceutical stocks might experience a great rally in 2008 and investors might willingly pay 25 times earnings, or $85, for Walgreen. Neither extreme would represent a state of price efficiency or a realistic appraisal of the company's worth. Without hesitation, we could conclude that Walgreen would be grossly overvalued at $85 and likewise undervalued at $27.

We can represent this pictorially, first with the payback table. With a growth rate of 13 percent and a P/E of 25, Walgreen's payback would be roughly 11.5 years according to the table. An investor would have to wait 11.5 years for the company to accumulate enough profits to equal the original investment. As I demonstrated earlier, such a prolonged payback is not desirable. Indeed, an investor should shun Walgreen at $87, or prices close to $87. But at a price of $27, payback would occur in the sixth year—a very desirable situation.

Many stocks behave exactly in this manner. Though earnings are steady, the stock nevertheless gyrates around the trendline of the company's growth rate, alternately reaching overvalued and undervalued price levels. Indeed, the best way to understand payback is to view it in the context of stock-price movements. We can depict this relationship graphically by comparing longer-term trends in earnings to longer-term movements in share price, as we did with Walgreen. Let's turn our attention to PepsiCo, the soft-drink and snack-food company, whose earnings and share-price growth moved in virtual lockstep over a 35-year period ending in 1994 (see Figure 7-3). Adjusting for past stock splits, PepsiCo rose from less than $0.75 in 1960 to just under $40 by the end of 1994. Running alongside the stock prices is a line showing trailing 12-months earnings. I adjusted the chart so that both prices and earnings could be put on the same scale. This helps to show the rate of change of both. PepsiCo traded at an average P/E ratio of 13 between 1960 and 1994, exactly what its annualized earnings growth averaged over that period. The fact that the stock rarely traded at exactly 13 times earnings shows that the market was constantly adjusting its perceptions of PepsiCo's expected growth rate. The market was willing to pay 35 times earnings for the company in 1973 and only 8 times earnings just two years later.

By early 1997, investors bid PepsiCo's shares to more than 30 times earnings again, far outreaching its historical growth rate. You can see that in retrospect, investors' perceptions of PepsiCo often were incorrect. Despite occasional earnings accelerations or decelerations, the actual long-term growth rate remained remarkably constant. What didn't remain constant was the share price, which weaved and bobbed around the earnings

FIGURE 7-3 PepsiCo 1960–1994.

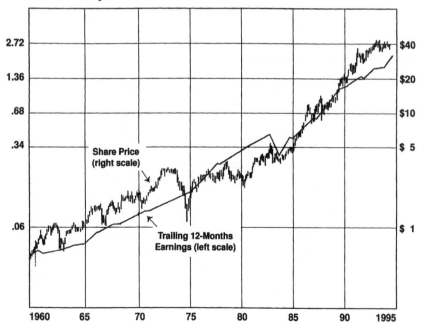

trendline. There were periods, such as the late 1960s and early 1970s, when the stock sold for an average of 20 times earnings. Alternately, the shares hovered below the earnings trendline for a number of years. That pattern holds for nearly all stocks. Periods of inflated prices will always be followed by periods of depressed prices and vice versa, with the earnings trendline forming the mean. Or as Peter Lynch once remarked:

> Often, there is no correlation between the success of a company's operations and the success of its stock over a few months or even a few years. In the long term, there is a 100 percent correlation between the success of the company and the success of its stock.[2]

As PepsiCo's chart shows, undervalued and overvalued conditions may persist for years, a fact that makes it difficult to pick the proper price at which to buy. Investors should generally avoid buying a stock well above its earnings trendline, where the risk of price decline is greatest. Such overvalued situations cannot exist indefinitely. Something must give: Either earnings accelerate faster than the market anticipates or the stock drops back to its trendline—or below. The further above the trendline the stock climbs, the more downside risk is inherent in the purchase. When a stock's P/E ratio rises well above the company's ability to generate suitable earnings, the payback period increases, and so does the eventual risk that sooner or later the company or its stock will fail to perform to your expectations.

THE VALUE OF BUYING GROWTH
When faced with two identically undervalued companies, an investor always should favor the one showing the best growth rate. By growth rate, I'm referring to the company's ability to generate higher and higher per-share earnings each year. Growth is the engine that drives P/E and provides the measuring stick for payback. Perhaps less understood is the fact that growth companies generate increasing rates of return on your original investment, as I showed in Chapter 5. Buying growth companies at depressed prices and holding the shares for extended periods will cause your yearly returns to reach astronomical levels.

Let's use the example of Philip Morris and assume the same earnings stream outlined earlier in this chapter. Instead of judging returns based on stock price fluctuations, we'll compare earnings to the original purchase price.

---

[2] Peter Lynch, *Beating the Street,* New York, Simon & Schuster, 1993, p. 303.

	Price Paid	EPS	P/E	Price/EPS	EPS Yield
1996	$45	$3.00	15	15.0	6.7%
1997		$3.45		13.0	7.7%
1998		$3.97		11.3	8.8%
1999		$4.56		9.9	10.1%
2000		$5.25		8.6	11.6%
2001		$6.03		7.5	13.3%
2002		$6.94		6.5	15.4%
2003		$7.98		5.6	17.9%
2004		$9.18		4.9	20.4%

As you can see, by the year 2004, Philip Morris would generate $9.18 in per-share earnings on your behalf. That translates into a 20.4 percent yearly return on your original $45 investment. In subsequent years, as Philip Morris earnings continue to grow, the rate of return will continue to grow too. Conversely, the rate of return P/E ratio will continue to fall. In 1996, you paid 15 times earnings to acquire Philip Morris at $45. By 2004, the implied P/E ratio has fallen to 4.9. In other words, the original purchase price was only 4.9 times the current earnings. Provided the company's growth rate remains constant, the rate of return increases to fantastic levels the longer you hold the shares. Investors who bought Philip Morris in 1984, when it traded for a split-adjusted price of $3, received in 1998 yearly earnings that exceeded their original investment. That's a 100 percent yearly return achieved without effort.

VALUING A COMPANY: ESTIMATING EARNINGS AND CASH FLOW

> "Value, under any plausible theory of capitalized earnings power, is necessarily forward looking."
>
> *James Bonbright[1]*

HAVING DISCUSSED THE MERITS and major principles of value investing in depth, we can now turn our study inward, to financial statements, which allow us to determine when a truly undervalued situation exists. We will start with a simple discussion of valuation and proceed in later chapters to more advanced methods of interpreting a company's performance.

When you pay cash for shares of stock, what are you really buying? The right to appoint senior management? A lien on the company's sales? A piece of the product line? A claim on the brand name? Actually, it's none of the above. It might surprise you to know that as an investor, you cannot claim any of the company's assets, whether cash, property, or intangibles. Civil courts have ruled that your status as an investor does not entitle you to the company's physical merchandise. You have the right, of course, to

---

[1] James C. Bonbright, *The Valuation of Property,* vol. I, reprint of 1937 ed., New York, The Michie Co, 1965, pp. 249–250.

demand that management protect the value of merchandise and use company assets to create earnings. Otherwise, you have no legal standing to claim a piece of the balance sheet. You cannot, for example, walk into Sara Lee's headquarters and demand six crates of frozen cakes. Nor would your 100 shares entitle you to a free set of Callaway golf clubs on demand.

YOU OWN THE EARNINGS!

Instead, your ownership interest entitles you to a share of the company's future earnings, a right most investors don't realize they have. Your claim on those earnings will be based on the size of your stock holdings. If Company X earns $1 million and you own 1 percent of the stock, you can claim $10,000 of those earnings. An easier way to calculate your share of the earnings is simply to multiply yearly earnings by the number of shares you hold. If Merck earns $3.50 per share and you own 200 shares, you can claim $700 of the company's total net income. The company has an obligation to return these earnings to you sooner or later, whether it exists as a private or public enterprise. An owner of a private company, for example, can pocket 100 percent of the yearly after-tax income. Those earnings constitute an owner's payback on the original investment and are the reason why the owner bought the company in the first place. The key to valuing a public company is to determine how much and how quickly a company can earn profits on your behalf.

> The key to valuing a public company is to determine how much and how quickly a company can earn profits on your behalf.

HOW MUCH WOULD YOU PAY FOR A SHARE OF YOURSELF?

For argument's sake, let's suppose your household was a public company with floating stock. Furthermore, let's assume you had the choice to invest in yourself or invest your money in another company or project. How would you begin evaluating the merits of both investments? First, start with some hypothetical assumptions:

Household salary: $75,000
Household spending: $65,000
Savings: $10,000

Household net worth: $80,000

Growth rate of salary: 5 percent annually

Outstanding debt: $175,000 (car loan and mortgage)

How would you value this enterprise? More important, what price would you pay for an ownership interest in this household? As you tried to think of the relevant criteria on which to value yourself, a thousand questions might run through your mind, among them:

- What is the likelihood that your salary will grow 5 percent a year? Can it grow faster? If so, how?
- What does your household do with its net income? Are all expenditures necessary? Are some expenditures temporary? Do any expenditures increase the household's net worth?
- What is your savings rate and what rate of return do you expect from your excess income? Are you plowing your disposable income into a 4 percent savings account or aggressive growth stocks?
- Are personal expenditures rising or falling? Are they rising at the rate of income?
- Is your salary predictable or cyclical? What are the chances you may lose your job or suffer a decline in income over the next few years? What are the chances your salary will double within five years?
- How fast is your net worth rising? Is your reported net worth realistic, or does it reflect assets that are declining in value?
- What are you doing with your leftover money each year? Are you using it to increase future years' income or spending it on luxury items and personal possessions?
- What are the terms of your car and home loans? When will you retire those debts? How much interest must you pay each year on those loans?
- What is the value of your home and auto? Are those values rising or falling?
- What additional expenses are you likely to experience the next few years that could detract from savings? Will you buy a new car? A more expensive home? Elective surgery? Have another child?
- How much would your yearly savings rise (or fall) if your income rose (fell)?
- Do you expect other sources of cash other than salary?
- Can you manipulate your tax burden to increase savings?

- What effects would a merger (getting married) or a demerger (divorce) have on your financial position?
- What is the value of your future income in today's dollars?

Each of these questions, as impersonal as they may sound, provides the clues you need to value yourself. Try this self-valuation exercise for fun, answering the questions above. As your mind works through the various valuation challenges posed here, you will eventually grasp how to value something as dynamic as a business. Truly, from an accounting standpoint, your household behaves much like a large corporation. The similarities between the two are striking. Like a company, you have income and expenses. You own property (an automobile, lawn mower, or furniture) that depreciates in value. You don't collect all your income or pay all your bills in cash, but occasionally do both on credit terms. You invest some of your excess income to increase net worth. You occasionally borrow money to meet short-term obligations. You must spend some of your excess income to maintain the condition of your property and personal possessions. You have *fixed expenses* such as phone and water service, food, property taxes, and insurance; *variable expenses* such as electricity, gasoline, medical and dental, and travel; and *nonrecurring expenses* such as plumbing and brake repairs. You likely pay interest on auto and home loans and collect interest from certificates of deposit, bonds, or bank accounts. Finally, you operate under a tax structure that allows you to take significant deductions to enhance your disposable income.

In fact, if you prepared financial statements based on your household's yearly activities, they would closely resemble statements corporations must report. They would include an income statement (a P&L), a balance sheet, and a statement of yearly cash flows. Figure 8-1 compares a typical American household with $75,000 in income with a company of the same size and net profit.

An investor who possesses no other information will be hard pressed to value a share of themselves or the corporation. Likewise, they could not reasonably deduce a fair price for the company's stock. Too many key pieces of data are missing. For example, you don't know whether the household's net income is growing or shrinking. You don't know whether the salary is flat or rising. You would need to see several years of income statements to determine whether this year's household expenses were average or abnormal. Past financial statements also would reveal whether interest payments are rising or falling relative to your salary.

Adding a balance sheet such as the one shown in Figure 8-2, provides more clues.

FIGURE 8-1   Income statement for a household.

Income Statement—Household		Income Statement—Corporation	
Salary	$75,000	Sales	$75,000
Other income	$0	Other income	$0
Total revenues	**$75,000**	**Total sales**	**$75,000**
Food	$8,500	Cost of goods sold	$26,000
Clothing	$2,000	Selling, administrative expenses	$5,200
Housewares	$2,000	Research & development	$1,800
Utilities	$2,000	Depreciation	$3,800
Medical	$1,800		
Insurance	$2,500		
Education	$3,000		
Other expenses	$2,000	Other operating expenses	$2,520
Operating expenses	$23,800	Operating expenses	$39,320
Operating income	**$51,200**	**Operating income**	**$35,680**
Interest income	$350	Interest income	$350
Interest paid on loans	$9,500	Interest expenses	$9,800
Income before taxes	$42,050	Earnings before taxes	$26,230
Federal/local taxes	$25,000	Taxes at 35% rate	$9,181
Disposable income	**$17,050**	**Net income**	**$17,050**
		Shares outstanding	10,000
		Income per share	$1.71

The balance sheets of the hypothetical household and corporation match up almost exactly. Indeed, many of the components of net worth are the same for both entities. But now that we have prepared a balance sheet, we get a clearer, albeit not complete, picture of the household's and corporation's financial health. For example, we can deduce that the corporation has a net worth of $8 per share ($80,000 divided by 10,000 shares outstanding). Hence, we can assume that the stock ought to sell for at least $8. We also see that both entities carry much debt. The majority of their assets ($180,000 out of $260,000) are owed to someone else. Thus, we can assume that both companies will be making interest and principal payments on their present debt for several more years. Knowing that, we can start to project their future expenses and profits.

The balance sheet also shows what the company's accumulated profits have been since it incorporated—$78,000. This $78,000 is the source of its net worth. Every dollar of profit that was "retained" (not paid out as a div-

FIGURE 8-2   Balance sheet of a household.

Balance Sheet—Household		Balance Sheet—Corporation	
Assets		**Assets**	
Cash	$1,000	Cash/short-term investments	$1,000
Short-term deposits	$2,500	Accounts receivable	$2,500
Investments	$25,000	Inventories	$25,000
Salary owed	$1,500	Prepaid expenses	$1,500
Home (FMV)	$175,000	Plant, property, equipment	$224,000
Auto (FMV)	$11,000	Other assets	$6,000
Personal possessions			
(FMV)	$38,000		
Other assets	$6,000		
Total assets	**$260,000**	**Total assets**	**$260,000**
Liabilities		**Liabilities**	
Outstanding bills	$3,000	Accounts payable	$3,000
Short-term debts	$2,000	Short-term notes	$2,000
Auto (unpaid principal)	$10,000	Current portion of	
		long-term debt	$10,000
Home (unpaid principal)	$165,000	Outstanding long-term debt	$165,000
Total liabilities	**$180,000**	**Total liabilities**	**$180,000**
		Paid-in capital	$2,000
		Retained earnings	$78,000
Net worth	**$80,000**	**Net worth**	
		(shareholders' equity)	**$80,000**

idend) bought something that increased the dollar value of assets. That's the key difference between a household and a corporation; the corporation exists to increase net worth. That's not the case with your household. Though you earned $17,050 after taxes, just like the corporation, you were free to spend the profits on anything you desired—a vacation, savings, a new car, recreation and leisure, or a new wardrobe.

To complete the picture, you need to determine how these entities obtain and spend their cash during the year. A statement of cash flows provides these answers. Figure 8-3 shows how both entities could have reported their cash flow.

The cash-flow statements show there is more to these entities than meets the eye. During the course of a year, a household or company can engage in numerous transactions that would not show up on a profit-loss statement, yet would affect the amount of cash you, as an owner, could claim. In our example above, both entities earned the same after-tax income, $17,050, yet produced radically different operating and net cash flows. The household, for example, drained most of its profits making discretionary purchases and maintaining its property. It offset discretionary spending by selling $7000 in stock and taking out a $12,000 home equity loan. In the end, the household was able to generate a total of $21,850 in cash flow during the year from a reported income of $17,050. By contrast, the business was able to generate $16,950 in operating cash flow, which

FIGURE 8-3   Cash flow statement for a household.

Cash Flow Statement—Household		Cash Flow Statement—Corporation	
Operating cash flow		**Operating cash flow**	
Net income	$17,050	Net income	$17,050
Maintenance on auto,		Depreciation	$3,800
home	($4,000)	Purchase of inventory	($2,500)
Purchase of personal		Change in accounts	($1,000)
possessions	($2,500)	receivable	
Vacation	($1,800)	Change in accounts	($400)
Recreation/leisure		payable	
spending	($2,200)		
Total operating cash flow	*$6,550*	*Total operating cash flow*	*$16,950*
Investing cash flow		**Investing cash flow**	
Purchase of stocks		Purchase of property,	
via 401 (k)	($6,000)	equipment	($3,500)
Proceeds from sale		Gain on sale of	
of stocks	$7,000	subsidiary	$7,000
Settlement of		Acquisition of XYZ	
insurance claim	$2,500	Company	($30,000)
Total investing cash flow	*$3,500*	*Total investing cash flow*	*($26,500)*
Financial cash flow		**Financial cash flow**	
Proceeds from home		Debt issued to pay	
equity loan	$12,000	for XYZ	$12,000
Prepayment of auto loan	($1,000)	Dividends paid	($1,000)
Tax refund	$800	Stock repurchased	($800)
Total financial cash flow	*$11,800*	*Total financial cash flow*	*$10,200*
Net cash flow	**$21,850**	**Net cash flow**	**$650**

nearly matched its net income. However, it spent $3500 on capital expenditures (purchase of property and equipment) and paid $30,000 cash to acquire XYZ Company. To obtain all the cash it needed to buy XYZ, it floated $12,000 in new debt. Still, the company created enough excess cash after all its expenses and discretionary purchases to pay a dividend and buy back some of its stock in the market.

We can see just how valuable cash flow statements are to an investor. They complete the portrait of our hypothetical entities. Armed with all three financial statements, you can hone your valuation, asking the following questions:

1. *Do the entities need to spend money each year to maintain aging equipment?* If so, how much? What percentage of net income is used up each year buying new machinery, or clothes and housewares? The more spent each year, the less cash flow left over for owners, which detracts from valuation. A household that nets $17,050 each year and spends $6000 a year replacing assets is worth less to a investor than one that nets $17,050 and needs to spend only $2000.

2. *Are certain sources of cash nonrecurring?* If they are, you should not include them when valuing the entity. The household, for example, boosted cash flow by selling $7000 in stock, settling a $2500 insurance claim, and taking out a home equity loan. Further, it received an $800 tax refund during the year. The company boosted its cash flow by selling a subsidiary for $7000.

3. *What role do loans or capital gains and losses play in generating cash flow?* Since each entity has engaged in substantial investment and financial activities, you need to measure the extent to which cash flow has been distorted.

4. *How much cash can the entities generate by manipulating their balance sheets?* Companies, for example, can increase cash flow by purchasing fewer inventories, paying their bills later, or collecting payments from customers faster. They likewise can exploit depreciation rules to cut their income taxes. Your household can use some of the same tricks. You can postpone car repairs or purchases of new clothing, defer the sale of stock into the next year, or itemize deductions to cut your tax bill. Or you can pay for a vacation with a credit card and defer payment until the following year. These maneuvers would not show up in your income statement, yet they would cause material changes to cash flow that would alter the household's value. A household can show a net profit each year but find itself in

a predicament if it defers payment of bills. Conversely, it might show a loss on paper but remain financially healthy if it obtains positive cash flow from other sources.

You can spot important trends in income and cash flow by obtaining several years of financial statements and walking through the company's or household's progress year by year. This allows you to see what happens to excess profits. Does the entity need all its profits to expand, or does it reinvest money, pay dividends, and repurchase shares? Have inventories been rising or falling? What effect is that having on cash flow? If you find that a company historically spends 3 percent of its revenues on capital expenditures, you can assume that ratio will hold in the future. If, by contrast, you find that an entity derives a substantial portion of its yearly cash flow from issuing debt, you might walk away from the enterprise.

Once you have a handle on interpreting these three statements, you can take the next step—determining how to value the entity.

FOUR WAYS TO ESTIMATE FUTURE EARNINGS

All intrinsic value exercises hinge on your ability to estimate future earnings or cash flow. Choose the wrong growth rate and your valuation will miss the mark by a wide margin. Admittedly, this is the most difficult aspect to valuing a business. Even seasoned analysts who scrutinize financial statements for months have been known to misjudge a company's growth potential completely. This is one reason why Warren Buffett loves companies that exhibit certainty; it allows him to avoid altogether the trap of estimating the unknown. Companies such as Gillette and Coca-Cola have exhibited such steady earnings growth over long periods that Buffett can make quick, yet reasonable, assumptions about their future earnings. Unfortunately, 99 percent of the world's companies display no such consistency, forcing investors to make reasoned judgments about future earnings. When confronted with this situation, an investor should use one of the following estimating methods.

1. *Recent growth rate.*

For companies with very steady profit histories, investors should apply past growth rates to the future. Studies have shown that past earnings growth best predicts future earnings growth. For example, a company that has attained annual earnings growth of 15 percent the past 35 years is not likely to post future results that deviate far from that level. Unfortunately, a small fraction of the thousands of public companies have attained this degree of consistency. They include Abbott Laboratories, Merck & Co., Philip Morris, McDonald's, Coca-Cola, Emerson Electric, Automatic Data Processing, and Walgreen, among others. If you were to chart their yearly earnings back to the mid-1960s, you would find a nearly consistent trend—earnings growing at steady rates during both strong and weak economies. Companies able to post this level of consistency over long periods should do the same in the future, for they have shown themselves to be immune from recession and have a track record of increasing sales year in and year out.

Investors sometimes make the mistake of assuming that a long and steady track record can be ignored. It cannot. A company that has generated 10 percent yearly growth for the past 50 years won't suddenly generate 14 percent growth. This is a mistake investors tend to make in frothy bull markets. The odds are stacked against an established company accelerating its earnings. In reality, the growth rate may actually slow over time as the company finds it more and more difficult to increase earnings from an ever-larger sales base. If Wal-Mart had continued to grow at rates experienced in the 1980s, sales would have grown to $1 trillion by 2005, clearly an impossibility.

Nevertheless, you can feel confident that a steady past growth rate can be duplicated. For example, consider a company that has attained earnings growth between 12 percent and 14 percent in each of the past 10 years. You can reasonably assume the company will attain the mean growth rate (13 percent) over the next 10 years. Thus, you can arrive at an intrinsic value rather quickly, because you can estimate the key component, future earnings, with a high level of confidence:

Example 1—Steady Growth Company

	EPS	Growth Rate
1987	$3.00	
1988	$3.39	13%
1989	$3.80	12%
1990	$4.33	14%
1991	$4.89	13%
1992	$5.48	12%
1993	$6.24	14%
1994	$7.06	13%
1995	$7.90	12%
1996	$9.01	14%
1997	$10.18	13%

Example 1—Steady Growth Company (*Continued*)

Estimated Earnings

1998	$11.50	
1999	$13.00	13%
2000	$14.69	13%
2001	$16.60	13%
2002	$18.76	13%
2003	$21.20	13%
2004	$23.95	13%
2005	$27.07	13%
2006	$30.59	13%
2007	$34.56	13%

During any given year, the company may experience a temporary acceleration or decline in earnings growth that causes your estimates to miss the mark. But chances are good that by 2007, the company's earnings will approximate your estimated level of $34.56 per share.

2. Weight past earnings.

Some valuation experts estimate future earnings or cash flow by assigning weights to recent past earnings. Typically, more weight is given to the previous few years' earnings on the premise that next year's earnings are more likely to resemble last year's than earnings attained five years ago. This "weighted-average" method is acceptable for companies showing highly cyclical earnings but whose near-term earnings are expected to hover close to last year's earnings.

With a weighted method, you apply variable weights to the past seven to 10 years of earnings and sum up the weighted averages to attain a yearly average you can apply to the future. For example, you might assign a weight of 10 to last year's earnings, 9 to the previous year's earnings, 8 to the prior year's earnings, and so on. The results give you an average that, mathematically speaking, will approximate recent year's earnings. The advantages of this method are that you avoid estimating future growth rates. In essence, you are using Graham's average earnings method. The result will be a conservative earnings estimate that likely will keep you from paying too much for the company. The disadvantage of weighting past earnings is that it may produce earnings estimates that prove too low and deter you from buying a company whose stock could rise tremendously. Investors desiring a margin of safety, however, should opt for this method.

Example 2—Weighted Earnings Method

	EPS	Weight	Weighted EPS
1988	$1.55	1	$1.55
1989	$1.25	2	$2.50
1990	$2.10	3	$6.30
1991	$3.65	4	$14.60
1992	$5.10	5	$25.50
1993	$4.80	6	$28.80
1994	$3.20	7	$22.40
1995	$2.10	8	$16.80
1996	$2.25	9	$20.25
1997	$2.90	10	$29.00
Sum		55	$167.70
Weighted average			**$3.05**

Estimated Earnings

1998–2007	$3.05

3. Take the average of past earnings.

Benjamin Graham put little faith in future estimates and believed that an investor should not attempt to project into the future what did not exist in the recent past. A conservative valuation, he said, "must bear a reasonable relation to the average earnings."[2] Hence, he remained skeptical of claims that a company could grow perpetually and tended to calculate intrinsic value using known, rather than predicted earnings.

In *Security Analysis,* Graham outlined the *average-earnings* method of forecasting, which says that future earnings should be based on the average of recent past earnings. By averaging a company's yearly earnings over, say, the past 7 to 10 years, you can determine with reasonable accuracy average future earnings as well. Graham further suggested that an investor should never pay more than 16 times a company's average earnings. Graham's method was highly appropriate in his day, when most listed companies were cyclical and few of today's growth industries existed. His concept applies best to cyclical companies—airlines, steel, oil, retailers, autos,

---

[2] Benjamin Graham and David Dodd, *Security Analysis,* reprint of 1934 ed., New York, McGraw-Hill, 1997, p. 452.

heavy equipment, etc.—whose earnings tend to ebb and flow with the economy. It works because cyclical companies tend to show little trendline growth over long periods. They post positive earnings for a number of years, then report losses during an economic slowdown. During the next expansion, earnings revive, perhaps to a new high, then nose-dive again in a recession. Over long stretches, earnings may course in a wavelike pattern.

The major advantage to averaging past earnings is that you can obtain a realistic appraisal for a cyclical company and avoid the trap of assuming upward-sloping earnings growth. Too often, investors chase cyclical companies when earnings peak on the presumption that future earnings can rise further. Using an averaging method, you will not overpay for recent growth. Another advantage is that you do not have to forecast movements in the economy; the averaging method does that for you. The key is to choose a long base period that includes a complete economic cycle of earnings, both peaks and troughs.

Example 3—Average Earnings

	EPS
1988	$1.55
1989	$1.25
1990	−$0.40
1991	−$0.90
1992	$0.10
1993	$0.85
1994	$1.60
1995	$1.85
1996	$2.25
1997	$2.30
Average	$1.05

Estimated Earnings	
1998–2007	$1.05

In the example above, investors might have been tempted to pay a steep premium for the company in 1996 and 1997, when earnings reached an all-time high. But the historical record of the company, which included consecutive yearly losses in 1990 and 1991, shows that you cannot trust the company to maintain the current level of earnings. Graham would have used $1.05 per share as a base in forecasting future earnings and likely would not have paid more than $17 for the stock. A growth investor, however, may have been misled by 1997 earnings and willing to pay upwards of $30 per share.

Be aware that the average-earnings method works only for cyclical companies. It grossly underestimates intrinsic value of growth companies, those with a proven track record of increasing sales and earnings. If we applied the average-earnings method to our steady growth company in our first example, the estimate of future earnings would have been $6.23 per share, the average of the past 10 years. That would have yielded a very low intrinsic value, so low you would have ignored the shares.

4. Estimate future shareholders' equity.

With this method, which I favor over the others, you estimate the growth of shareholders' equity over a period of years, then determine the earnings needed to cause the equity account to reach this level. Shareholders' equity, discussed in detail in Chapter 10, represents the company's net worth (assets minus liabilities) at a fixed point in time. You can roughly approximate each year's ending equity by taking the previous year's equity and adding current year's retained earnings. For example, if Company X began the year with $10 million in shareholders' equity and earned $1 million during the year, its end-of-year equity should be roughly $11 million, provided the company paid no dividends. If it paid $200,000 in dividends, ending equity would approximate $10,800,000 ($10 million plus $1 million minus $200,000). My experience shows that this method of estimating future equity works for many types of companies, especially consumer products companies—Cola Cola, General Foods, Philip Morris, PepsiCo, and others—that tend to post predictable yearly returns on equity.

Estimating future shareholders' equity is a two-step process. First, calculate average return on equity (ROE) for the past 10 years or more to capture a full economic cycle. Next, project the average ROE into the future. Figure 8-4 shows how to project ROE using the example of Genuine Parts, the auto parts wholesaler. Its 30-year consistent track record lends itself to a quick analysis of equity growth.

In recent years, Genuine Parts has paid about 50 percent of its earnings out as dividends, the reason why yearly equity has not increased as much as net income. Nevertheless, Genuine Part's yearly returns on equity were remarkably consistent when you consider that it attained these results during three recessions. Thus, an investor could confidently use the 18.7 percent average ROE to project future earnings. Assuming a 50 percent

FIGURE 8-4 Genuine Parts—return on equity and forward projections.

30-Year Returns

	Net Income	Beginning Equity	Ending Equity	ROE
1967	$7,491,411	$47,308,163	$55,679,256	14.5%
1968	$8,794,941	$55,679,256	$63,649,275	14.7%
1969	$10,778,467	$63,649,275	$77,437,679	15.3%
1970	$13,290,852	$77,437,679	$85,290,945	16.3%
1971	$16,535,006	$85,290,945	$95,476,147	18.3%
1972	$17,567,931	$95,476,147	$108,053,465	17.3%
1973	$20,341,677	$108,053,465	$121,548,638	17.7%
1974	$24,005,057	$121,548,638	$137,156,965	18.6%
1975	$29,981,108	$137,156,965	$163,092,941	20.0%
1976	$37,763,166	$163,092,941	$206,861,402	20.4%
1977	$42,243,015	$206,861,402	$233,641,292	19.2%
1978	$50,263,000	$233,641,292	$275,127,000	19.8%
1979	$61,715,000	$275,127,000	$320,706,000	20.7%
1980	$67,833,000	$320,706,000	$359,889,000	19.9%
1981	$77,543,000	$359,889,000	$410,689,000	20.1%
1982	$100,167,000	$410,689,000	$581,915,000	20.2%
1983	$103,634,000	$581,915,000	$636,218,000	17.0%
1984	$119,667,000	$636,218,000	$701,113,000	17.9%
1985	$126,241,000	$701,113,000	$729,231,000	17.7%
1986	$121,552,000	$729,231,000	$758,493,000	16.3%
1987	$148,292,000	$758,493,000	$760,256,000	19.5%
1988	$181,373,000	$760,256,000	$863,159,000	22.3%
1989	$199,488,000	$863,159,000	$971,764,000	21.7%
1990	$206,596,000	$971,764,000	$1,033,100,000	20.6%
1991	$207,677,000	$1,033,100,000	$1,126,718,000	19.2%
1992	$219,788,000	$1,126,718,000	$1,235,366,000	18.6%
1993	$257,813,000	$1,235,366,000	$1,445,263,000	19.2%
1994	$288,548,000	$1,445,263,000	$1,526,165,000	19.4%
1995	$309,168,000	$1,526,165,000	$1,650,882,000	19.5%
1996	$330,076,000	$1,650,882,000	$1,732,054,000	19.5%
1997	$342,397,000	$1,732,054,000	$1,859,468,000	19.1%

30-Year Average	**18.7%**
Shares Outstanding	**179,592,000**

FIGURE 8-4   Genuine Parts—return on equity and forward projections.
(*Continued*)

10-Year Forward Projections

	Net Income	Beginning Equity	Ending Equity	ROE	Est. EPS
1998	$365,000,000	$1,859,468,000	$2,041,968,000	18.7%	$2.03
1999	$400,000,000	$2,041,968,000	$2,241,968,000	18.7%	$2.23
2000	$439,000,000	$2,241,968,000	$2,461,468,000	18.7%	$2.44
2001	$482,000,000	$2,461,468,000	$2,702,468,000	18.7%	$2.68
2002	$530,000,000	$2,702,468,000	$2,967,468,000	18.7%	$2.95
2003	$582,000,000	$2,967,468,000	$3,258,468,000	18.7%	$3.24
2004	$639,000,000	$3,258,468,000	$3,577,968,000	18.7%	$3.56
2005	$702,000,000	$3,577,968,000	$3,928,968,000	18.7%	$3.91
2006	$771,000,000	$3,928,968,000	$4,314,468,000	18.7%	$4.29
2007	$846,000,000	$4,314,468,000	$4,737,468,000	18.7%	$4.71

dividend payout and starting with a beginning equity of $1.859 billion, you can calculate future years' ending equity and the earnings per share required to generate an 18.7 percent ROE.

One quick way to estimate future earnings is to use the assumed ROE (18.7 percent) and multiply by the dividend payout ratio (in this case, 50 percent). The result, 9.35 percent, will closely approximate the growth rate of earnings. When estimating future earnings this way, it's important that you account for dividends and subtract them from ending equity, since dividends are paid from retained earnings. If Genuine Parts paid no dividends, its yearly ROE would have been much lower, since its equity base would have been much larger.

ATTACHING VALUE TO A BUSINESS

The value of our mock household, or any company, is based on what you as a shareholder could expect to take out of the entity over time. Whatever the household or company earns or generates in cash flow eventually belongs to you. Either the enterprise returns its profits immediately in the form of dividends or retains them for reinvestment. The value of the enterprise to you will be the sum total of all economic benefits it will generate going forward. If your household generates $10,000 in after-tax profits each year and will do so for the next 50 years, a shareholder would be entitled to her or his portion of the $500,000 in aggregate profits.

In theory, the household might be worth $500,000 to investors. In reality, the household's intrinsic value is nowhere near $500,000. Why? For one, inflation will erode the value of future profits. Stated in today's dollars, $10,000 a year in profits would erode steadily. Since you are paying today's dollars for the stock, it follows that the value assigned to future earnings should also be stated in today's dollars. Assuming our household earns $10,000 per year for 50 years, the sum total of its profits, adjusted for inflation, would fall considerably short of $500,000. At an inflation rate of just 3 percent per year, the value of the household's future earnings is reduced to $257,298, or just over half the reported earnings. Higher rates of inflation reduce the value of future earnings even more.

THE "DISCOUNT RATE"

Adjusting earnings only for inflation doesn't fully account for the lost *opportunity costs* of the money invested. Opportunity costs represent the rate of return you gave up to invest in the entity. It represents what you could have earned on your money in a similar investment bearing the same risk. For example, say you had the opportunity to invest in an office development that offered a potential 15 percent yearly return, or you could buy shares of a railroad stock selling for $50. Both ventures carry equal risk. To determine the value of the railroad, you must estimate its future yearly earnings or cash flows and "discount" them by 15 percent each year. If the result yields a value greater than $50 per share, you should invest in the railroad. If you arrive at a value of less than $50 per share, the stock is over-valued and the office development offers the better investment.

The discount rate is made up of two components, the risk-free rate (the yield on a government bond held to maturity) and a premium that accounts for the risks you take. The discount rate already takes into account inflation, since inflation is priced into government bond yields. So if the risk premium is, let's assume, 8 percent a year and government bonds yield 7 percent, your discount rate will be the sum, 15 percent per year.

APPLYING A DISCOUNT RATE

To discount, you simply divide each future year's earnings, or cash flow, by your chosen discount rate. For example, supposing the enterprise is expected to earn $10,000 a year over the next five years and the opportunity costs are 15 percent, this is how you would discount the five-year stream of earnings.

Discounting an Enterprise's Yearly Income (Discount Rate = 15%)

Year	Income	Divided by	= Discounted Value
1	$10,000	1.15	$8,696
2	$10,000	$(1.15)^2$	$7,561
3	$10,000	$(1.15)^3$	$6,575
4	$10,000	$(1.15)^4$	$5,718
5	$10,000	$(1.15)^5$	$4,972
Sum	**$50,000**		**$33,522**

In the first year, you divide the $10,000 profit by 1.15 to reflect the 15 percent discount rate. The resulting figure, $8696, shows what those profits really would be worth to you. In the second year, you have to discount $10,000 twice by a factor of 1.15. Thus, you divide $10,000 by the square of 1.15. In the third year, profits are divided by the cube of 1.15, and so on. As you can see, the value of $10,000 shrinks considerably over time since the discounting factor compounds.

After five years, $10,000 in profits is worth only $4972 in today's dollars, and the enterprise has generated a total of $33,522 in discounted profits for shareholders. Assuming the enterprise remained in business only five years, its intrinsic value would be $33,522, the total amount that investors could expect.

The value of the enterprise is the sum total of all future discounted earnings. In our example above, we found the enterprise to be worth $33,522, assuming a five-year operating life. If we assumed a 10-year life, the enterprise would be worth considerably more because the cumulative total of yearly profits would be greater.

That's the major trap of discounting. Forecasting too many years into the future makes a company increasingly valuable on paper, up to thousands of dollars per share! Unfortunately, corporations are considered perpetual entities that will exist hundreds of years into the future. When valuing them, you must try to discount perpetual earnings decades from now. Fortunately, mathematics permits you to do this within a few minutes. The solution is to estimate future earnings in two stages. The first stage should project 10 years into the future. In the second stage, you should project the *continuing value* of all subsequent years' earnings. The total value is the sum of the two stages.

CALCULATING CONTINUING VALUE

Step 1—Estimate earnings in the 11th year. In our example, we
assumed $10,000 in earnings every year, so 11th year earnings
would be identical to 10th year earnings.

*Step 2—Divide 11th year earnings by the difference between your dis-
count rate and the company's growth rate.* If your discount rate is
15 percent (or 0.15) and you expect 5 percent earnings growth in
the second stage, you would divide earnings by 0.10 (0.15 minus
0.05).

*Step 3—Divide the result of Step 2 by the discount factor in the 10th
year—in this case, 1.15^{10}.* The result will be the continuing value.

In our example, we assumed flat earnings of $10,000 a year perpetually—
no growth. Our result is a continuing value of $16,479 and a total value of
$66,667.

Discounting in Two Stages (Discount Rate = 15%)

Year	Income	Divided by	= Discounted Value
1	$10,000	1.15	$8,696
2	$10,000	$(1.15)^2$	$7,561
3	$10,000	$(1.15)^3$	$6,575
4	$10,000	$(1.15)^4$	$5,718
5	$10,000	$(1.15)^5$	$4,972
6	$10,000	$(1.15)^6$	$4,323
7	$10,000	$(1.15)^7$	$3,759
8	$10,000	$(1.15)^8$	$3,269
9	$10,000	$(1.15)^9$	$2,843
10	$10,000	$(1.15)^{10}$	$2,472
First Stage Value			**$50,188**
Continuing Value			
($10,000/.15)/$(1.15)^{10}$			$16,479
Value of the Enterprise			**$66,667**

What happens if the household's yearly income grows by, for example, 5
percent after 10 years? Obviously, the value of the household grows. In this

case, you would go back to Step 2 of the continuing-value calculation and
subtract the 5 percent growth rate from the 15 percent discount rate and
divide the result (0.10) from 11th year earnings, now calculated to be
$10,500. The household is now worth $74,906.

First Stage Value	$50,188
Continuing Value	
($10,500/.10)/(1.15)^{10}	$24,718
Value of the Enterprise	$74,906

WHAT DISCOUNT RATE SHOULD YOU CHOOSE?

Your valuation depends ultimately on choosing an adequate discount rate.
If you select a high discount rate, the result will be a low valuation and you
might shun an otherwise rewarding company. An artificially low discount
rate yields a high valuation and may prompt you to buy overvalued stock.
Unfortunately, no standard exists for determining an appropriate discount
rate. Below are the most commonly used methods.

1. *Weighted average cost of capital.* The majority of valuation experts
set discount rates using a *weighted average cost of capital* (*WACC*) method,
which sums up and weights the opportunity costs of owning the company's
stocks and bonds. The opportunity costs of a company's bonds are merely
the current yield of the bonds in the marketplace adjusted for taxes paid on
interest. The opportunity cost of the company's stock is the long-term
annual rate of return investors expect from the stock. Let's assume that
investors expect a 10 percent annual rate of return on a company's stock
and an *after-tax return* of 5 percent on its bonds. If stocks constitute 70 percent of the company's capital (debt plus equity), and debt makes up 30 percent, the WACC will be:

$$WACC = (.10)(70\%) + (.05)(30\%)$$
$$= .07 + .015$$
$$= .085, \text{ or } 8.5\%$$

Determining a company's cost of capital is difficult and requires you to
make subjective judgments about the returns of the entire market as well as
the stock's historical correlation with the market. Suffice it to say, most
investors might wish to determine a reasonable rate of return on the market
as a proxy.

2. *Market return.* Some valuation firms estimate the long-term annual
rate of return on stocks—10 percent—and use that as their discount rate.

Because stocks have a tendency to beat inflation by six percentage points a year (see Chapter 5), the 10 percent annual rate of return on stocks, one could argue, already reflects inflation and the risk premium on inflation. This method only holds, however, if we can rely on 10 percent annual returns going forward, a truism discussed in Chapter 2.

3. *Treasury bond yields.* The simplest—and most controversial—method is to use the yield on 10-year or 30-year government bonds as the discount rate. If a 30-year Treasury bond currently yields 6.5 percent, you would discount the company's future earnings by 6.5 percent. If bond yields fall, a higher valuation would result; conversely, higher yields result in a lower valuation. Of all the methods, discounting earnings to Treasury yields makes the most intuitive sense for value investors. Since you are buying good companies at the cheapest possible price, you already are removing much of the risk built into traditional discount rates. Moreover, this method removes the burden of forecasting. To calculate WACC, recall that you need to estimate the market's future returns. You must also estimate the risk premium put on the business's earnings, as well as the market's expected returns on the company's bonds. To a purist, this method relies too heavily on forecasting random events. Finally, discounting earnings to current bond yields forces you to buy "certainty." Recall from Chapters 4, 5, and 6 that you can remove business risk and thereby virtually eliminate the risk premium in a discount rate by buying a company with highly stable earnings and/or at a cheap price. A company that has increased earnings by, say, 10 percent annual rates for the past 40 years possesses very little business risk. If you could buy such a company for seven times its earnings, you have removed almost all risk from your discount rate and can confidently use the yields on government bonds.

4. *Your own hurdle rate.* Another relatively straightforward method is to discount future earnings at the rate of return you require on the stock. For example, if you bought a stock under the premise that it would climb 15 percent a year, use 15 percent as your discount rate.

Whichever of the four methods you choose, make sure that you choose a discount rate that *exceeds* the company's growth rate. If you don't, your valuation will be skewed and the results will have no meaning. If a company grows 20 percent a year and you discount earnings at only 6 percent rates, your valuation will be unrealistically high and could approach infinity. Practically speaking, it makes sense to choose a discount rate higher than the growth rate. If you expect a company to grow at 10 percent annual rates, you should expect the stock to grow by at least 10 percent a year since stock prices tend to grow at the same rate as long-term earnings.

SUMMING IT ALL UP

You need to make one more adjustment when valuing future earnings: Subtract the company's long-term debt, found on the balance sheet, from the discounted value of earnings. Thus, the final formula for determining an entity's value can be expressed as follows:

Intrinsic value = discounted first-stage earnings
                          + continuing value – the value of debt

Let's return to our hypothetical household, which, as you recall, reported a $17,050 yearly profit and $21,850 in cash flow in 1997. For argument's sake, let's base our valuation on yearly cash flow, using $21,850 as our base going forward. Let's assume, too, that cash flow grows at an 8 percent annual rate. To finish our valuation, we need to assign a discount rate to future cash flow. Applying a discount rate of 15 percent yields the following cash flow stream.

Calculating Final Household Value (Discount Rate = 15%)

Year	Income	Divided by	= Discounted Value
1	$23,598	1.15	$20,520
2	$25,486	$(1.15)^2$	$19,271
3	$27,525	$(1.15)^3$	$18,098
4	$29,727	$(1.15)^4$	$16,997
5	$32,105	$(1.15)^5$	$15,962
6	$34,673	$(1.15)^6$	$14,990
7	$37,447	$(1.15)^7$	$14,078
8	$40,443	$(1.15)^8$	$13,221
9	$43,678	$(1.15)^9$	$12,416
10	$47,173	$(1.15)^{10}$	$11,660
First Stage Value			**$157,213**
Continuing Value			
$(\$50,947/.07)/(1.15)^{10}$			**$179,904**
Value of the Household			**$337,117**
Minus Value of Debt			$175,000
Total Value			**$162,117**

After diligent analysis of the household, we have determined its value to an investor at $162,117, or 6.9 times 1998 cash flow. An investor who bought all of your shares should be willing to pay that amount if he or she wished to claim your future profits. In determining this value, we assumed an 8 percent growth rate in cash flow and a 15 percent discount rate. We then subtracted $175,000 in owed principal on the household's automobile and home.

Just how much an investor would pay for a fraction of this household depends on the number of shares outstanding. Assuming the existence of 10,000 shares, each would have an intrinsic value of $16.21. At prices above $16.21, an investor would not purchase any shares. At prices below $16.21, your household is a bargain.

C H A P T E R

ANALYZING A COMPANY'S DIVIDEND RECORD

"The most important objective of an investor is a rewarding total return."

Geraldine Weiss[1]

THE IMPORTANCE OF DIVIDENDS in the historical record of Wall Street has been memorialized in the minds of most investors. Take away the dividends public companies have paid over the past 70 years and yearly returns on investment fall dramatically. From 1928 to 1997, for example, the Dow Jones industrial average, the most publicized market benchmark, rose a compounded 4.86 percent a year, not the oft-quoted 9 percent to 10 percent cited by the media. Dividends made up the difference. The average yearly dividend yield of the 30 DJIA stocks was 4.4 percent between 1928 and 1997. It's only when you add together the capital gains returns of 4.86 percent and dividend yields of 4.4 percent that compounded stock returns look respectable again.

THE GROWTH FACTOR OF DIVIDENDS
To belittle the importance of yearly dividends is clearly unsound, since dividends have not only provided a major source of investors' profits but also

[1] Geraldine Weiss and Gregory Weiss, *The Dividend Connection,* Chicago, Dearborn Financial Publishing, 1995, p. 2.

offered a degree of comfort in poor markets. Stocks paying high dividends tend to decline less in poor markets. One cannot overlook, either, their role in providing inflation-beating returns (recall that concept from Chapter 5). A company that continually improves its earnings and dividends offers compelling short-term returns that can beat bond yields. Over the long term, a growth company offers stock-price returns that can beat the market as a whole.

One need only look at two dividend-paying growth companies, Merck & Co. and Philip Morris, to see how dividends can benefit investors over long periods. Assume an investor bought Philip Morris and Merck in 1980 at split-adjusted prices of $1.90 and $3.90, respectively, and held the shares. By 1997, the yearly dividends for both companies constituted a huge return on the original investment (see Figure 9-1). Likewise, yearly

FIGURE 9-1   Philip Morris and Merck

	Philip Morris (Bought at $1.90)				Merck & Co. (Bought at $3.90)			
	EPS	Div.	EPS Yield	Div. Return	EPS	Div.	EPS Yield	Div. Return
1980	$0.20	$0.06	10.5%	3.2%	$0.28	$0.12	7.2%	3.1%
1981	0.22	0.08	11.6%	4.2%	0.30	0.14	7.7%	3.6%
1982	0.26	0.10	13.7%	5.3%	0.31	0.16	7.9%	4.1%
1983	0.30	0.12	15.8%	6.3%	0.34	0.16	8.7%	4.1%
1984	0.35	0.14	18.4%	7.4%	0.37	0.17	9.5%	4.4%
1985	0.42	0.17	22.1%	8.9%	0.42	0.18	10.8%	4.6%
1986	0.52	0.21	27.4%	11.1%	0.54	0.21	13.8%	5.4%
1987	0.65	0.26	34.2%	13.7%	0.74	0.27	19.0%	6.9%
1988	0.74	0.34	38.9%	17.9%	1.02	0.43	26.2%	11.0%
1989	1.01	0.42	53.2%	22.1%	1.26	0.55	32.3%	14.1%
1990	1.28	0.52	67.4%	27.4%	1.52	0.64	39.0%	16.4%
1991	1.51	0.64	79.5%	33.7%	1.83	0.77	46.9%	19.7%
1992	1.82	0.78	95.8%	41.1%	2.12	0.92	54.4%	23.6%
1993	1.35	0.87	71.1%	45.8%	2.33	1.03	59.7%	26.4%
1994	1.82	1.01	95.8%	53.2%	2.38	1.14	61.0%	29.2%
1995	2.17	1.22	114.2%	64.2%	2.70	1.24	69.2%	31.8%
1996	2.56	1.47	134.7%	77.4%	3.20	1.42	82.1%	36.4%
1997	3.00	1.60	157.9%	84.2%	3.82	1.69	97.9%	43.3%

earnings for Philip Morris and Merck provided astounding inflation-beating returns.

These companies have been particularly generous, returning 40 percent to 50 percent of their yearly earnings to investors, while reinvesting the rest to increase the equity account. Because both companies grew consistently, they were able to raise their dividends nearly every year. By 1997, Philip Morris's dividends alone provided an 84.2 percent return on an investor's 1980 investment. Merck's dividends provided a 43.3 percent return on a 1980 investment. Their dividends have provided returns that beat inflation by a wide margin.

But to achieve these types of annual returns, you had to have been discriminating. For one, you had to buy both stocks at relatively cheap prices. Philip Morris was priced at an average of 10 times earnings in 1980; Merck at 14 times earnings. Second, you had to choose companies capable of improving their earnings consistently over long periods, which in turn permitted strong dividend growth. Finally, you had to hold these stocks long enough to allow the earnings and dividend yields to surpass the rate of inflation. A long holding period also enabled you to optimize the stocks' appreciation potential. Had you held Philip Morris or Merck only two to three years, you might have suffered a drop in value in the stock. Anything can happen over a short period. Over 17 years, however, you were assured of share-price growth that kept up with the growth in earnings. By the end of 1997, Philip Morris traded at $45, a 2268 percent return on your original investment. Over the same period, Philip Morris's earnings grew 1400 percent. Merck traded at $106, a 2618 percent return. Its earnings increased 1264 percent.

The presence of dividends signifies more than management's generosity. It is a by-product of the firm's success.

To be sure, the presence of dividends signifies more than management's generosity. It is a by-product of the firm's success. A company must make money to afford a dividend. And it must earn much more than it pays as dividends if the company is to grow internally, for a company that pays all of its earnings to shareholders as dividends has no retained earnings left over at the end of the year to reinvest in new plants or acquire assets from other companies' shareholders. Dividends also reveal management's continued confidence in the future. When a company raises its dividend, management is making a statement about the expected course of earnings. It is a delicate matter for companies to cut their dividends, and very few do. Thus, by raising the dividend, management has committed the company to years of higher payouts, thereby signaling it expects future earnings to grow enough to more than compensate.

DIVIDENDS AS HOLDOVERS OF THE "PACK-RAT" AGE

As enchanting as dividends may appear, they do not by themselves guarantee good annual returns. Too many investors embrace dividends as their savior on the belief that only respectable companies pay dividends. Further, they have been persuaded by financial planners to divide their portfolios between bonds, dividend-paying stocks, and nondividend-paying stocks, with an emphasis on securities offering guaranteed returns. This desire for dividend income stems from the post-crash Depression era, a time when investors were fearful of stock declines and demanded—and received—ever-more generous dividend payouts from companies.

The influential finance textbooks of that time emphasized the need to buy and hold dividend-paying stocks, as opposed to so-called "speculative" issues, because of their relative safety. A company that could afford to pay a dividend, these books contended, was less likely to liquidate and its stocks were less likely to decline should another crash occur. Many academic studies have been predicated on this concept, and later generations of finance students were taught to value companies based on their expected dividends. Older investors, too, have been coached to look upon dividends as some kind of financial messiah that would deliver them through retirement. In the same way that these Americans learned to covet their jobs and houses, staying rooted to one location for decades, and accumulate tools and furniture that later filled the attic, so, too, did they latch onto stocks that paid dividends.

Benjamin Graham was as much a product of this Depression-era mindset as any analyst. His models for valuation invariably stressed companies capable of earning yearly profits and returning them to investors. To Graham and legions of academics who followed in his footsteps, a dividend in the hand was worth more than a promise of capital gains in the fist. They believed that given the inherent risk of investing, it was better to receive money from the company now than have to depend on its ability to generate future profits on their behalf. To quote Graham:

> Until recent years the dividend factor was the overshadowing factor in common-stock investment. This point of view was based on simple logic.

The prime purpose of a business corporation is to pay dividends to its owners. A successful company is one which can pay dividends regularly and presumably increase the rate as time goes on. Since the idea of investment is closely bound up with that of dependable income, it follows that investment in common stocks would ordinarily be confined to those with a well-established dividend. It would also follow that the price paid for an investment in common stocks would be determined chiefly by the amount of the dividend.[2]

To accept such a partisan view toward dividends runs counterintuitive to financial logic. There are many compelling reasons why companies do not and should not pay dividends. Graham clarified his view of dividends, acknowledging that there may be times when it is prudent for a company to withhold payouts from investors. He listed three instances in which they might do so: (1) to strengthen cash flow, (2) to increase productive capacity, or (3) to "eliminate an overcapitalization" (repurchase shares).

All three events should improve the intrinsic worth of the company *to the benefit of shareholders.* Indeed, when a company can make better use of its cash internally than investors can externally, prudence demands that the company retain its earnings and suppress its dividends. Graham believed that if a company successfully reinvests its earnings to expand production or shore up shaky finances, the company will be in a better position to pay future dividends. By sacrificing $1 in dividends now, investors may benefit more if the company can reinvest the money and increase its intrinsic value by more than $1. Sooner or later, academics argue, that $1 will come back to investors as a dividend.

Many modern-day value investors, including Warren Buffett, gently part ways with Graham and accept this more flexible view of dividends. They argue that dividends may pose little economic benefit to investors today, especially in light of tax-law changes, and will probably even detract from a stock's potential return. Buffett's Berkshire Hathaway portfolio displays his bias against dividends, except in cases when the company has a history of appropriating earnings wisely (see Figure 9-2). Buffett's major holdings at the end of 1997 consisted of several large-cap growth companies that paid far less than 50 percent of their earnings as dividends (the market average was around 38 percent in 1997). The dividend yield on those stocks averaged less than 1 percent.

Investors seeking dividends need to understand the relationship

---

[2] Benjamin Graham and David Dodd, *Security Analysis,* reprint of 1934 ed., New York, McGraw-Hill, 1997, p. 325.

FIGURE 9-2   Berkshire Hathaway's largest stock holdings, 1997.

	1997 EPS	1997 Div.	Payout	12/31/97 Yield
American Express	$4.15	$0.90	22%	1.0%
Coca-Cola	$1.67	$0.56	34%	0.8%
Walt Disney	$2.75	$0.48	17%	0.5%
Federal Home Loan Mtg.	$1.90	$0.40	21%	0.9%
Gillette	$1.91	$0.86	45%	0.9%
McDonald's	$2.20	$0.32	14%	0.7%
Washington Post	$26.23	$5.00	19%	1.0%
Wells Fargo Bank	$25.62	$5.20	20%	1.5%

between internal returns and external (shareholder) needs. In this regard, companies must be selfish. They should avoid slavishly giving in to demands for ever-higher dividends. Instead, management should willingly withhold dividends—even for years—if it can show a pattern of successful reinvestment with shareholders' money. If the company can generate a better return on shareholders' money than shareholders can when reinvesting their dividends, the company should retain its earnings.

> Management should willingly withhold dividends—even for years—if it can show a pattern of successful reinvestment with shareholders' money.

Let's assume that General Motors earns $10 million in profits and has the option of returning some, none, or all of the $10 million to shareholders. The choice will hinge on GM's *hurdle rate,* the return it expects to obtain by reinvesting the money internally. If GM can buy a new $10 million plant that generates a 25 percent return on yearly investment, it likely will retain all of the $10 million. Under such circumstances, the choice is obvious. GM will pay dividends only if investors have the opportunity to obtain rates of return that exceed 25 percent. Rarely does the stock market offer such high guaranteed rates of return. But if the new plant can return only 10 percent a year, the choice becomes more difficult for GM. Because some investors can beat a 10 percent return on their own, the company may choose to spend only $5 million of its profits on the plant, return the extra $5 million as dividends, and take out a $5 million loan to finance the rest of the expansion. If the new plant is expected to generate an even lower return on investment, say, 5 percent, the company is likely to return all of the money as dividends and take out a $10 million loan to finance the project.

As you can see, a company cannot take the subject of paying dividends lightly. Management must integrate dividend-paying policies with the company's long-term financial and capital expansion plans. In practice, corporate America has followed these general principles. The evidence lies in the relationship between dividends, earnings growth, and returns on assets exhibited by companies. The fastest-growing companies, those attaining the highest rates of return on assets, pay no dividends whatsoever and likely won't for years to come. They include hundreds of small-cap companies, as well as name-brand growth companies such as Microsoft, Oracle, Cisco Systems, Gateway 2000, Dell Computer, 3Com, Boston Scientific, Outback Steakhouse, and Office Depot. The slowest growing companies, those attaining low rates of return on internal investments, return nearly all of their earnings as dividends. They include, most notably, electric and gas utilities. Most other companies lie somewhere in between, paying dividends equal to 10 percent to 60 percent of their yearly earnings. For the most part, their dividends provide insight to the company's internal hurdle rate. Companies paying relatively small dividends—less than 10 percent of earnings—likely generate very high internal growth rates. Companies paying large dividends—40 percent to 60 percent of their yearly earnings—return the money because their businesses are mature and because fewer growth opportunities are available. This group includes consumer products companies such as Philip Morris and Kellogg, major drug companies, and banks.

No doubt, many companies have become so attuned to the public's desire for dividends that they continue to pay them long after it is judicious. They shower investors with dividends during periods of earnings declines in an empty attempt to provide a psychological prop to the share price. In these cases, management not only has acquiesced to shortsighted demands but consumed valuable cash assets that could have been marshaled more effectively elsewhere. A number of mining companies, for example, wrongly maintained their dividends in 1997, after gold, copper, silver, and mineral prices crashed and these companies' profitability was in serious doubt.

Conversely, some financially strong companies offer dividends even when there is no doubt they should abstain. Most likely, these companies pay dividends just to satisfy fund managers' desire for income. Dozens of mutual funds are prohibited from buying stocks in nondividend-paying companies and have been forced to shun some of the fastest-growing companies in America as a result. High-growth companies such as Charles Schwab, Wal-Mart, Walt Disney, Cracker Barrel Old Country Store, and Callaway Golf pay modest dividends simply to attract more institutional investors to their stock. A quick glance at these companies' financial performance confirms that they should not pay dividends at all and likely do so for unsound reasons. Callaway Golf, as I point out in Chapter 10, attains such high annual returns on its assets and equity that it should continue to retain all of its earnings rather than pay them out to investors. Its yearly dividend yield traditionally has been less than 1 percent, a return so insignificant that investors should avoid buying the stock for that very reason. Cracker Barrel's 1998 dividend of $0.02 per share constituted 1.4 percent of its yearly earnings. From a financial standpoint, there can be no justification for a company dangling such small carrots before investors unless its motives are impaired. If the company can attain a high return on its assets, it should plow all of its profits back into the company every year rather than squander those profits on investors, subjecting them to yearly taxes.

I show this relationship in Figure 9-3, which compares dividend payout ratios (the percentage of earnings management wishes not to reinvest) to return on assets for select large-cap companies. It should be immediately evident that dividend policies differ widely among companies, even among those in the same industry. At first glance, the dividend policies of these companies would appear to be random. But payout ratios tend to follow a trendline related to returns on assets. In general, the higher a company's return on assets, the less it should pay out to investors as dividends. Likewise, companies experiencing very low returns on assets, that is, showing little profit, should likewise retain their earnings rather than return such a precious commodity to shareholders. When a company enjoys a high return on equity but chooses to return the majority of its earnings to investors, it has acted illogically.

DIVIDENDS AND INDUSTRIAL "LIFE CYCLES"

Why do some companies return only 10 percent of their earnings as dividends and other companies 60 percent or more? As we stated earlier, the answer mostly relates to the company's investment opportunities. When opportunities abound, companies should retain as much of their earnings as

FIGURE 9-3   Dividends and internal returns of select S&P 100 companies as of December 31, 1997.

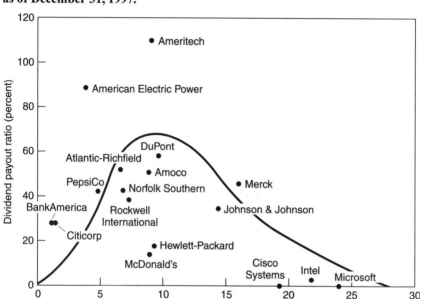

possible under the premise that a dollar retained can be turned into more than a dollar in shareholder equity. Only when such investment opportunities vanish should a company begin returning earnings to shareholders. Precisely when this shift occurs is difficult to pinpoint. But as the chart above suggests, companies do link their dividend policies to internal rates of return. The chart also suggests that dividend policies are linked to growth rates—more specifically, to the company's life cycle. Companies generally course through four cycles before they are liquidated or sell their assets. In each cycle, a company's reinvestment and dividend policies differ. These phases can be described briefly.

1. *Initial growth phase.* In their earliest growth phase, companies tend to be cash-starved and retain all of their earnings to support research efforts, make acquisitions, or build manufacturing facilities. This phase is characterized by high annual growth rates—at times 100 percent or more—sustained for a period of several quarters, if not a few years. Companies in this stage must focus all their resources on exploiting new markets and technologies and fending off potential competitors.

2.   *Expansion phase.* In this stage of the company's life, growth slows
     somewhat but remains very strong. The company's products take
     hold in the market, modest cost efficiencies are reached, and rapid
     expansion emerges as the goal. New stores, plants, and regional
     headquarters are built and the company's payroll and administrative
     costs rise in line with sales. These companies are characterized by
     high returns on assets and equity and relatively high profit margins.
     Most companies in this phase choose to pay only modest dividends,
     since investors tend to be better off deriving their returns from capi-
     tal gains.

3.   *Mature growth phase.* Most big-name American companies—
     Bristol-Myers Squibb, Coca-Cola, Walt Disney, Procter & Gamble,
     DuPont, Citicorp, Ford Motor, etc.—lie in this stage, which is char-
     acterized by "mature growth." After years, or decades, of successful
     expansion, these companies have built a sizable war chest of
     resources they use to win incremental market share. Because of
     their size, they are less likely to show double-digit sales gains, but
     use their operating leverage (covered in Chapter 11) to drive earn-
     ings growth. New investment opportunities are more limited at this
     point, and most companies in the mature phase generate more cash
     flow than they require to maintain the business. They return most of
     this excess cash flow to investors as dividends. In this phase, divi-
     dends may approach 60 percent of yearly earnings.

4.   *Period of stabilization or decline.* Companies in this phase experi-
     ence little or no growth in output and use their cash flow to replace
     aging equipment. Earnings growth stalls and the company is able to
     find few if any alternatives for its excess profits. As a result, the
     enterprise will, and should, return the bulk of its earnings to
     investors.

Investors who track a company's performance over many years will see predictable changes in growth rates and dividend policies. Wal-Mart, the $120
billion-a-year retailer, presents a textbook example of how a company
changes its financial priorities as it matures. By 1997, Wal-Mart's growth
potential had clearly peaked and was slowing. Wal-Mart's sales didn't actually cease growing, but the rate of change of external growth had. The company began building fewer new stores and spent larger and larger sums
refurbishing existing stores rather than erecting brand-new facilities. Given
the huge amounts of capital needed to build a store and the difficulty Wal-
Mart faces finding new communities able to support a 190,000-square-foot

FIGURE 9-4   Wal-Mart's dividend history.

FY	Earnings per Share	Return on Assets	Return on Equity	Dividends	Payout Ratio
1992	$0.70	12.0%	26.0%	$0.08	11.4%
1993	$0.87	11.1%	25.3%	$0.10	11.5%
1994	$1.02	9.9%	23.9%	$0.13	12.7%
1995	$1.17	9.1%	22.8%	$0.17	14.5%
1996	$1.19	7.8%	19.9%	$0.20	16.8%
1997	$1.33	7.9%	19.2%	$0.21	15.8%
1998	$1.56	8.3%	19.8%	$0.27	17.3%

store, Wal-Mart concentrated more of its resources overseas. In December 1997, Wal-Mart acquired 21 stores owned by German retailer Wertkauf, a clear sign that its U.S. expansion had reached a mature stage. An investor who dissected Wal-Mart's yearly results would have seen that the company's rate of return on new U.S. stores appeared to be falling. In other words, it was taking longer for new stores to break even. One look at the balance sheet confirms this trend. Wal-Mart's returns on assets and equity fell consistently in the 1990s (see Figure 9-4). Because Wal-Mart's existing stores continued to prosper and the company built fewer new stores, Wal-Mart's operating cash flow improved dramatically, turning positive for the first time in 1997. Management found itself flush with excess cash and responded with a series of dividend increases. This was the sensible course of action given Wal-Mart's declining returns. Rather than continue to retain all of its earnings, Wal-Mart wisely chose to return a higher percentage of its earnings to shareholders each year and allow them to decide how to spend the proceeds.

TAX LAWS AND DIVIDENDS

Paying and raising dividends may seem like a routine matter for corporations, but it constitutes a major policy decision that impacts future earnings, rates of return on assets, and share prices. Companies view dividends as a use of cash that competes with other investments. When examining whether to pay a dividend, management compares whether investors will be better off taking cash now or waiting, perhaps for years, for the company to return its accumulated wealth. Another factor weighing on the minds of management is its mandate to increase stock price. The higher the dividend relative to earnings, the less you can expect the stock's price to rise, holding other factors equal. A company that pays out 100 percent of its earnings as dividends will see its stock ascend far less than one that retains all earnings for reinvestment. Most companies have neither 0 percent nor 100 percent payout ratios. Instead, they seek a middle ground that satisfies both their need for reinvestable cash and investors' desire for dividend income. Moreover, investors have been showing an increasing preference for capital gains over dividends, and as such, corporations have been hesitant to raise dividends sharply. After all, no company should increase its dividends if the public is not clamoring for them. Where once corporations paid out more than 60 percent of their yearly earnings as dividends, by late 1997, they were paying less than 40 percent.

To understand why this trend occurred, shareholders should view dividends in the context of corporate finance. Starting in the late 1980s, the dividend picture changed dramatically. Interest rates declined steadily for several years, pushing up bond and stock prices and causing a drop in yields. Investors accustomed to collecting 8 percent and 9 percent yields suddenly faced the unhappy prospects of buying their favorite income stocks at yields of 3 percent or less. While this was taking place, subtle changes in tax laws lessened some of the advantages of passive dividend income. The 1993 Budget Reconciliation Act was the major driver toward lower dividend payouts, raising the top ordinary income tax rate to 39.6 percent and widening the gap between the tax rate on dividends and the tax rate on capital gains, which was capped at 28 percent. The 11.6 percentage point differential made it far less advantageous to hold dividend-producing stocks.

Seen in the context of tax policy, the reduction in dividend payout ratios that took place in the 1990s is perfectly rational. Because corporations exist to maximize returns to investors, it makes sense that they adopt policies that make their shares as attractive as possible. Before the mid-1980s, when tax brackets were higher and viewed as confiscatory, companies could maximize investor returns by paying their earnings back as dividends and allowing shareholders to determine the best use of the proceeds. Since that time, and especially starting in the mid-1990s, the very opposite has occurred.

Consider the choices facing General Motors, which for the sake of example, has earned $10 million in excess profits and has the option of paying that $10 million out as dividends or reinvesting the money and returning it to shareholders at a later date. Let's also assume that GM and its investors can invest the $10 million in Treasury bonds yielding 6 percent. How will GM decide? By comparing its tax rate to shareholders' rates and the after-tax returns to both the company and its shareholders. It must allocate the money in a way that maximizes the returns to shareholders.

When GM's tax rate is the same as the top tax bracket of shareholders, it doesn't matter how the $10 million is disbursed. The net return to shareholders will be the same. If GM bought $10 million in bonds and let them compound at 6 percent annual rates, the bonds would generate $3,382,256 in interest after five years. Each year, GM will pay taxes equal to 35 percent of the interest. At the end of five years, it will have collected $2,198,466 in interest. If it sells the bonds, it has $12,198,466 to distribute back to shareholders as dividends. Of course, as soon as investors receive the money, they will lose 35 percent in taxes too. The net to them will be $7,929,003.

The other alternative is for GM to give the entire $10 million to investors up front and let them invest it. Should that happen, investors would pay a 35 percent tax on $10,000,000, which would net them $6,500,000. Assuming they invest the $6,500,000 in bonds that pay 6 percent a year, their after-tax proceeds from the interest and from selling the bond in the fifth year would be the same: $7,929,003.

The decision for GM changes when tax rates change. If GM's effective tax rate drops to 34 percent, investors will be better off, albeit only slightly, if GM hoards all $10 million, buys the bonds, and pays the proceeds out in five years as a dividend. Similarly, if the top individual tax rate climbs to 37 percent, investors will net more money if GM reinvests the $10 million. Thus, an important corollary: *When individual tax rates are higher than corporate tax rates, companies generally serve investors better by reinvesting profits rather than immediately returning them to investors as dividends. When corporate tax rates are higher than individual tax rates, companies best serve individuals by paying out their excess profits as dividends.*

When Congress lowered the capital gains tax rate on stock investments in 1997, it handed corporations an added inducement to avoid paying dividends. Likewise, investors were treated to special incentives as an enticement to shun dividend-paying stocks. Congress lowered the capital-gains tax rate to 20 percent from 28 percent for those investors willing to hold a stock at least 18 months. The measure gave corporate boards further incentive to favor higher stock prices over higher dividends and to take actions that would maximize capital gains to investors. In the long run, this will discourage companies from raising dividends as fast as earnings.

Adding complexity to this process is the fact that most Americans do not pay the stated tax rates, in other words, their *effective rate* often is much lower. The effective rate for a typical family in the 31 percent tax bracket that takes standard exemptions and itemizes deductions for medical bills, mortgage payments, state and local taxes, and charitable contributions may be 20 percent or less. To these families and those in lower tax brackets, whose tax rates on dividends may be only 15 percent, it would make more sense for a company to pay dividends now than to reinvest its earnings. Unfortunately, a company cannot pick and choose to whom it pays dividends. It must create blanket dividend policies based on average tax rates. Now that capital-gains tax rates have been lowered further and corporate tax rates remain below the highest individual income tax rates, investors must look beyond dividends for a financial savior.

Another factor to keep in mind is that dividends slow the pace of a corporation's growth. Every dollar reinvested in the company should add one dollar to the company's net worth and at least one dollar to its intrinsic value. However, as I indicated above, there is a tradeoff between dividends and share-price growth. The more dividends returned to investors, the less appreciation potential in the stock. If a company pays all of its earnings as dividends, it may never increase its net worth. If earnings do not grow, the stock may trade like a bond, fluctuating up and down only in response to changes in interest rates. If earnings steadily climb, the stock is still likely to carry a lower P/E ratio than a nondividend-paying stock with the same growth rate. This is so for two reasons: First, the net worth has not changed, and second, the company's annual after-tax return would be substantially less to investors.

> Every dollar reinvested in the company
> should add one dollar to the company's
> net worth and at least one dollar
> to its intrinsic value.

ARE DIVIDEND-REINVESTMENT PLANS LOGICAL?

The lessons of history suggest that investors should maintain open minds when it comes to dividends. They should not automatically chase dividend-paying companies out of fear of buying "speculative stocks." Further, it is incorrect to focus on dividend stocks without determining whether the dividend really enhances after-tax returns. Conversely, investors should not automatically shun dividend-paying companies in an effort to avoid paying annual taxes, for some of the finest growth companies pay dividends with little or no adverse effect on their stock prices. In short, no overriding strategy will apply to all companies. Nevertheless, you always should weigh the after-tax value of dividends when determining whether a company is suitable to own.

Investors should apply the same diligence when evaluating *dividend-reinvestment* strategies. Over the past decade, the media has devoted considerable coverage to "dollar-cost averaging" and the strategy of reinvesting a company's dividends. For many investors, the allure of these strategies is immense, and today millions of Americans routinely plow their quarterly checks back into companies without so much as a question. More than 1000 public companies have joined this fray and have crafted programs that allow investors to bypass brokers, buy stocks directly from the company, and have their dividends reinvested. Companies have found these plans helpful in retaining investor loyalty. It also allows the entity to diffuse the shareholder base; it can place more shares directly in the hands of buy-and-hold investors rather than institutions and offer a low-cost way to issue new shares to the public.

Dividend-reinvestment strategies are appealing, and they certainly provide tremendous convenience for investors. In many cases, however, these plans are fundamentally flawed for the reasons cited above. When companies pay dividends, they are, in effect, encouraging you to take your money and spend it elsewhere. After all, if the company believed its own assets offered a superior investment, it would retain its earnings and pay no dividend. Intel pays a minuscule dividend because every dollar it plows back into the company has been returning more than 30 percent a year. As long as Intel continues to earn high rates of returns on reinvested earnings, it will provide greater benefit to shareholders by holding onto earnings.

But when a company returns most of its earnings to investors, it is in essence conceding that it cannot earn enough return on the money and as such, is encouraging you to find an investment paying higher returns. Knowing this, why would you plow that money back into the same company? Yet this is exactly what investors do when they reinvest dividends. The strategy, if it can be called that, is all the more senseless when applied to high-dividend-paying companies such as electric utilities, most of which now offer self-directed dividend-reinvestment plans. The typical utility pays out 80 percent to 90 percent of its yearly earnings as dividends, which suggests that utilities can find few profitable internal projects in which to reinvest your earnings. What can they possibly do with your money that they haven't done already? More often than not, proceeds from dividend-reinvestment plans have been used to issue more shares, which dilutes the earnings of the same company to which you entrusted more of your money. Reinvesting a dividend in low-growth companies such as electric utilities is like frequenting a restaurant whose service is poor or mediocre at best and tipping the waiter each time!

10

MEASURING A COMPANY'S INTERNAL PERFORMANCE

"Correctly judging the difference between image and reality opens the door to very substantial returns."

Robert Metz[1]

I N A PERFECT WORLD, a business could sell its goods for whatever price it set, operate for years without competition, stay immune to higher costs, and never feel compelled to invest in research and development. For most companies, such an Elysian field existence— if it exists at all—is short-lived at best. Particularly now, as we approach a new millennium, companies have been forced to rethink their strategies for survival. The proliferation of technology and the emergence of overseas competition have allowed start-up firms to successfully challenge market leaders on price and quality. Resources and capital move virtually unimpeded across boundaries, and competitors can overcome technological disadvantages within months. Companies are fully exploiting regional discrepancies in wages, interest rates, taxes, and currencies to steal

---

[1] Robert Metz and George Stasen, *It's a Sure Thing,* New York, McGraw-Hill, 1993, p. 117.

market share in formerly concentrated industries such as steel, apparel, drugs, banking, semiconductors, and telecommunications.

In reality, harsh conditions have existed for decades and will continue to exist for businesses. Financial writers at the turn of the century and again in the 1940s and 1950s lamented that companies were unable to retain their monopolies because of competition. The situation has never improved; it's only gotten worse. Corporations must adapt constantly and keep vigilant watch on their internal performance if they wish to increase market share and reward shareholders. Those that maintain vigorous operations despite the increasing demands of competition have brought outstanding returns to investors.

This chapter looks at three critical measures of success—return on equity, retained earnings and productivity—and how they assist you in evaluating companies.

RETURN ON EQUITY

The 1990s have witnessed some spectacular corporate achievements—continued improved earnings, better productivity, a reduction of overhead costs, and strong top-line sales gains, to name just a few. The tools companies used to produce these results, restructurings, layoffs, share buybacks, and management's success in utilizing assets, also have fueled improvements in return on equity (ROE), the often-overlooked benchmark of capital utilization. The majority of investors and most seasoned analysts fixate on earnings, but a company's ability to maintain high returns on owners' capital is crucial to long-term growth. An investor should pay as much attention to ROE as a yardstick of progress as earnings per share since earnings can be manipulated in any number of ways. Warren Buffett said as much in his 1979 annual report to shareholders:

> The primary test of managerial economic performance is the achievement of a high earnings rate on equity capital employed (without undue leverage, accounting gimmickry, etc.) and not the achievement of consistent gains in earnings per share. In our view, many businesses would be better understood by their shareholder owners, as well as the general public, if management and financial analysts modified the primary emphasis they place upon earnings per share, and upon yearly changes in that figure.[2]

---

[2] From the 1979 annual report of Berkshire Hathaway.

Calculating returns on equity is fairly straightforward. It is the ratio of yearly profits to the average equity needed to produce those profits:

$$ROE = \frac{\text{net income}}{(\text{ending equity} + \text{beginning equity})/2}$$

If a company earned $10 million—started the year with $50 million in shareholders' equity and finished with $60 million—its return on equity would be roughly 18.2 percent.

$$ROE = \frac{\$10 \text{ million}}{(\$60 \text{ million} + \$50 \text{ million})/2}$$

$$= 0.1818, \text{ or } 18.2\%$$

This figure shows that management obtained an 18.2 percent return on the resources you gave it to generate profits. Investors provide capital to management when they buy stock or loan the company money through a bond issue. Shareholders' equity, assets minus liabilities, represents investors' stake in the net assets of the company. It is the sum total of the capital contributed to the company and the company's earnings to date on that capital, minus a few extraordinary items. High ROEs signify success in utilizing assets to investors' benefit. Theoretically, returns on equity also serve as a useful predictor of dividends and the company's growth rate. A company that consistently posts an ROE of 20 percent and retains 50 percent of its earnings should experience dividend growth close to 10 percent. Merck's return on equity has hovered between 30 percent and 35 percent in the 1990s, and the company typically retains about 53 percent of its earnings. If those trends held, an investor could expect dividends to grow 16 percent to 19 percent a year.

Returns on equity for the S&P 500 companies have averaged between 10 percent and 15 percent for most of this century, but they rose sharply in the 1990s (see Figure 10-1). Indeed, one of the reasons U.S. companies traded at such premiums to their book values in the mid-1990s was that they enjoyed historically high returns on equity. Under such conditions, rich stock valuations are justified—as long as companies can maintain these high returns.

Companies able to sustain high returns on equity are remarkable enterprises, to be sure, and should be purchased when their stocks trade at attractive levels. The difficulty in maintaining high ROEs can be seen in this hypothetical example of a company earning $10 million initially and attaining a consistent 25 percent ROE.

Year	Base Equity	Net Income	Ending Equity	ROE
1998	$35,000,000	$10,000,000	$45,000,000	25%
1999	$45,000,000	$12,855,000	$57,855,000	25%
2000	$57,855,000	$16,525,000	$74,380,000	25%
2001	$74,380,000	$21,242,888	$95,622,888	25%
2002	$95,622,888	$27,307,733	$122,930,621	25%
2003	$122,930,621	$35,104,090	$158,034,711	25%
2004	$158,034,711	$45,126,308	$203,161,019	25%
2005	$203,161,019	$58,009,869	$261,170,887	25%
2006	$261,170,887	$74,571,686	$335,742,574	25%
2007	$335,742,574	$95,861,903	$431,604,477	25%
2008	$431,604,477	$123,230,476	$554,834,953	25%

Because each year's net income is added into equity and becomes a component of next year's calculation, it becomes considerably more difficult to generate sufficient net income to keep the ROE at 25 percent. In fact, our hypothetical company must increase its net income and equity by 28.6 per-

FIGURE 10-1   Return on average equity—Dow Industrials.

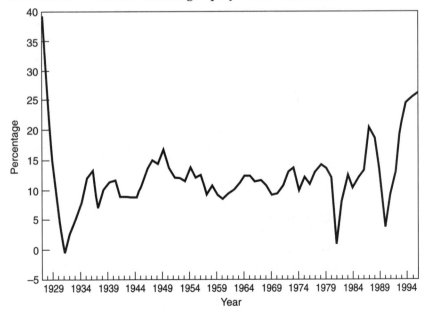

cent annually to maintain a 25 percent ROE. This poses an interesting axiom: *High returns on equity should be accompanied by even higher increases in net income.* Look what happens to our hypothetical company's ROE when net income grows by only 15 percent annually.

Year	Base Equity	Net Income	Ending Equity	ROE
1998	$35,000,000	$10,000,000	$45,000,000	25%
1999	$45,000,000	$11,500,000	$56,500,000	23%
2000	$56,500,000	$13,225,000	$69,725,000	21%
2001	$69,725,000	$15,208,750	$84,933,750	20%
2002	$84,933,750	$17,490,063	$102,423,813	19%
2003	$102,423,813	$20,113,572	$122,537,384	18%
2004	$122,537,384	$23,130,608	$145,667,992	17%
2005	$145,667,992	$26,600,199	$172,268,191	17%
2006	$172,268,191	$30,590,229	$202,858,419	16%
2007	$202,858,419	$35,178,763	$238,037,182	16%
2008	$238,037,182	$40,455,577	$278,492,760	16%

Wall Street clearly favors stable earnings growth, but as you can see, it leads to a gradual decline in ROE and a decline in the growth rate of shareholders' equity. If management wishes to maintain a company's ROE at 25 percent, it must find ways to create more than $1 in shareholder equity for every dollar of net income produced. Indeed, when net income does not grow as fast as equity, management has not maximized use of the extra resources given it. To quote Buffett:

> Most companies define "record earnings" as a new high in earnings per share. Since businesses customarily add from year to year to their equity share, we find nothing particularly noteworthy in a management performance combining, say, a 10 percent increase in equity capital and a 5 percent increase in earnings per share. After all, even a totally dormant savings account will produce steadily rising interest earnings each year because of compounding.[3]

Focusing on companies producing high ROEs is rarely a losing proposition. High ROEs necessarily lead to strong earnings growth and a steady increase in net worth and intrinsic value. In our hypothetical example above, we would expect the company's stock price to increase an average of

[3] From the 1977 annual report of Berkshire Hathaway.

at least 28.6 percent a year, mirroring the growth in shareholders' equity. If the company's net worth is increasing at 28.6 percent annual rates, the value of the business should be increasing by at least that amount. When evaluating two nearly identical companies, the one producing higher ROEs will almost always provide better returns for you over time. Five other points are worth considering when evaluating ROEs.

Focusing on companies producing high ROEs is rarely a losing proposition. High ROEs necessarily lead to strong earnings growth and a steady increase in net worth and intrinsic value.

1. *A high return on equity attained with little or no debt is better than a similar ROE attained with high debt.* Debt levels are a major determinant of shareholders' equity, although it's not always clear whether debt contributes to or detracts from returns. Holding other factors constant, the more debt added to the balance sheet, the lower the company's shareholder equity, since debt is subtracted from assets to calculate equity. Companies employing debt wisely can greatly improve ROE figures because net income is compared against a relatively small equity base. But higher debt is rarely desirable, particularly for a company with very cyclical earnings. Callaway Golf generated ROEs averaging 43 percent between 1993 and 1997 while it was retiring all of its long-term debt. That's no small feat. Callaway's asset base is quite small, however, and the company's return on assets has been extraordinarily high—34 percent in 1997. Figure 10-2 shows the 1997 ROEs for the 30 companies comprising the Dow Jones industrial average. Many of them attained high ROEs because of their high debt level.

2. *High returns on equity must be understood in their proper context.* Drug and consumer-products companies tend to possess higher-than-average debt levels than are typical and consequently post higher returns on equity. They can bear higher levels of debt because their sales are much more consistent and predictable than those of cyclical manufacturers. Thus, they can safely use debt to expand, rather than worry about having to meet interest payments during an economic slowdown.

FIGURE 10-2   1997 returns on equity for the Dow Industrials.

	ROE	Debt/ Equity		ROE	Debt/ Equity
AlliedSignal	24.4%	120%	IBM	25.0%	120%
Alcoa	11.5%	150%	International Paper	3.2%	140%
American Express	22.2%	NM	Johnson & Johnson	26.6%	40%
AT&T	29.1%	90%	McDonald's	17.7%	70%
Boeing	10.0%	70%	Merck	32.4%	60%
Caterpillar	33.1%	180%	Minn. Min. & Mfg.	24.3%	50%
Chevron	16.7%	70%	Morgan (JP)	13.5%	NM
Coca-Cola	56.7%	40%	Philip Morris Cos.	44.3%	180%
DuPont	34.0%	150%	Procter & Gamble	27.5%	60%
Eastman Kodak	27.2%	90%	Sears Roebuck	25.2%	330%
Exxon	17.2%	70%	Travelers Group	16.9%	NM
General Electric	23.4%	450%	Union Carbide	26.9%	140%
General Motors	19.6%	790%	United Technologies	18.5%	100%
Goodyear Tire & Rubber	3.1%	110%	Wal-Mart Stores	17.8%	70%
Hewlett-Packard	19.2%	30%	Walt Disney	11.4%	80%

NM—not meaningful.

3. *These days, a high ROE may be the result of stock buybacks.* Companies can greatly manipulate ROEs through share buybacks, ESOPs, and the granting of options. General Electric pioneered new territory in November 1989 when it announced a $10 billion share buyback program with the stated intention of improving return on equity. Since then, hundreds of companies have used repurchases to their advantage. By retiring shares, companies reduce shareholders' equity, and improve per-share earnings, a double bonus to ROE. Schering-Plough, the pharmaceutical company, posted an unusually high ROE of 65.9 percent in 1996. The figure seems astonishing given that Schering-Plough had virtually no debt. Schering-Plough bought back 142 million shares that were sitting in the treasury for reissue. The cost basis of the shares ($3.56 billion at the end of 1996) was subtracted from shareholders' equity, thereby inflating ROE. Had Schering-Plough not been banking stock, its 1996 ROE would have been 23.3 percent, more in line with competitors. Hoarding shares is not necessarily bad for shareholders. Companies rich enough to buy back substantial blocks of stock are better able to boost ROE and earnings over time.

Schering-Plough was experiencing strong sales trends, improving profit margins, and its capital expenditures represented just a fraction of net income. As such, the company was well positioned for repurchasing shares each year to improve ROE.

4. *Returns on equity tend to peak and trough with the year-over-year growth in earnings.* A cyclical company posting a high ROE isn't likely to maintain the rate. Between the 1990–1991 recession and 1996, DuPont's return on equity fluctuated between 38.9 percent in 1996, a year of record earnings, and 4.9 percent in 1993, when earnings bottomed.

5. *Companies that can attain high ROEs without the benefit of charges, assets sales, or special gains are preferable.* Any decision by the company that decreases the value of assets, such as a restructuring charge or the sale of a division, also decreases the dollar value of shareholders' equity, but it gives an artificial boost to ROE. Conversely, a company increasing ROE without these crutches is legitimately growing its earnings. It's difficult to keep improving ROE when the equity base is huge, but a number of companies managed to do just that in the mid-1990s—AlliedSignal, Atlantic Richfield, Banc One, Bank of New York, Coca-Cola, Dell Computer, Emerson Electric, Exxon, General Electric, Honda, McDonald's, Merck, and Procter & Gamble.

ROE AND ITS PREDICTIVE ABILITIES

Many academic studies have looked at the predictive qualities of return on equity ratios; that is, they have pondered whether a company's ROE could serve as a good forecaster of future financial performance. In fact, there is some correlation between the trend of a company's ROE and the trend of future earnings, a point Warren Buffett has repeated often in his annual reports. If yearly returns on equity are climbing, earnings should be rising as well. If the ROE trend is steady, chances are that the earnings trend will likewise be steady and much more predictable. By focusing on ROE, an investor can more confidently make assumptions about future earnings. Indeed, one method of improving the accuracy of earnings forecasts is to back your way into it. You estimate future returns on equity, then determine the earnings necessary to produce those results. Recall, again, our hypothetical example above. Starting with a 1997 net income of $10 million and a predicted yearly ROE of 25 percent, an investor can predict future net income and equity. By 2007, yearly profits will have grown to $123.3 million, or 12.3 times present levels. If the number of shares outstanding remains constant, then earnings per share will rise 1233 percent over the next decade.

Year	Base Equity	Net Income	Ending Equity	ROE
1998	$35,000,000	$10,000,000	$45,000,000	25%
1999	$45,000,000	$12,855,000	$57,855,000	25%
2000	$57,855,000	$16,525,000	$74,380,000	25%
2001	$74,380,000	$21,242,888	$95,622,888	25%
2002	$95,622,888	$27,307,733	$122,930,621	25%
2003	$122,930,621	$35,104,090	$158,034,711	25%
2004	$158,034,711	$45,126,308	$203,161,019	25%
2005	$203,161,019	$58,009,869	$261,170,887	25%
2006	$261,170,887	$74,571,686	$335,742,574	25%
2007	$335,742,574	$95,861,903	$431,604,477	25%
2008	$431,604,477	$123,230,476	$554,834,953	25%

You can use ROE figures to predict potential downturns in earnings as well. Academic studies have shown that returns on equity successfully predict earnings slowdowns when recent ROEs are unusually high. If a company typically experiences an ROE between 10 percent and 15 percent and suddenly reports 20 percent, chances are good that the company will experience a reversal in earnings in the next reporting period. We would expect this relationship to hold for the market in general, and, indeed, it does. Years in which corporate ROEs have surged historically have been followed by periods in which earnings declined, as the graph of DJIA companies showed earlier in this chapter.

GROWTH IN RETAINED EARNINGS

Nothing measures the value of management better than its track record of investing money. Management's role, you recall, is to increase the value of the firm. It can do so by creating profits from its sales and by successfully reinvesting those profits to maximize shareholders' returns. I explained in Chapter 9 that management sometimes has no choice but to return its earnings as dividends, for only by doing so can the company maximize value to shareholders. In other instances, when profit opportunities abound, the company should—indeed it must—retain all of its profits.

In his 1924 book, *Common Stocks as Long-Term Investments,* Edgar Lawrence Smith first postulated that common stocks should rise in value if the company does not pay out all its earnings as dividends. Every dollar retained by the company, Smith argued, increases shareholders' equity, which increases net worth and should cause identical upward movements in the market value of the company. If Company X earns $5 million in profits, pays out $2 million as dividends, and retains $3 million, the "book value" of the company has increased by $3 million. A company with 10 million shares outstanding should see a $3.33 rise in the stock.

It didn't take long for Wall Street to exploit Smith's breakthrough. In the late 1920s, speculators exploited Smith's theories to support their frenzied thirst for equities. In the public's mind, as long as a company was retaining money—any money—it was increasing its intrinsic value, and, therefore, the company could keep increasing in value. It did not matter whether the underlying assets supporting the stock were worth the present price. Nor did it matter whether the company could maintain its growth rates in earnings or retained earnings. The market rewarded growth companies with ever-higher valuations and overlooked slow-growth companies that were adding just as much value to their retained earnings each year. Benjamin Graham wrote that by 1929, investors were so fixated on future earnings they ignored the historical records of companies and bid up stocks based on what retained earnings might be years down the road. Nevertheless, Smith's notion that business value rises with retained earnings is credible. If a company earns $1 per share and retains it all, the value of the company should rise by at least $1. If it doesn't, then value has been destroyed somewhere. That's where a careful analysis of financial statements can help.

The line item "retained earnings" is merely an accounting adjustment on the balance sheet. It is the sum of all accumulated profits since the time the company was formed minus dividends paid. If a company's net income over the past 50 years was $20 billion and it paid $10 billion in dividends, retained earnings would be $10 billion. That doesn't mean that the company is sitting on $10 billion in cash. Rather, it means management has had at its disposal over the past 50 years $10 billion in excess profits to reinvest. Most of the money likely was spent building new plants, hiring workers, researching products, expanding into new markets, or buying other companies.

Companies are investment conduits; they exist to generate a return on shareholders' money.

Though retained earnings exist as a paper account, the line item is nevertheless important, for it tells you the source of the company's increase in net assets. To explain this concept, let's take the hypothetical example of an individual who saves $20,000 over three years.

	Year 1	Year 2	Year 3
Income	$50,000	$55,000	$60,000
Expenses	$45,000	$50,000	$50,000
Savings	$5,000	$5,000	$10,000

This individual's balance sheet would show $20,000 in accumulated savings. Now, let's assume the following:

Assets

House	$100,000
Car	$15,000
Personal Possessions	$5,000
Total Assets	$120,000

Liabilities

House (unpaid principal)	$90,000
Car (unpaid principal)	$10,000
Total Liabilities	$100,000
Net Worth	$20,000

We can see that this person did not sock the $20,000 under the mattress. He bought a $100,000 house on which he still owes $90,000. He also bought a $15,000 car and has paid off $5000 of the loan as well as $5000 in personal possessions against which he has no outstanding liabilities. The $20,000 he created in net worth exactly matches his three-year savings. As a corporation, he would have to itemize the source of his net worth on a balance sheet. In this case, he would list $20,000 in "retained earnings." The $20,000 in cash no longer exists, but instead has been turned into $20,000 in unencumbered assets.

The key for this individual and for all companies is whether he spent the $20,000 wisely. For retained earnings to have value to a company, they must be reinvested in projects that offer suitable rates of return. Otherwise, a company should not retain anything and return all earnings to investors. If our individual were a corporation, he would have to obtain a suitable return on the car and home or else spend his savings on possessions offering a higher return. Clearly, this is not practical or advisable for individuals. Companies, however, are investment conduits; they exist to generate a return on shareholders' money. Thus, they must show a track record of spending their retained earnings wisely and over long periods. If not, then Edgar Lawrence Smith's theory of value has little meaning. What good are retained earnings, after all, if the firm spends them on projects providing inferior returns? In such cases, retained earnings may rise, but the stock may not, because the market has wisely recognized that management failed to maximize value.

Indeed, what if our hypothetical person reported a net worth below $20,000? He destroyed value. The $20,000 in profits did not translate into $20,000 in net worth. What happened? For one, the house or auto may have declined in value, indicating a poor investment. In addition, he may have had to plow money back into his existing assets just to maintain their value. His $5000 collection of possessions may include a rack of business suits that need replacing every season, the backyard fence may have been destroyed during a recent storm and needed replacing, or the transmission on his car may have inexplicably failed. Any of these foreseen or unforeseen circumstances could have forced him to spend excess profits to restore the lost value of his assets.

Thus, when you study retained earnings, you essentially are hunting for evidence that the company has wisely reinvested its profits. Checking to see that a company has passed these three tests will help ensure this.

1. *Return on equity is high.* If the company's ROE is higher than its industry average, it is doing a better job of reinvesting resources than its competitors. The higher the ROE, the more earnings the company should retain each year, within reason. Some companies boast exceptional ROEs but nevertheless return a good portion of their yearly earnings to investors because they cannot find enough suitable investment opportunities. These companies include Philip Morris, for example, most drug manufacturers, and food companies such as PepsiCo and Coca-Cola. Some companies, too, report high ROEs because they pay large dividends. Recall that dividends reduce retained shareholders' equity.

2. *Capital expenditure needs are low.* A company may earn a high return on equity, but if all of its yearly profits are used to replace aging equipment, it has done little to increase intrinsic value and its retained earnings are illusive. Regional and long-distance telephone companies, for example, spend the bulk of their yearly earnings upgrading networks, buying switching equipment, and maintaining tens of thousands of miles of phone lines. Every dollar of earnings they spend on maintenance is a dollar not spent on expansion, which is where you want retained earnings directed. High levels of capital expenditures are acceptable only if the company is building new stores or increasing capacity.

3. *The company's market value rises with retained earnings.* No investor can track accurately a company's historical use of retained earnings. Doing so requires that you collect decades of annual reports and comb through financial statements to check how retained earnings have grown. But you can rely on the market to make sensible judgments about a company's reinvestment policies. The value of the firm should rise at the rate of retained earnings; it follows that successful companies can increase their intrinsic value faster than retained earnings. Over long periods, the market will accurately reflect a company's growth history. If the market value of the company's stock has tended to climb faster than retained earnings, you can reasonably deduce that management has created excess value through its use of assets.

PRODUCTIVITY: GETTING BETTER RETURNS FROM YOUR PHYSICAL AND HUMAN ASSETS

Productivity growth is the chief reason why real wages and corporate earnings in the United States have grown faster than wages in many other countries. In broad terms, Americans have continued to produce more on a per-hour basis, making their labor all the more valuable in world markets. Historically, higher productivity has had positive implications for companies, workers, and shareholders. From an investor's perspective, productivity improvements lead to better returns on a company's resources, better profit margins, and better bottom-line earnings. Productivity growth in the United States, however, has not been consistent. Factory output per hour was rising 3 percent to 4 percent a year in the 1950s and 1960s but has grown at rates well below 2 percent since.

Figure 10-3 provides insight as to why this is the case. Workers generally are able to produce more when given more advanced equipment. When companies cut back on equipment outlays, productivity growth can slow. That occurred in the 1970s and 1980s. In 1966, as the chart shows, capital spending was growing more than nine times as fast as the labor force. The typical company, in fact, was increasing its equipment purchases 9.4 percent for every 1 percent increase in employees. By 1971, however, companies had scaled back equipment purchases and the ratio had dropped below 1.0. Beginning in 1991, the pace of capital equipment purchases picked up dramatically again. Companies began adding equipment faster than they added employees. By June 1996, the capital equipment/labor growth ratio had climbed back to 6.8, a 30-year high (Figure 10-3). This trend helps explain not only the surge in industrial companies' earnings since 1991 but also why the mid-1990s stock market rally had real staying power.

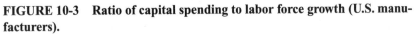

FIGURE 10-3   Ratio of capital spending to labor force growth (U.S. manufacturers).

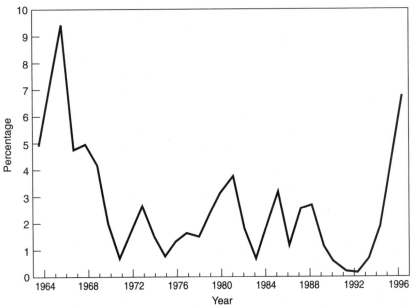

Calculating exact productivity gains for an individual company is difficult for an investor. In fact, many companies lack the resources to measure their own inputs and outputs. But a few simple calculations will tell you, in general, whether the enterprise is getting more out of its equipment and employees. The easiest method is to calculate the company's sales per employee. The data needed to calculate this ratio is found in most annual reports, usually organized in a convenient table. To calculate the ratio, divide annual sales by the average number of workers the company employed during the year. For example, if a company began the year with 10,000 employees, finished the year with 11,000 employees, and reported sales of $500 million, the average employee generated $47,619 in sales for the company. Of course, not every employee actually contributes to a company's revenues, but this calculation reveals approximate productivity levels across the full range of jobs at a given company.

Productivity figures can't be isolated; they need to be studied over a number of years. Only then can an investor gauge whether the company is experiencing meaningful improvements in its use of resources and whether they contribute to better earnings. Figure 10-4 showcases 27 diverse companies exhibiting exceptional productivity growth in the 1990s. It was pre-

FIGURE 10-4   Productivity growth of selected companies.

	Sales/ Emp. 1991 ($000)	Sales/ Emp. 1996 ($000)	Annualized % Change	Sales Growth 1991–1996	EPS Growth 1991–1996
Air Products & Chem.	$205.0	$267.2	5.4%	6.5%	9.9%
AlliedSignal	115.9	169.2	7.9	3.4	23.5
Armstrong World	121.1	179.7	8.2	1.3	35.4
Andrew	126.7	191.3	8.6	13.5	33.6
Equifax	79.3	128.0	10.1	10.6	29.9
Emerson Electric	106.9	129.1	3.8	8.5	9.9
Dover	109.1	155.0	7.3	11.1	22.0
Dow Chemical	254.6	502.6	14.6	4.9	17.4
Donnelley (R.R.)	138.3	168.1	4.0	11.0	4.6
Frontier	175.8	326.0	13.1	18.1	10.3
Hewlett-Packard	194.9	358.6	13.0	21.5	26.5
Honeywell	104.5	141.8	6.3	3.4	6.2
Johnson & Johnson	151.0	252.0	10.8	11.7	14.6
International Paper	195.6	261.3	6.0	8.8	−4.7
Kellogg	337.8	460.4	6.4	2.9	3.4
Lubrizol	282.1	356.6	4.8	1.6	4.5
Merck & Co.	230.6	420.6	12.8	18.2	11.8
Morton International	164.7	238.4	7.7	13.6	19.3
Motorola	113.4	199.1	11.9	19.8	17.2
Pall	103.5	135.3	5.5	7.9	11.9
Philip Morris Cos.	338.1	453.8	6.1	4.2	11.1
PPG Industries	168.3	230.6	6.5	4.9	33.0
Russell	54.0	70.0	5.3	9.1	8.9
SBC Communications	144.5	209.7	7.7	8.0	12.4
Schering-Plough	185.3	277.9	8.4	10.2	16.9

pared from annual reports, from information any investor could have easily found. The correlation between productivity growth and earnings growth for these companies is no coincidence. When plants are more productive, they can generate the same output at less cost, that is, each dollar of new sales translates into incrementally better earnings.

An indirect way to study productivity growth is to measure the growth of capital expenditures, costs which companies must list in the statement of cash flows. As a test, compare what a company spends on capital spending during one year with the dollar growth in sales experienced in the next. This gives you a ballpark estimate of its return on capital spending. For example, if Hewlett-Packard spent $2 billion on capital equipment last year and this year's sales increase by $4 billion, it saw a twofold return on its expenditures. Comparing this ratio over a number of years will help you see trends in a company's efficiency.

Finally, compare the growth rate of capital spending over several years with the growth rate in employees. As I pointed out above, when capital spending grows much faster than head counts, high rates of productivity—and profit improvement—can usually be counted on to follow. Between 1991 and 1996, Equifax, the credit and data services company, increased its capital spending at 26 times the rate that it added employees. As a result, profits grew at 29 percent annual rates over that period. The stock rose 500 percent. In the same five-year period, Andrew Corp.'s head count rose 34 percent, while sales rose 88 percent. Capital expenditures grew at more than three times the rate of employees. As a result, Andrew posted a respectable 8.6 percent annual productivity growth rate. From 1991 to 1996, sales per employee at Johnson & Johnson rose 67 percent, an annualized rate of 10.8 percent. Over that same time, net income grew at 14.6 percent annual rates and the stock tripled.

11

DISCOVERING HIDDEN
VALUE IN PROFIT MARGINS

"Hardly ever are business people blessed with a market so strong or isolation so great that price is unrelated to cost."

Gary Sutton[1]

PROFIT MARGINS ARE AMONG the most meaningful barometers of business performance. They measure a company's internal efficiency, its ability to take top-line sales and translate those sales into profits for investors. For sales only have meaning to an investor if turned into hard earnings. Hence, businesses only have value if they can create profits from their sales. If a company generates $5 billion in sales but breaks even each year, it may be worth no more to an investor than a business with $5 million in sales and no profits. Owners of either enterprise cannot take any profits out of the business at the end of the year to compensate them for their time, investment, or the amount of risk taken.

Once you have studied profit margins, you will quickly discover that no two companies enjoy identical efficiencies. However, profit margins do tend to correlate closely within industry groups. Software makers tend to experience much higher profit margins than automakers. Drug and food companies enjoy profit margins that are twice as high as banks. Margins for regulated companies such as electric utilities tend to be fairly constant because the government places caps on their profitability. Cyclical compa-

---

[1] Gary Sutton and Brian Tarcy, *Profit Secrets from a No-Nonsense CEO,* Career Press, 1995, p. 28.

nies experience profit margins that fluctuate over the business cycles. In boom times, margins are high; in bust periods, negative margins—losses— are common. Supermarkets and food distributors experience extremely low margins—often below 1 percent—because they rely on volume to generate acceptable levels of net income.

In examining profit margins, it is wise to audit a company's performance over time, usually 10 years or more. Analyzing a decade of results allows you to spot trends that may emerge and cause a company's profitability to change. At the least, it will show you the range of possibilities. Within a 10-year period, you are likely to see a full economic cycle, which is helpful in understanding how margins expand and contract with the economy.

Profit-margin analysis is relatively easy to perform once you grasp the basic terminology.

Gross profit margin (GPM)—This measures what remains of a company's profits after deducting the cost of goods sold from revenues. GPM reveals how much the company paid for labor, materials, and other resources to produce the items sold during the quarter or year. If General Motors sold $25 billion in automobiles one quarter and spent $20 billion in costs directly attributable to those vehicles, its gross profit would be $5 billion and its gross profit margin would be 20 percent ($5 billion divided by $25 billion). Many factors determine a company's GPM, including the sales price of the goods sold, the price the company paid for raw materials (which may fluctuate daily), and the costs of paying employees. Another key factor is how the company decides to spread its costs over the reporting period. If General Motors buys a batch of wheels for $200 each and another batch for $150, it can choose which batch to assign to revenues in the quarter. By assigning the $150 batch to the sold autos, it will report a higher profit margin. In the next reporting period, however, it may have little choice but to assign a $200 wheel cost to each new car sold. This will result in a decline in GM's gross profit margin from the previous reporting period.

Operating margin—This is the most important ratio to study in a profit-loss statement. A company's operating margin reflects the true, unadjusted costs of producing output, and it is the biggest determinant of profits. To calculate operating margins, subtract from sales the cost of goods sold, selling and administrative expenses, depreciation and amortization, and outlays for research and development. These expenses are readily found in income statements and footnotes. When calculating operating margins, you should disregard nonoperating expenses such as interest, nonrecurring gains or losses, restructuring charges, and contributions and costs from discontinued operations. This is important, because it will allow you to make unencumbered observations about the company's efficiency. Once you have set aside these items, you can make multiyear margin comparisons and rank the company against its peers in the same industry. If significant differences exist between the company's operating and pretax profit margins, they should be investigated. The differences likely are the result of charges, high interest expenses, nonrecurring events, or boilerplate items such as "other income." If these items recur regularly and/or cause a significant change in the company's reported margins, you must adjust for them when valuing the company.

Net profit margins (NPM)—These measure the percentage of sales brought to the bottom line. NPM includes all sources of revenues and all costs, whether fixed, variable, or nonrecurring. You calculate NPM by subtracting all reported costs from revenues and dividing the results by revenues. Or you can simply divide net income by sales. This figure is important because it reveals how much assets the company used up to expand sales. When viewed over a number of years, net profit margins reveal whether the company has become more efficient or less efficient at producing goods.

The relationship between the three profit margins can be seen in the table below, which shows IBM's 1997 quarterly earnings. IBM reported no charges and included no unusual items during the year. Its steady improvement in profit margins, therefore, came from aggressive cost-cutting, sales gains, and from a lower effective tax rate, not from one-time events.

	4Q-97	3Q-97	2Q-97	1Q-97
Revenues	$23,723	$18,605	$18,872	$17,308
Cost of Goods Sold	14,205	11,507	11,471	10,716
Gross Income	**9,518**	**7,098**	**7,401**	**6,592**
Selling and Administrative Costs	5,060	3,932	3,958	3,684
Research & Development	1,425	1,162	1,221	1,069
Operating Income	**3,033**	**2,004**	**2,222**	**1,839**
Other Income	173	162	137	185
Interest Expense	194	183	179	172
Income Before Taxes	**3,012**	**1,983**	**2,180**	**1,852**
Taxes	919	624	734	657
Net Income	**2,093**	**1,359**	**1,446**	**1,195**
Gross Profit Margin	40.1%	38.2%	39.2%	38.1%
Operating Margin	12.8%	10.8%	11.8%	10.6%
Effective Tax Rate	30.5%	31.5%	33.7%	35.5%
Net Profit Margin	8.8%	7.3%	7.7%	6.9%

Historically, the best-performing companies have been those with wide profit margins or those able to maintain or improve their profit margins over time. Microsoft enjoys some of the highest profit margins in the world. Once it sinks resources into creating new software and applications, Microsoft spends next to nothing incorporating programs onto millions of floppy disks and selling them to computer manufacturers and retailers. Microsoft derives a large share of its revenues from royalties and licensing fees on software whose costs were sunk in previous quarters or years. In a typical quarter, Microsoft reports gross profit margins of 90 percent, operating margins of 50 percent, and net profit margins of 30 percent to 35 percent.

> Historically, the best-performing companies have been those with wide profit margins or those able to maintain—or improve— their profit margins over time.

FINDING CLUES IN QUARTERLY PROFIT STATEMENTS

To acquire a true understanding of a company's operations, you need to study quarterly profit-and-loss statements. The line items on these statements often yield a valuable clue that the enterprise may be experiencing a reversal of trend that could result in improved or impaired earnings going forward. The following examples show the variety of information you can glean from the examination of a few simple ratios.

Harrah's Entertainment.   In the mid-1990s, Harrah's Entertainment, the casino and riverboat company, began experiencing operating difficulties when a number of states issued licenses for new riverboats and gaming facilities. Harrah's holds the largest U.S. share of the gaming market, with 20 casinos in every major gambling outpost—northern and southern Nevada, New Jersey, Illinois, Mississippi, and Missouri. The presence of new competition began pinching Harrah's performance, as evident by its dwindling sales and operating margins. By early 1997, Harrah's riverboats as well as its Las Vegas and New Jersey casinos were exhibiting no sales growth and a sharp decrease in operating margins. Without doubt, this indicated that Harrah's was (1) experiencing a decline in traffic at its facilities and (2) needing to spend more on advertising and to discount its services (reduce the rate for rooms) to once again lure customers. This trend would not have been evident unless an investor analyzed Harrah's operating segments. By maintaining a vigil on these numbers, an investor was in a position to avoid the huge sell-off in the stock in 1996 and spot any reversals of trend. In the fourth quarter of 1997, for example, year-to-year sales growth climbed to 6.6 percent, which included large gains at riverboats and in southern Nevada. This was the first sign that Harrahs was emerging from its troubles.

	4Q-97	3Q-97	2Q-97	1Q-97	4Q-96	3Q-96	2Q-96	1Q-96
Revenues								
Riverboats	158,110	171,311	169,512	157,313	150,199	160,994	165,801	152,148
Atlantic City	79,509	98,954	88,412	82,635	80,385	98,725	80,978	78,501
Northern Nevada	65,916	88,918	71,676	61,241	67,086	89,758	71,852	70,479
Southern Nevada	83,900	70,918	68,729	64,613	67,515	71,541	75,102	75,626
Indian and Other Gaming	10,535	8,147	10,564	8,297	8,160	7,708	7,333	6,129
Total	**397,970**	**438,248**	**408,893**	**374,099**	**373,345**	**428,726**	**401,066**	**382,883**
Operating Profit								
Riverboats	27,298	35,518	32,189	29,154	26,637	33,421	40,216	40,967
Atlantic City	12,629	25,614	20,112	14,925	15,700	26,887	17,716	14,709
Northern Nevada	4,691	22,957	11,701	5,184	10,510	26,339	12,537	10,367
Southern Nevada	13,326	7,291	10,424	10,900	15,186	14,357	18,894	19,532
Indian and Other Gaming	522	552	1,345	3,789	2,314	−1,099	−1,131	−3,420
Total	**58,466**	**91,932**	**75,771**	**63,952**	**70,347**	**99,905**	**88,232**	**82,155**
Sales Gains								
Riverboats	5.3%	6.4%	2.2%	3.4%	1.1%	0.2%	13.2%	10.4%
Atlantic City	−1.1%	0.2%	9.2%	5.3%	−1.5%	0.9%	−4.4%	1.6%
Northern Nevada	−1.7%	−0.9%	−0.2%	−13.1%	−10.3%	−4.8%	−11.8%	8.4%
Southern Nevada	24.3%	−0.9%	−8.5%	−14.6%	−6.5%	−5.5%	−2.4%	4.6%
Indian and Other Gaming	29.1%	5.7%	44.1%	35.4%	570.0%	−380.0%	−3730%	50.0%
Total	**6.6%**	**2.2%**	**2.0%**	**−2.3%**	**−1.3%**	**0.7%**	**3.0%**	**7.4%**
Operating Margin								
Riverboats	17.3%	20.7%	19.0%	18.5%	17.7%	20.8%	24.3%	26.9%
Atlantic City	15.9%	25.9%	22.8%	18.1%	19.5%	27.2%	21.9%	18.7%
Northern Nevada	7.1%	25.8%	16.3%	8.5%	15.7%	29.3%	17.5%	14.7%
Southern Nevada	15.9%	10.3%	15.2%	16.9%	22.5%	20.1%	25.2%	25.8%
Indian and Other Gaming	5.0%	6.8%	12.7%	45.7%	28.4%	−14.3%	−15.4%	−55.8%
Total	**14.7%**	**21.0%**	**18.5%**	**17.1%**	**18.8%**	**23.3%**	**22.0%**	**21.5%**

Seattle FilmWorks.   The study of profit margins will sometimes lead you to discover other potential red flags in a company's operations. One such example is Seattle FilmWorks, a high-end photofinishing company that markets and processes color film through the mail. Its unique accounting system to measure costs proved to be its downfall in 1997 and 1998. To draw new customers, the company traditionally conducts direct-mail campaigns in which it ships complimentary rolls of films. Recipients shoot the film and mail it back to Seattle FilmWorks, which processes and returns the pictures, along with new rolls of free film.

To its credit, Seattle FilmWorks created an excellent sales foundation by creating a chain of repeat usage. The problem came when the company had to record the costs of its direct-mail campaigns. Most companies would expense these costs immediately, but Seattle FilmWorks amortized the costs over a three-year period. Thus, if it cost $5 to win the average customer, that $5 was spread evenly over 12 quarters. In the first quarter, for example, the company would record $0.42 in acquisition costs and charge it against current earnings. It then would shift the remaining $4.58 to the balance sheet as a liability called "capitalized acquisition costs."

This pyramidlike cost shifting works well as long as sales are growing as fast or faster than the costs that are being deferred. But when sales growth slows, the proportion of balance sheet costs shifting back to the income statement grows larger and larger. This is what started to take place in 1996. Within the span of eight quarters, Seattle FilmWorks' sales growth fell from 45 percent to about 6 percent. At the same time, the amortized costs of those previous sales were being piled onto each successive quarter's income statement and dragged earnings down. By the end of 1997, the reported level of expensed acquisition costs were growing more than three times the rate of sales, and the level of capitalized marketing costs still on the balance sheet had grown to 67 percent of current sales. Clearly, the company was in trouble and the stock price reflected that. The shares dropped to $4 by mid-1998, well off its 1996 high of $15.

	4Q-97	3Q-97	2Q-97	1Q-97	4Q-96	3Q-96	2Q-96	1Q-96
Revenues	$22,471	$32,743	$25,553	$21,657	$21,236	$27,133	$22,509	$17,821
Acquisition Costs	$4,164	$4,231	$4,289	$3,762	$3,482	$3,233	$2,974	$3,236
Capitalized Costs	$15,121	$13,882	$15,865	$13,139	$12,675	$11,334	$10,900	$9,645
Sales Growth	5.8%	20.7%	13.5%	21.5%	27.3%	24.3%	42.5%	45.0%
Acquisition Cost Growth	19.6%	30.9%	44.2%	16.3%	37.2%	37.8%	36.6%	60.4%

Charles Schwab.   The period 1996–1997 was a very important one for Schwab, as the company came to rely less on trading commissions as a source of profits and more on fees paid from mutual funds. Through its OneSource mutual fund "supermarket," Schwab markets hundreds of mutual funds to customers and is paid a royalty from each fund based on the dollar amount of investments made in the fund by Schwab customers. Schwab's costs to maintain OneSource are relatively minor. Most of the quarterly revenues paid by mutual funds drop straight to the bottom line.

Schwab's income statements reveal another interesting facet of the business—its variable cost structure. Notice how increases in revenues correlate closely to increases in net income, earnings per share, expenses, and other items. When sales, costs, and net income are all growing at nearly identical rates quarter after quarter, nearly all the company's costs are *variable* in nature (a term discussed further below). Moreover, we can conclude that the company is successful at managing its cost chain. From an investor's perspective, a cost structure such as Schwab's makes it much easier to predict future earnings. If you can reasonably estimate that Schwab's revenues will grow at 20 percent annual rates over the next five years, you can conclude with a fair amount of certainty that net income will grow at near 20 percent rates as well.

	4Q-97	3Q-97	2Q-97	1Q-97
Revenues				
Commissions	315,000	322,679	261,396	274,919
Mutual Fund Service Fees	119,000	112,155	101,824	94,698
Net Interest Revenue	100,400	94,013	82,485	76,723
Principal Transactions	64,000	61,252	63,598	69,135
Other	22,200	21,740	21,481	20,179
Total	**620,600**	**611,839**	**530,784**	**535,654**
Expenses, Excluding Interest				
Compensation and Benefits	261,700	255,104	224,119	220,838
Communications	45,700	45,790	45,511	45,701
Occupancy and Equipment	41,000	39,279	38,490	35,414
Commissions Floor Brokerage	20,900	26,290	22,217	22,444
Depreciation & Amortization	32,300	34,948	29,686	27,773
Advertising Expenses	38,500	29,303	25,954	35,835
Professional Services	19,300	19,865	16,573	13,881
Other	39,400	34,320	22,491	23,448
Total	**498,800**	**484,899**	**425,041**	**425,334**

(*continued*)

	4Q-97	3Q-97	2Q-97	1Q-97
Income Before Taxes	121,800	126,940	105,743	110,320
Taxes	41,200	50,415	41,781	43,585
Net Income	80,600	76,525	63,962	66,735
Shares Outstanding	263,800	273,001	271,637	271,238
Basic EPS	0.3055	0.2803	0.2355	0.2460
Year-Over-Year Changes				
Net Income	35.02%	34.09%	–8.75%	42.16%
EPS	38.11%	32.32%	–9.68%	40.64%
Revenues	28.67%	42.28%	7.93%	19.89%
Expenses	30.19%	45.38%	13.93%	15.86%
Commissions	30.19%	53.58%	0.09%	14.12%
Fund Fees	37.49%	39.68%	35.07%	37.57%
Compensation	31.82%	48.61%	11.79%	12.84%

Maverick Tube. Usually, a strong relationship between costs and earnings becomes evident when studying a company's financial performance over a multiyear period. With enough historical data, an investor can discover useful trends in profit margins and determine when it is best to purchase shares. Let's use the example of Maverick Tube, a $300 million-a-year manufacturer of steel pipe for the oil and gas industries. Maverick's earnings have advanced and declined, like any cyclical company, on the ebbs and flows of the economy, the level of well-drilling activity in North America, and the prices of steel and crude oil. The impact on Maverick's cost structure from these events becomes apparent when you dissect several years of performance.

Maverick Tube's Operating Performance and Leverage

	Sales	Cost of Goods Sold	Selling Expenses	Operating Income
1997	291,060	252,803	13,966	24,291
1996	204,182	182,042	10,198	11,942
1995	167,896	159,865	7,728	58
1994	124,843	117,833	4,896	1,722
1993	133,729	121,596	6,059	5,330
1992	98,941	92,342	4,783	(3,258)
1991	126,029	115,507	5,172	5,350
1990	123,255	109,100	4,211	9,944
1989	67,249	61,632	2,994	2,623

	Change in Sales	Gross Profit Margin	Change in Operating Income
1997	42.5%	13.1%	103.4%
1996	21.6%	10.8%	20489.7%
1995	34.5%	4.8%	−96.6%
1994	−6.6%	5.6%	−67.7%
1993	35.2%	9.1%	−263.6%
1992	−21.5%	6.7%	−160.9%
1991	2.3%	8.3%	−46.2%
1990	83.3%	11.5%	279.1%

We can see, first, that large percentage increases in sales usually lead to higher profit margins, as we would expect. The company spreads more revenues over the same fixed costs and thereby can boast a larger accounting profit on every piece of tubing shipped. Second, we see that selling expenses tend to be fairly constant, hovering between 4 percent and 6 percent of sales each year. The key to Maverick's performance lies in its GPM, which reflects both the level of sales and the prices Maverick pays for steel. When cost of goods sold rises above 93 percent of sales, that is, GPM is below 7 percent, Maverick has a difficult time earning a profit. Its operating income falls sharply and after-tax income, which takes into account interest expenses, is mildly positive at best. But when cost of goods sold falls below 87 percent, that is, GPM is above 13 percent, Maverick swims in profits.

Maverick shows the extent to which raw materials costs—in this case, steel—can impact the bottom line for shareholders, especially for companies that spend most of their revenues covering fixed and variable costs. When studying a manufacturer whose profit margins rely heavily on raw materials prices, you need to understand the relationship between commodity prices and earnings. Sometimes, as in Maverick's case, the profit margin reveals an opportunity to purchase the company. In 1996, quarterly gross profit margins began to climb above 10 percent, an indication that bottom-line earnings were ready to explode. A combination of lower steel prices and rising crude oil prices, which spurred demand for new wells, helped Maverick, which as late as 1995 was barely operating in the black. Sure enough, Maverick's profits soared, and the stock rallied from $5 in 1995 to $50 by mid-1997. A state of extreme overevaluation resulted, yet another example of how exuberance over short-term profits leads to irrationality, and investors began to dump shares. By mid-1998, Maverick's stock traded around $10 again, though profit margins were still rising. Thus, investors were given two opportunities to take advantage of Maverick's profit-margin expansion.

OPERATING LEVERAGE—
WHEN EARNINGS RISE FASTER THAN SALES

These examples show that changes in a company's cost structure, whether yearly or quarterly, can cause large swings in earnings and influence your valuation of the enterprise. The extent to which earnings are affected depends on the nature of the company and the industry in which it operates. Drug, tobacco, and consumer-products companies such as PepsiCo, Coca-Cola, Merck, Pfizer, Procter & Gamble, Colgate-Palmolive, and Philip Morris have very stable cost structures. When sales rise 10 percent, their earnings likely climb about 10 percent, a one-to-one relationship. Similarly, when sales fall 10 percent, you can anticipate a roughly 10 percent decline in per-share profits. When earnings react this closely to sales, the company's cost structure is heavily weighted toward *variable costs.* A variable cost is an expense that changes with respect to units of output. It includes labor costs and benefits, raw materials, distribution and warehousing costs, marketing, advertising and travel expenses, sales force commissions, and other items deemed essential to producing each unit of product. When a company's orders double, it presumably needs to purchase twice as many units of raw materials, may require twice the amount of labor to produce the added quantity, and may have to double its marketing and sales efforts. Likewise, when orders drop, the company should not need to spend as much on labor, raw materials, and the like.

Companies with high variable costs tend to be less sensitive to economic cycles. When sales slow, most of their operating expenses lessen, and their per-unit costs of production don't drop nearly as much. Thus, companies such as Coca-Cola and Merck tend to have very stable profit margins, even during peaks and troughs in the economy. By contrast, a company with high *fixed costs* is characterized by profit margins that are highly sensitive to sales changes. Fixed costs are those expenses borne every day by a company, whether it operates at full capacity or its plants sit idle. They include interest costs on debt, utility costs, rents and leases, administrative overhead for accounting, legal and clerical staff, maintenance for buildings and corporate headquarters, and salaries of executive officers and personnel whose wages cannot be assigned to a specific product. Fixed costs, as the name implies, do not fluctuate with output. For accounting purposes, they are prorated over the firm's yearly production. If a firm produces 1000 engines a year and bears fixed costs of $1 million a year, it will spread the $1 million over those 1000 units, adding $1000 to the accounting cost of each engine. If the company produces 2000 engines, it spreads its fixed costs evenly over twice as many units, thereby reducing the per-unit overhead to $500—and increasing its profits by $500 per unit. If sales drop to 500 units, however, the company will have to assign $2000 of overhead costs to each engine, and per-engine profits will drop by that amount.

Obviously, a company's profit margins depend very much on its particular blend of fixed and variable costs. Companies carrying a high percentage of fixed costs see a sharp decline in profit margins when sales drop. Conversely, their profits soar when sales rise. A company that experiences a disproportionate increase in earnings relative to sales is said to possess *operating leverage,* a key concept to understanding profit margins and estimating a firm's earnings potential. Companies with operating leverage use their mix of fixed and variable assets to their benefit during expansion phases. For every 1 percent increase in sales, they will report an above 1 percent rise in earnings. Their operating leverage ratio will be greater than 1.0. If earnings rise at twice the rate as sales, a company will exhibit an operating leverage ratio of 2.0. A ratio of 3.0 means that earnings rise three times as fast as sales, and so on. The higher the ratio, the higher a company's fixed costs relative to variable costs.

Quantifying the effects of operating leverage on the bottom line can be tough given that companies do not break out enough information in their financial statements to identify fixed and variable costs. Lacking precise data, an outsider must, at best, guess the percentage of a company's costs that are fixed or variable. But you can approximate these percentages with sufficient accuracy. The simplest method is to compare the changes in yearly revenues to changes in costs. The ratio of these changes will approximate the company's mix of fixed and variable costs. The formula is:

Variable costs as a % of sales

$$= \frac{\text{total costs (this year)} - \text{total costs (last year)}}{\text{sales (this year)} - \text{sales (last year)}}$$

Fixed costs as a % of sales = (1 − variable costs as a % of sales)

A company's variable cost ratios can vary greatly from one reporting period to the next and should be expected. When a company experiences a sales slowdown and is slow to cut costs, it will experience a temporary surge in the variable expense ratio. An investor should try to evaluate many quarters of data and average them to get a better profile of the company's cost structure. Charles Schwab's variable costs, for example, typically average about 90 percent of all costs; fixed costs constitute the remaining 10 percent. Once you have calculated the fixed and variable cost ratios, you can reasonably calculate a company's operating leverage and determine how earnings will change relative to sales. To calculate operating leverage, simply multiply the fixed cost percentage by the company's operating profit margin.

$$\text{Operating leverage (OLE)} = \frac{\text{fixed costs as a percentage of sales}}{\text{return on sales (operating margin)}}$$

If a company's OLE is above 1.0, operating leverage exists. An increase in sales will cause a disproportionate jump in earnings. If a ratio below 1.0 persisted, earnings would not grow at the same rate as revenues. In Schwab's case, operating leverage is absent because most of its operating costs are variable. They include brokerage commissions, which increase only if account trading activity increases; payroll expenses, which increase as the number of customer accounts increase; marketing expenses, which rise with revenue increases; and technology costs, which tend to increase as numbers of employees increase.

Studying a firm's profit margins and operating leverage provides an important tool in forecasting future earnings and cash flow. Over time, you will learn to spot trends in these ratios and adjust your analysis accordingly. In general, companies tend to show two distinct operating leverage trends, cyclical and steady. Below are examples of both.

Hypothetical Leverage Ratios for Two Companies

	Drug Company	Airline
1989	0.95	0.65
1990	0.93	0.92
1991	1.01	1.45
1992	1.03	2.90
1993	0.92	2.25
1994	0.92	0.83
1995	0.97	−0.40
1996	1.04	−1.35
1997	1.00	−0.97
1998	0.97	0.68

We can see immediately that the drug company exhibits far more predictable operating performance than the airline. Historically, the drug company's operating leverage has hovered around 1.0, which means that you can expect a 1 percent increase in earnings for every 1 percent increase in sales. For the sake of expediency, you may choose to average the 10-year trend and use the result to estimate future earnings growth. This is not possible—or prudent—with an airline. Greater care must be taken to ensure that you avoid extrapolating recent operating performance into the future. The past record shows a highly cyclical leverage ratio, undoubtedly due to the airline's high fixed costs. In some years, the example shows, sales increases led to sharp increases in earnings. In other years, increasing sales actually caused earnings to fall.

Does that make the airline an inferior investment to a drug manufacturer? No, but it does mean you must evaluate an airline differently, making sure to avoid buying the company at the top of the leverage cycle. The most

FIGURE 11-1   Increase in earnings based on a company's costs and sales growth.

Fixed Costs as a Percentage of Sales

Sales Increase	10%	20%	30%	40%	50%	60%	70%	80%	90%
2%	2.2%	2.5%	2.9%	3.3%	4.0%	5.0%	6.7%	10.0%	20.0%
4%	4.4%	5.0%	5.7%	6.7%	8.0%	10.0%	13.3%	20.0%	40.0%
6%	6.7%	7.5%	8.6%	10.0%	12.0%	15.0%	20.0%	30.0%	60.0%
8%	8.9%	10.0%	11.4%	13.3%	16.0%	20.0%	26.7%	40.0%	80.0%
10%	11.1%	12.5%	14.3%	16.7%	20.0%	25.0%	33.3%	50.0%	100.0%
12%	13.3%	15.0%	17.1%	20.0%	24.0%	30.0%	40.0%	60.0%	120.0%
14%	15.6%	17.5%	20.0%	23.3%	28.0%	35.0%	46.7%	70.0%	140.0%
16%	17.8%	20.0%	22.9%	26.7%	32.0%	40.0%	53.3%	80.0%	160.0%
18%	20.0%	22.5%	25.7%	30.0%	36.0%	45.0%	60.0%	90.0%	180.0%
20%	22.2%	25.0%	28.6%	33.3%	40.0%	50.0%	66.7%	100.0%	200.0%
22%	24.4%	27.5%	31.4%	36.7%	44.0%	55.0%	73.3%	110.0%	220.0%
24%	26.7%	30.0%	34.3%	40.0%	48.0%	60.0%	80.0%	120.0%	240.0%
26%	28.9%	32.5%	37.1%	43.3%	52.0%	65.0%	86.7%	130.0%	260.0%
28%	31.1%	35.0%	40.0%	46.7%	56.0%	70.0%	93.3%	140.0%	280.0%
30%	33.3%	37.5%	42.9%	50.0%	60.0%	75.0%	100.0%	150.0%	300.0%

prudent times to buy the airline, in fact, would have been in 1989 and 1996–1997, when operating leverage ratios hit bottom and were likely to improve. The best time to sell the stock, by contrast, would have been in 1992–1993, when fixed costs imparted the maximum benefit to earnings.

I have summarized the relationship between costs, sales, and earnings in Figure 11-1, which shows the range of profit gains a company can attain based on its cost structure and sales growth. Let's assume, for example, that a company's sales were $100, that all costs were fixed, and that costs were 70 percent of sales, or $70. Thus, operating profits are $30. But if sales grow 10 percent to $110 and costs remain at $70, profits rise to $40, or 33.3 percent. The company "levered" its high cost structure and obtained a growth in earnings far in excess of its growth in sales. Earnings grew 3.3 times as fast as sales, a very attractive ratio. Had costs been 80 percent of sales, operating profits would rise 50 percent, a five-to-one ratio. Had costs been 30 percent of sales, profits would increase only 14.3 percent.

12

ANALYZING THE FINANCIAL RATIOS THAT MATTER

"The trouble with broad generalizations when applied to stock evaluation is not that they are without some truth, but that too much of the truth has been left out of them."

Arnold Bernhard[1]

BERNARD APTLY ADDRESSES a problem that too many investors share, which is the tendency to fixate on indicators of value at the expense of actual value. The majority of investors try to boil down investing to a few easily understood principles. Most lean toward *ratio analysis,* buying and selling stocks based on mathematical relationships between price and earnings, price and volume, price and growth, etc. These methods hold merit, as I pointed out in Chapter 2. Many studies have upheld the wisdom of buying stocks trading at price-to-earnings, price-to-book, or price-to-sales ratios below that market average. Problems arise when investors wrongly interpret these ratios or, conversely, ignore their potency.

---

[1] Arnold Bernhard, *The Evaluation of Common Stocks,* New York, Simon & Schuster, 1959, p. 4.

INVESTING BY BOOK VALUE

Benjamin Graham spent several years trying to determine what factors were most useful in determining value. He settled on just a handful, the most prominent of which was the company's net asset or *book* value. Graham found that stocks trading for less than their liquidation values—tangible assets minus liabilities divided by shares outstanding—tend to provide the best returns. In Graham's day, when most U.S. companies were manufacturers whose assets were tied up in factories, machinery, and inventory, a company's liquidation value constituted its minimum worth. No matter how out of line a company's stock traded relative to its earnings, it should not, he postulated, ever trade below the company's net worth unless the company was in financial distress. A stock that trades below its own book value is akin to a dollar bill selling for 85 cents or a house selling for less than the cost of the materials needed to build it.

> A stock that trades below its own book value is akin to a dollar bill selling for 85 cents or a house selling for less than the cost of the materials needed to build it.

Graham correctly assumed that such an undervalued condition could not continue indefinitely. Either the stock eventually would rise above its book value or the company would choose to liquidate. If management cannot take the steps necessary to raise the value of the stock above its own minimum value, it has an obligation to break the company up, sell off the pieces for their liquidation price, and return the money to shareholders as a special dividend, Graham said:

> There can be no sound reason for a stock's selling continuously below its liquidating value. If the company is not worth more as a going concern than in liquidation, it should be liquidated. If it is worth more as a going concern, then the stock should sell for more than its liquidating value.[2]

This theory of "liquidating value" became one of the early pillars of value investing. It assumed that any stock valued at less than the company's assets

[2] Benjamin Graham and David Dodd, *Security Analysis,* reprint of 1934 ed., New York, McGraw-Hill, 1997, p. 499.

must rise in value, thereby guaranteeing a positive return to shareholders. When presented with a choice between buying a fairly valued company, thereby taking the risk that the stock might not rally further, and one trading below its book value, an investor should opt for the undervalued stock every time, Graham believed.

> Stocks selling below liquidation value are in many cases too cheap, and so offer an attractive medium for purchase. We have thus a profitable field here for the technique of security analysis.[3]

DEFINING BOOK VALUE

Book value is the company's net equity per share (recall the definition of *shareholders' equity* in Chapter 10). Investors can readily calculate book value—or a reasonable approximation of it—within minutes by studying the balance sheet. For example, let's say that Fruit of the Loom's balance sheet shows $100 million in shareholders' equity and that the company issues 10 million shares of stock. Its book value, then, is $10 per share ($100 million divided by 10 million). If shareholders' equity rises to $125 million, then book value increases to $12.50 per share. If shareholders' equity is $100 million and Fruit of the Loom issues 20 million shares, Fruit of the Loom's book value is only $5 per share.

What do these figures represent? Literally, they reflect the company's "reported" net worth, what Fruit of the Loom's investors could expect to receive if the company sold its assets, paid off creditors, and distributed the proceeds. Book value is compiled by adding the current value of all assets (cash, investments, receivables, land, equipment, inventories, buildings, etc.) and subtracting the company's short- and long-term liabilities. If the common stock trades for less than this fire-sale value, the company is being offered in the market at a bargain.

You must exercise caution when calculating book values. A value investor is wise to apply the following two adjustments to reported balance sheet values.

1. *Adjustment for intangibles.* When one company acquires another at a premium to book value, this creates "goodwill" that must be carried on the balance sheet. This goodwill is an intangible asset whose value is deducted from yearly earnings until used up. If Gannett pays $40 million for a local newspaper whose balance sheet assets are valued at only $30 million, $10 million in goodwill has been created. Obviously, this $10 million is not backed by any asset; it represents the premium to book value that

---

[3] Ibid. p. 499.

Gannett is forced to pay to acquire the enterprise. So Gannett's subsequent balance sheets will carry an asset called goodwill or *intangible assets*. The purpose of the entry is to balance the ledger. Gannett used up $40 million in equity to buy the newspaper, so an offsetting $40 million transaction must show up elsewhere on the balance sheet. In this case, it will show up as a $30 million increase in hard assets—plant, machinery, inventories, etc.—and $10 million in goodwill.

Graham placed little merit in goodwill, for to him, the value of goodwill was hard to quantify. As such, he recommended that investors deduct it when performing book value calculations, because doing so can significantly reduce book value for some companies. In the example above, if Fruit of the Loom holds $200 million in hard assets, $25 million in goodwill, and $100 million in liabilities, its book value is only $75 million ($175 million minus $100 million), not $100 million.

Discretion is allowed when evaluating goodwill. Many value investors, Buffett included, part company with Graham on this issue and believe goodwill has value. To them, goodwill is a residual value tacked onto the purchase price to reflect the "excess" returns the company presumably generates over companies with a similar combination of assets. It represents, at least theoretically, the capitalized value of those excess returns. Indeed, for many companies, goodwill is a real asset. Consider a drug company that holds dozens of patents. If Merck bought Eli Lilly and paid $30 per share more for the stock than the book value of Lilly's assets, you can assume that at least part of the $30 reflects the long-term value of Lilly's patents.

But for other companies, goodwill often turns out to be a mirage. It's not uncommon for companies to write off their goodwill after an acquisition, declare a newly acquired asset impaired, or later concede they overpaid for the assets based on optimistic earnings projections. In such cases, goodwill represents merely the premium management *believed* it had to pay to wrest control of the target company from shareholders. Thus, it may have no long-lasting value for a buyer.

> The fact that an intangible asset originated in an acquisition does not guarantee that it will have continuing value any more than if the intangible assets were self-generated.[4]

To be safe, investors should neither exclude goodwill in their book value calculations nor incorporate it completely. Applying 50 percent of the

---

[4] White, Sondhi, and Fried, *The Analysis and Use of Financial Statements,* New York, John Wiley & Sons, Inc., 1994, p. 910.

goodwill to your book value analysis will yield a closer approximation of its actual value.

2. *Adjustment of values for their likely sale prices.* A balance sheet does not reveal the exact price at which assets can be sold in a liquidation. Rather, it reveals *management's approximation* of an asset's fair value. The first rule in calculating liquidating value, Graham instructed, is to assume that all liabilities are real but that all assets are of "questionable value." Accounting rules mandate that companies carry their liabilities at real costs, so they can be deducted at face value when making book value calculations. The stated value of assets, on the other hand, is arbitrary. Assets are valued either at their *historical cost,* the price the company originally paid, which may differ widely from their value today, or based on management's estimates of today's fair market value.

But what management says assets are worth and what a buyer is willing to pay for those assets are two different things. The Limited, for example, valued its merchandise inventories at $1.1 billion on June 30, 1997, but it's doubtful any apparel dealer would pay anywhere near that amount had The Limited liquidated. More likely, the merchandise—mostly clothing— would have sold for 25 cents on the dollar, perhaps less. Likewise, General Electric would have had only a faint chance of fetching the $25.9 billion it claimed its plants and equipment were worth at the end of 1996.

To value assets more appropriately, Graham devised a quick table that remains useful to this day. He suggested that investors value most assets at a fraction of their reported value to reflect more realistic sales prices.

Valuing Balance Sheet Assets

	% of Face Value	Average
Cash, Marketable Securities	100%	100%
Receivables	75%–90%	80%
Inventories	50%–75%	67%
Fixed Assets (plants and machinery)	1%–50%	15%

If Hewlett-Packard, for example, values its inventories at $500 million, an investor should mark them down to between 50 percent and 75 percent of their reported value. For valuation purposes, Hewlett-Packard's inventories should be realistically valued between $250 million and $375 million. If the company reports fixed assets of $4 billion, investors should value them between $40 million and $2 billion, a wide discrepancy, to be sure.

Graham's adjustments seem reasonable. Cash and marketable securities are highly liquid; the company can sell these assets at any time for roughly the value posted on the balance sheet. Receivables, the money due from merchandise sold on credit, should be valued at slightly less than their book value because of the risk of nonpayment and because several months may elapse before all payments are collected. In generally, the longer it takes the company to collect its receivables, the lower their carrying value. Investors should value inventories and fixed assets for far less than their stated values owing to their rapid obsolescence.

VALUING BALANCE SHEET ASSETS

Graham's figures are not carved in stone. They require you to make several judgment calls. Let's apply Graham's calculations to two unique enterprises, Wendy's International and Giant Cement Holding Co., so that we can evaluate the types of adjustments you may need to make when valuing assets. Wendy's balance sheet on Dec. 31, 1996, revealed the following.

Wendy's International

	Reported Value	Adjustment	Realistic Value
Cash	$218,956	100%	$218,956
Short-Term Investments	4,795	100%	4,795
Accounts Receivable	53,250	98%	52,185
Notes Receivable	11,003	95%	10,453
Inventories	17,000	50%	8,500
Other Short-Term Assets	31,959	75%	23,969
Property and Equipment	$1,207,944	50%	$603,972
Other Assets	236,527	90%	212,874
Total Assets	$1,781,434		$1,135,704
Shares Outstanding	133,785		133,785
Per-Share Value of Assets	**$13.31**		**$8.50**

As you can see, I took some liberties with Graham's adjustments to demonstrate the unique valuation circumstances of a restaurant. Rather than value accounts receivables between 75 percent and 90 percent, it seems more reasonable to value Wendy's receivables at around 98 percent of their reported value. Wendy's accounts receivables typically constitute a small fraction of total sales. These receivables are mostly payments owed from franchisees for delivery of food and materials. Unless the franchisees are in financial distress, chances are excellent these receivables will be paid, and within a very short time.

Wendy's inventories—essentially food—should be valued at the low end of Graham's suggested range owing to their perishability. In fact, they may be worthless to a buyer in a liquidation. Property and equipment, however, should be valued at the high end of Graham's suggested range, in this case, at least 50 percent of their reported value. Wendy's restaurant properties tend to be newer buildings that could be sold to other franchisees at prices closer to their fair real estate values. The other meaningful adjustment comes in the other assets account, which, as you can see, I valued at 90 percent of their stated worth. The footnotes in Wendy's annual report showed that the majority of other assets were notes receivable—loans that Wendy's carried on the books at their current trading value.

Nevertheless, we have significantly reduced Wendy's per-share value of assets by $4.81, from $13.31 to $8.50. Had we marked the food inventories down to zero, the restated book value would be even lower than $8.50. Had we, however, valued the restaurants at more than 50 percent of their stated value, book value would have been higher.

In our other example, Giant Cement Holding Co., a commodity manufacturer, posted year-end 1996 assets as such.

Giant Cement Holding Co.

	Reported Value	Adjustment	Realistic Value
Cash	$10,432	100%	$10,432
Accounts Receivable	14,897	80%	11,918
Inventories	17,656	50%	8,828
Other Short-Term Assets	2,071	50%	1,036
Property and Equipment	$70,418	25%	$17,605
Other Assets	3,142	75%	2,357
Total Assets	$118,616		$52,176
Shares Outstanding	9,833		9,833
Per-Share Value of Assets	**$12.06**		**$5.30**

In this case, I reduced the per-share value of assets by 56 percent, from $12.06 to $5.30, because of their presumed low fire-sale value. The largest reduction occurs in the "inventories" account, which footnotes reveal were comprised mostly of supplies, coal, and repair parts of little value to a buyer. The rest presumably is cement that was ready for delivery. I reduced the value of accounts receivable to 80 percent of their stated worth based on the fact that Giant Cement's receivables constituted 14 percent of sales, meaning the company takes about 49 days to collect its payments. This lag increases the risk that some payments may not be received.

USING GRAHAM'S ADJUSTMENTS TO VALUE A COMPANY

While Graham's calculations do not reveal a company's true breakup value, they do come closer to a proper figure than simply using shareholders' equity. Care must be exercised, however, when using Graham's method. His 15 percent valuation factor for fixed assets would seem too low considering that many fixed assets appreciate in value. Consider a company that purchased a plant in 1960 for $1 million and depreciates it over 40 years. By the year 2000, the reported book value of that plant is zero, for all the depreciation has been used up. But if the company maintained the plant in decent working order, the facility will likely have appreciated in value because of inflation, a phenomenon hardly present when Graham wrote.

A similar problem exists when valuing inventories. A coil of steel may fetch 80 percent of its stated value in a liquidation, an article of clothing only 10 percent. One million obsolete microchips may have no value. Investors will have to make subjective judgments on a case-by-case basis. Warren Buffett once learned the hard way the difference between liquidating value and accounting value. When he auctioned Berkshire Hathaway's last textile mill in New Bedford in 1985, Buffett raised only a fraction of the mill's stated book value. Some of the huge looms purchased for $5000 four years earlier sold for just $26 apiece.[5]

When Kmart sold its Builder's Square chain in September 1997 to private investors, it received only stock warrants and $10 million in cash for the entire company, which included 162 giant stores stocked with merchandise. Builder's Square assets had been rendered nearly worthless because its market share had eroded and the stores lost money. As such, they were worth more to a new owner closed than open. Previously, Kmart had taken a $500 million charge against earnings and wrote down the value of Builder's Square's assets to zero.

[5] Peter Lynch, *One Up on Wall Street,* New York, Penguin Books, 1989, p. 208.

USING BOOK VALUE TO THINK LIKE A CEO

The premise underlying Graham's methodology, which has gone mostly ignored in the 1990s, is that you should evaluate a company's true worth as if you were the one sitting in the CEO's seat making the choice whether to buy the company. Just as you should never buy a *private* business without reasonably valuing the assets, so should you place some value on a *public* company's worth. When applied right, the book value tool keeps you from chasing and possibly getting burned by an outrageously overvalued stock.

> Just as you should never buy a private business without reasonably valuing the assets, so should you place some value on a public company's worth.

What would Graham say today? The average S&P 500 stock traded at more than six times its book value in mid-1998, the highest valuation ever. In other words, investors were paying an average of $6 for every $1 of net assets they purchased a claim against. By comparison, large-cap stocks traded at close to their book values throughout most of this century. Indeed, while book value remains a sound guiding principle for investors—and one of the easiest to calculate, it lacks the relevancy today that it had in Graham's time, a fact that Warren Buffett is quick to acknowledge. Relying on book value alone can lead investors to pass up worthwhile investments.

Knowing the pitfalls of book value analysis can prevent you from egregious mistakes. In addition, book value can be deceptive in certain industries, most notably retailing. These enterprises necessarily carry high levels of inventory that turn over quickly. On a typical day, Sears, Roebuck & Co. may have $5 billion in goods sitting on its shelves and in warehouses. Having that amount of merchandise on hand inflates the asset side of the balance sheet and gives the company a deceptively high book value. But if the inventories aren't selling, the company might have serious cash management problems that book value figures would necessarily mask.

Book value also has less relevance when studying cash-rich, debt-free companies with highly liquid operations, such as Microsoft. On Microsoft's balance sheet, for example, cash constituted two-thirds of assets for most of 1997 and 1998. The company enjoys such excrescent profit margins and turns over its merchandise so quickly that it can finance all of its day-to-day operations from recent sales. Graham would have ignored Microsoft. It traded for an unheard-of 25 times book value in 1998. Obviously, today's investors must be more flexible. For companies such as Microsoft, the relevant measure of net worth is the earning power of its cash and such intangibles as employee education and know-how, not the liquidation value of its hard assets, which book value measures. That's why the market has tolerated Microsoft trading at extraordinary price-to-book ratios.

Conversely, stated book values may be deceptively low for asset-rich companies such as homebuilders, whose asset values can jump dramatically. Homebuilders buy parcels of land and often bank them for two to three years before beginning construction. Over that time, the value of the land may rise appreciably. An astute builder will buy as much land as possible during a recession and wait until the real estate market rallies before developing the parcels. Until the builder sells the homes, the properties will list on the balance sheet at their historical, recession-low prices. In a hot economy, then, the company's book value will be highly understated. If you can find stock of a builder trading below book value in a strong economy, buy it! Chances are good its assets are worth considerably more than their reported value.

The restructuring craze has distorted book value figures, too, and as a result, it has made them less reliable. Many old-line manufacturers have closed plants, spun off subsidiaries, taken restructuring charges, and sold poor-performing assets in an effort to become leaner. Such moves often improve the company's outlook, but they usually lower the value of the company's assets—and book value—thus making the stock appear more inflated than it is. Stock buybacks, in which companies repurchase previously issued shares, also diminish book value because they reduce shareholders' equity. At the same time, buybacks inflate the company's return on equity. Dozens of major corporations have retired shares and boosted their balance sheet returns as a result.

Still, any time you can locate a stock trading below its book value, prudence demands that you examine it closely, for holding all other factors equal, *a stock trading below the company's liquidating value is always a safer investment than one trading above its "book."* To be sure, book value still has practical use when evaluating financial or old-line industrial companies whose major expenses are inventories, machinery, factories, and debt-financing. If you track historical stock prices this becomes evident. A close correlation has historically existed between share price and book value for the auto, banking, and insurance sectors. Until the mid-1990s, these types of stocks usually traded near their book values. As earnings and book value rose, so did the share price.

If you have used book value before, hold onto it as a good yardstick. Just be sure to recognize its present-day limitations, make needed adjustments, and remember the context in which Graham had found it useful. A company's book value doesn't predict how high a stock could or should trade. Rather, it reveals the minimum level to which the stock can drop and acts to cushion the shares from further decline. The bottom line is that it is eminently sensible to buy stocks trading close to their book values.

PICKING BY P/E RATIOS

When appraising any business, an investor's first objective is to attach a reasonable multiple to the company's bottom-line earnings. Starting with a base of recent earnings, investors should develop some criteria to determine what premium they are willing to pay for what the company earned on their behalf. If a company earns $2 per share, you can safely assume the company is worth at least $2 per share. It could be worth more or less than $2, depending on several factors: (1) whether the company is growing or contracting, (2) whether its earnings are growing or contracting, (3) whether the rate at which earnings are growing or contracting is up or down, and (4) whether that $2 in earnings represents an average, peak, or trough based on recent history.

Choosing stocks solely on earnings multiples is risky; the market is replete with seemingly contradictory premiums. One company earning $2 per share may trade at $20, while another trades at $50. A company earning $0.01 per share may list for $3, while another in the same industry trades for $60. The disparities usually arise because of the four factors listed above. A company generating $2 in earnings and growing at 20 percent rates is presumed to be worth more than a company generating $2 in earnings and growing at 5 percent. As I showed in Chapter 7, faster growth rates translate into faster payback. Hence, any analysis of a company must conclude by placing some reasonable multiple to the company's current or recent average earnings. In addition, whatever multiple you determine is fair should be based on your own appraisal, not the market's. Don't allow yourself to be misled by the premium other investors are willing to pay for a stock. If the market values a company at 20 times its earnings and you determine the fair multiple to be only 15, listen to yourself and refrain from buying the shares.

UNDERSTANDING P/E

Investors cannot initiate an appraisal of a company's fair market value without looking first at the market's baseline indicator of worth, the price-to-earnings (P/E) ratio. A P/E ratio shows the premium you pay for every dollar of a company's earnings. To calculate the ratio, divide the current stock price by the company's per-share earnings over the past four quarters. If a stock sells for $80 and the company earned a combined $4 per share over the past four quarters, divide 80 by 4 and you'll see the stock's P/E is 20.

> Investors cannot initiate an appraisal of a company's fair market value without looking first at the market's baseline indicator of worth, the price-to-earnings (P/E) ratio.

When you buy a stock selling at 20 times earnings, you're essentially stating that you're willing to pay $20 for every $1 the company earned on your behalf. If the stock sells at 35 times earnings, a stock must generate 35 times its current earnings to pay back your investment. To some extent, P/E ratios are a testament of faith in that they reflect consensus opinions about a company's prospects. The higher the P/E, the more faith investors have in the company's ability to generate profits. When buying a stock with a P/E of, say, 50, investors must hope that earnings grow fast enough to recoup their investment over a reasonable time. When Presstek peaked at $200 in early 1996, it traded for a prodigious 700 times earnings, so enamored were investors of its profit potential. That potential never materialized, however. Investors once willing to pay $70 for every $0.10 of earnings unfortunately soon learned the folly of their ways. Presstek collapsed under the weight of its own overvaluation and dropped $160 within three weeks.

As stated in Chapter 7, P/E ratios play a crucial role in calculating payback. Without knowing where a stock trades relative to its tangible returns, it's next to impossible to determine when—indeed, if—the company can return your investment within a reasonable time. And because P/E ratios are widely tracked and used, they are a useful barometer for measuring investor sentiment, the market's perceptions of future returns, and how the market currently values assets.

As I showed in Chapter 2, investing in a group of low P/E stocks typically will provide better returns than a basket of high P/E stocks over extended periods. The assumption is that earnings of low P/E companies will surprise Wall Street to the upside, whereas high P/E companies can only meet traders' expectations or fall short. During the mid-1990s, an era thought to have favored glamour and momentum stocks, low P/E stocks actually outperformed their peers by a wide margin. Indeed, investors get plenty of upside leverage when picking low P/E stocks, as many investors in bank stocks found out between 1995 and 1997. A stock whose P/E moves from 6 to 10—still a low valuation—gains 66 percent in price, holding earnings constant. During a two-and-a-half year stretch ending in May 1997, Wells Fargo's stock rose from a P/E of 9 to 22 and gained $170 along the way.

WATCHING OUT FOR THE PITFALLS OF P/E

Before using this yardstick for determining value, investors should understand the pitfalls associated with relying on P/E ratio exclusively. The P/E ratio, remember, has two components, price and earnings. When the stock of a large company such as Ford, Chrysler, or DuPont trades at only four times its earnings, something has to give. The stock either must be bid up in recognition of its undervalued state or the market has correctly predicted that earnings will fall. Often, it's the latter. Ford traded at six times earnings for much of 1995, primarily because analysts and traders feared the company's profits would drop in the following months. If Ford's stock had stayed at a fixed price and earnings fell 50 percent, the P/E ratio would have doubled to 12. And that's why many cyclical stocks—banks, autos, and steel, in particular—traded at low P/Es in 1994, 1995, and 1996. It wasn't that these stocks were steals. On the contrary, traders were expecting a sluggish economy and believed these types of companies would experience a sharp decline in profitability. But here was a classic case of investors caring too much about future projections and paying too little attention to the attractive value Ford and the others offered. Once investors realized their mistake in early 1997, Ford's stock shot up 40 percent within six months.

But there are times when a low P/E translates into extraordinary value. In July 1996, Novellus Systems, which produces the deposition equipment that creates microchips, fell to $32, or six times earnings, on panic selling and fears of a dramatic slowdown in semiconductor sales. Even as the stock plummeted, analysts believed that Novellus was capable of 25 percent to 30 percent annual earnings growth. The stock bottomed one afternoon, turned on a dime, and surged above $100 within a year. In 1997, Western Digital, one of the largest makers of disk drives for computers, fell to $27, six times earnings, on fears of a potential price war among disk-drive manufacturers. Whether a price war developed was, in retrospect, immaterial to investors. Western Digital's earnings had been rising at triple-digit rates. The stock doubled in value within three months.

PLACING P/E IN CONTEXT

To be sure, a P/E ratio is not a frozen yardstick; it's a very dynamic one. For it to have any meaning to a value investor, it must be understood in context. A stock's P/E ratio should be compared to its own historical average, to P/E ratios of other stocks in the sector, and to the P/E of a broad market index. Using the ratio as a gauge, you can determine when an individual stock— even the entire market—is undervalued or overvalued. P/E ratios peaked, for example, just before market crashes in 1972 and 1987.

Industries tend to trade within distinct P/E ranges, which renders comparisons across industries impractical. Judging railroad, semiconductor, and food stocks by their P/E ratios ignores the different dynamics inherent in each segment. Banks, utilities, and insurance companies historically have traded at P/Es of between 8 and 13 because of the nature of their businesses. Most of their assets are tied up in cash or intangible financial products whose value can fluctuate greatly over a short time. Their earnings also tend to be more cyclical than, say, Kellogg's. This adds an element of risk to their growth trends. Consumer products stocks such as Procter & Gamble, Philip Morris, and Clorox tend to trade in a P/E range of 15 to 25. During inflated bull markets, consumer products stocks may trade at near 30 times earnings. During bear markets, the earnings multiple may fall to the low teens. High-tech or aggressive growth companies often trade at P/Es above 30.

A high P/E may inaccurately reflect the company's performance if the company took a significant accounting charge against earnings. For example, several telephone companies took enormous charges in 1995 to speed up the depreciation of their equipment. On paper, some of them posted minuscule profits for the year, which inflated their P/Es to more than 100. If you didn't factor out those charges, you might have ignored otherwise decent stocks because they appeared overvalued. On the flip side, a very low P/E ratio like four or five may indicate unusual factors, such as a one-time boost to earnings. The company may have sold a division for a profit or recognized gains due to a change in accounting methods.

In either case, a little extra digging on your part will separate deceptive P/Es from genuine figures.

INTERPRETING PRICE-TO-SALES (P/S) RATIOS

The financial press occasionally emphasizes this ratio, particularly when spotlighting small-cap growth companies. In theory, the relationship between share price and sales should be direct. If a company's share price is not keeping up with the growth in sales, the stock may be undervalued. Some fundamental analysts, including Charles Allmon, believe sales are the primary driver of stock value. Like many value investors, Allmon questions the credibility of reported earnings and focuses on top-line revenues.

> I consider company sales (revenues) more important than profits when searching for stock market values. Common sense says that in the long run no company can grow faster than its sales. There is a finite limit to expanding profit margins. I would guess that 98 percent of investors focus on profits, with nary a glance at the revenue stream, the lifeblood of every company.[6]

When private businesses are listed for sale, the asking price usually is expressed as a multiple of yearly revenues. Normally, businesses sell for one to two times their yearly sales. A local newspaper with $2 million in revenues may sell for $2 million, or as is common in this industry, at a multiple to circulation. If the paper has 10,000 subscribers, for example, it may sell for $200 per subscriber. In either case, sale price is calculated based on the stream, or expected stream, of revenues generated. The price/sales ratio, or P/S, offers a quick measure for assessing worth. Its calculation is relatively simple:

$$(\text{Stock price} \times \text{shares outstanding}) / \text{yearly revenues}$$

For example, let's assume Sears' stock sells for $50, that there are 400 million shares, and revenues total $50 billion. The ratio then becomes:

$$(\$50 \times 400{,}000{,}000) / \$50{,}000{,}000{,}000 = 0.4$$

The ratio shows that the market value of Sears' stock is four-tenths of its annual sales. Is that a favorable ratio? Many stock pickers would say yes. Historically, companies whose stocks are valued at less than their yearly sales have tended to outperform the market, sometimes by a wide margin (as I discussed in Chapter 2). But investors will find many exceptions to this rule and must be careful when deciphering a P/S ratio. Retailers tend to trade at deep discounts to their revenues, as do distributors, oil companies,

---

[6] Charles Allmon, *Growth Stock Outlook,* 15 August 1997, p. 1.

steel manufacturers, automakers, and commodity manufacturers. What do these companies have in common? They all have commodity product lines, high production costs, intense competition, and low profit margins.

LINKING P/S RATIOS TO PROFIT MARGINS

To successfully interpret the price-to-sales ratio, you must evaluate it within the context of profit margins. My research has found a high correlation between the P/S ratio of a stock and the company's profit margin. In general, the lower a company's profit margin, the lower its P/S ratio. Companies showing higher levels of profitability tend to trade at higher P/S ratios. Intuitively, this makes perfect sense. Higher profit margins result in higher earnings generated and faster payback. A company generating extremely low profit margins requires significantly more time to generate suitable profits for its owners.

To successfully interpret the price-to-sales ratio, you must evaluate it within the context of profit margins.

Fleming Cos., the $16 billion food distributor, offers an illustration. Here's a company whose extraordinarily low P/S ratio masked its low level of profitability.

Fleming Co.'s Margins and Valuation

	1996	1995	1994
Revenues ($mil.)	$16,487	$17,502	$15,724
Cost of Sales	$16,432	$17,416	$15,611
Net Income	$26	$42	$56
EPS	$0.71	$1.12	$1.51
Profit Margin	**0.2%**	**0.2%**	**0.4%**
Revenues/Share	$436	$466	$422
Avg. Share Price	$16.19	$24.50	$26.31
Price/Sales	**0.04**	**0.05**	**0.06**
Average P/E	22.8	21.9	17.4

Note the lines highlighted in bold. Fleming traded at a P/S ratio of roughly 0.04 in 1996, or ½₇th of its yearly sales. But as is evident from the P/E figures, the stock in no way could be considered undervalued. Why? Because Fleming delivered abnormally low profit margins, far lower than 1 percent. Supermarket and food distribution companies subsist on the lowest profit margins of practically any industry. They make their profits from volume. Fleming needs to generate more than $16 billion a year in revenues to earn $40 million to $50 million in income for shareholders.

Look at the data above and ask yourself this question: If you could buy all of Fleming and also pay yourself from the yearly profits, what would you bid? Would you pay $16.5 billion (one times annual sales), a typical multiple for a private business? If your answer is yes, you are throwing away your money. With such low profit margins, Fleming's yearly earnings would be unable to return your $16.5 billion investment for more than a century. Why would you spend $16.5 billion for a yearly return of $26 million? Let's put that in simpler terms: For every $100,000 you invest in the company, Fleming would put back $158 in your pocket.

Without looking any farther than these figures, we can state confidently that Fleming was more fairly valued at $16 in 1996 than if it had sold for one times sales, or $436 a share. At a price of $16, Fleming traded for 22 times 1996 earnings and 14 times average earnings. Both of these are reasonable valuations.

We can conclude, then, that P/S ratios are essentially an indirect play on profit margins. When buying stocks trading at less than their annual sales, care must be taken to choose those with the highest average profit margins, for they will return your investment more quickly. Faced with the choice of buying two or more companies with identical P/S ratios, the company with the higher profit margin will be the more undervalued. Occasionally, it is wiser to buy a company with a higher P/S ratio if profit margins are disproportionately higher, as the table below shows. Here, three equally sized and capitalized companies are compared based on their profit margins. Note that the stock carrying the highest P/S ratio offers the most compelling P/E ratio because of its higher profit margin:

	Revenue	Shares	Price	P/S	Margin	EPS	P/E
Company A	$1,000	100	$5	0.5	3%	$0.30	16.7
Company B	$1,000	100	$5	0.5	5%	$0.50	10.0
Company C	$1,000	100	$8	0.8	10%	$1.00	8.0

C H A P T E R

13

ASSESSING A COMPANY'S INTANGIBLE VALUE

"With a common stock, few of us are rich enough to afford impulse buying."

Philip Fisher[1]

F EW COMPANIES EXHIBIT perfect track records. An enterprise that manages to increase earnings at consistent rates over long periods is truly rare. Rarer still are those that retain the same top managers year after year, increase worldwide market share at constant rates, maintain the same capital structure and balance sheet ratios, and retain the same narrow product lines year in and year out. Such companies can be analyzed in short order. Simply look at what they've done over the recent past and project sales, earnings, cash flow, and dividends at the same rates. If the market misprices the company and you perceive it to be a value, you should buy the stock. A few consumer-products companies do come close to the perfect company I've described above—pharmaceutical and nutritional products concern Abbott Laboratories, Coca-Cola, Gillette, chewing gum manufacturer William Wrigley, and Walgreen. Still, the thousands of remaining public companies have exhibited enough inconsistency over their lives that investors must not only evaluate financial statements for physical evidence of performance but look for

[1] Philip A. Fisher, *Common Stocks and Uncommon Profits,* reprint of 1958 ed., New York, John Wiley & Sons, Inc., 1996, p. 103.

intangible factors that make the company worth owning. I devote this chapter to five of these intangibles.

FIRST INTANGIBLE: RATIONAL MANAGEMENT

The adage "buy a company any idiot can run because sooner or later one will" is often appropriate in this business. Outstanding managers in business, as in any endeavor, are a rarity. We all would like to believe that CEOs are akin to the cream that rose to the top, that they are the most knowledgeable, creative, diligent, and sharpest people of the hundreds or thousands employed at the enterprise. Experience, however, proves otherwise. The psychological profile of CEOs tends to reflect society at large, with its share of leaders, tyrants, overachievers, geniuses, egotists, and dolts. On the one hand, we have too many mediocre managers who rise to the top because of dumb luck. Perhaps they hired into a great company and ascended on the backs of the talented employees below them. Rarely should these managers be credited for possessing individual gifts. Some CEOs rise to the top—like politicians do—because they are survivors of the selection process. They displayed the stamina necessary to endure a highly political, promotion-oriented obstacle course that took 10 to 20 years to navigate.

Fortunately, good products don't necessarily require good managers to execute. You could have chosen any of 100 top CEOs to run Procter & Gamble over the past decade and the company would have earned large sums of money, so deep is P&G's product line. Likewise, Walt Disney could be run profitably by any of 100 executives who understand the entertainment business. Some may have done better than current CEO, Michael Eisner, some worse. To heap all the plaudits on Eisner for Disney's success is to idolize on face value. Disney owes its earnings rebound in the 1990s as much to a strong economy and high levels of consumer spending as anything else. Not to take anything away from Eisner, but he just happened to be there when it all happened. The quality of Disney's programming and filmmaking and the allure of its new theme parks have played subdominant roles. Had the economy been mired in a recession, Disney's bottom-line performance would have been abysmal.

The same holds for Citicorp. It's been fashionable to praise CEO John Reed for the turnaround of this once near-bankrupt financial powerhouse. But a strong economy and the Federal Reserve's tight-fisted policy on interest rates has allowed the big banks to reliquefy in the 1990s and rejuvenate their balance sheets. We can apply this same argument to many fields, particularly sports. Was Mike Ditka really a great football coach, or was he blessed in 1985 with one of the greatest assemblages of talented players pro football has ever seen? Could a basketball coach other than Phil Jackson have achieved consecutive NBA championships with a roster that included Michael Jordan, Scottie Pippen, and Dennis Rodman? Likely, yes.

Isolating the real contributions of management is nearly impossible unless you have the opportunity to see firsthand how they execute their strategies. Many executives, it must be acknowledged, rise to the top based on seniority, aggressiveness, office politics, or their skills in self-promotion, not because of strong financial or strategic-planning skills, as we might desire. In fact, many CEOs have little financial experience when they assume the top post. They likely have spent their earlier years in sales, served as paid consultants to the company, headed up engineering teams, or managed a few of the corporation's subsidiaries. The majority of them have no experience making the types of financial and capital-allocation decisions that impact investors. Thus, as an owner in the company, it is best to save yourself the disappointment of expecting miracles from top managers. Rather, you should expect only that they (1) keep the company on a clearly defined upward path, (2) steadily increase the value of the company, and (3) *act rationally* when setting financial policy.

> Isolating the real contributions of management is nearly impossible unless you have the opportunity to see firsthand how they execute their strategies.

What do I mean by "rationally"? Given the opportunity, many managers will occasionally take actions that are contrary to the best wishes of the owners. They are human, after all, and suffer from the same irrepressible emotions as everyone else. Like many investors, CEOs have a tendency to act in concert with their peers, or spend corporate money on projects when it's fashionable, and not necessarily financially prudent. If these actions are repeated over time, don't wait for the market to discover the mistakes, consider another company to own. What are examples of rational behavior that signals the company is worth buying?

A wise acquisition policy.   The stock market often rewards acquisitions by bidding up the stock of the acquirer because it accepts management's incessant argument that the deal will improve earnings. But history is riddled with examples of companies buying competitors and later regretting the action. In most cases, the deal soured because management paid a rich premium for the target or issued too many shares and diluted shareholders' basis. AT&T's 1991 acquisition of NCR qualifies as one of the biggest wastes of shareholder money on record. Westinghouse's takeover and subsequent spinoff of CBS constitutes another huge squandering of financial resources. In a matter of two years, CBS went from being public and independent to a private subsidiary of Westinghouse to a publicly traded broadcasting company again. The fees and debt incurred during these consecutive transactions detracted greatly from the value of CBS. In retrospect, the events were merely a group chest-thumping exercise by top Westinghouse management to gain control of a television network. Such lemminglike behavior also is evident in the health-care field, where medical technology and hospital/clinic chains brought financial difficulties upon themselves by overplaying the merger game. Each acquisition has brought fewer bottom-line gains than the one before it, as management has been forced to pay ever-higher premiums for the few remaining properties.

The pace of bank, brokerage, and insurance mergers in the mid-1990s will likely haunt those acquiring companies as well. It was bad enough that these companies paid upwards of five times book value for assets. Adding insult to injury, they financed the acquisitions mostly through stock issuance, hence diluting earnings for current shareholders on the false belief that they could cut enough costs at the target company to raise growth rates at the new combined bank. Unfortunately, there exists a mammoth junkyard of deals like these that never pan out the way management envisioned. But many deals do work, and they do because management (1) obtained the target at a reasonable price, (2) purchased a business vital to their own product lines, (3) purchased a direct competitor and reduced the costs inherent in competing, or (4) financed the deal wisely. Paying cash for a takeover target usually is preferred, since no debt is incurred and shareholders' interest is not diluted. When a company routinely issues shares to finance takeovers, it is essentially giving away part of the company to another group of shareholders, thereby reducing everyone's stake in the company and their share of future earnings. It also is putting too much pressure on itself to find enough cost-reducing synergies to offset the larger float. Stock deals make sense only if the acquiring companies' shares are overvalued and the target company possesses better financial prospects.

Successful companies stick to their core competencies and rarely require the steroid boost of an acquisition. Coca-Cola has remained a syrup company since its inception. For a brief period, it dabbled in consumer products (it once owned Columbia Pictures), but Coke's strategy through-out has been to produce soft drinks, period. Some of the most successful banks in the United States are small, local institutions that generate high returns on assets and equity year after year serving healthy, demographi-cally sound markets. An investor usually does better owning one of these gems that return 15 percent a year on equity than a conglomerate superre-gional bank that can barely return 9 percent because of past acquisitions. The point is, if you commit to a value investing philosophy, you should look for managers being similarly committed when they invest on your behalf.

Successful companies stick to their core competencies and rarely require the steroid boost of an acquisition.

An understanding by management of their companies and limitations. If top management has a long ownership stake in the company, there's a better chance they possess a high level of industry sophistication and are running the company more effectively than outside managers. Several hun-dred companies are still headed by their founders or cofounders, including such large concerns as Intel, Microsoft, Cisco Systems, and Oracle. Share-holders benefit when the same people who built a company from scratch head the chain of command, for they know the product lines, industry mechanics, employees, and markets inside and out. What you should eschew is an endless chain of CEOs, especially if they are chosen from out-side the industry. Success in one field rarely translates into success in others. Unless you are "Chainsaw" Al Dunlap, given a mandate to cut employees and close plants, your knowledge and skills likely do not serve more than one industry. A closer look at some of the acquisition-happy medical companies today would reveal that they are headed by lawyers, for-mer consultants to the industry, and accounting partners, not the people you would expect to remain still and patiently stay the course.

The extent to which managers commit themselves financially to the company is just as important. It's reasonable to expect that top managers, particularly at smaller companies, own a considerable amount of the com-pany's stock, at least 5 percent to 10 percent. They must reveal their owner-ship stakes in the yearly proxy statement, an important document sent to all shareholders in advance of the annual meeting. The proxy statement reveals the largest shareholders—mutual funds are likely to own the biggest stake in the company—as well as the experience of top management and board members, their compensation, and options packages. At larger companies such as AT&T, Citicorp, Merck, General Electric, and Hewlett-Packard, insiders typically will own less than 1 percent of the stock. This doesn't reflect poorly on management. These businesses have existed for upwards of a century, and the original founders departed long ago. Through the years, the number of shares outstanding may have risen a hundredfold, and the CEO's office may have been occupied by more than a dozen people.

Management's repurchasing of shares at fair prices.   Few things should irk an investor more than managers who blow shareholders' cash by repurchasing stock at inflated prices. This problem reached epidemic proportions in 1997 and 1998, a time when prices for the top industrial companies had climbed to generous levels based on traders' overly optimistic earnings expectations. As management found it increasingly difficult to meet these high earnings expectations, they began to rely on stock buybacks to boost bottom-line earnings. Microsoft repurchased shares trading at 40 to 50 times earnings, while Procter & Gamble bought back shares at 30 times earnings. In Procter & Gamble's case, top managers sold some of their personal holdings in the market at the same time they sanctioned stock repurchases for the company they controlled. This behavior by P&G management not only defied reason but posed a serious conflict of interest that should have infuriated shareholders.

In traditional finance, share repurchases are considered wise. When a company generates more after-tax cash than it can use to maintain and grow the business, it should return some of that cash to investors. Historically, companies practiced raising their dividends to provide an immediate payback to shareholders. More recently, companies have opted to repurchase shares in the open market, a move that has the effect of decreasing the stock outstanding, raising per-share earnings, decreasing shareholders' equity, and raising the company's return on equity. Stock buybacks are most effective when shares are repurchased at low prices. Buying shares after a price decline not only displays management's confidence in the company but can provide an opportunity for the company to acquire undervalued assets. If management buys back shares at $30 and the company's intrinsic value is $50, it is buying assets for 60 cents on the dollar. If it cannot find an alternative investment that is as attractive, management should repurchase as much stock as it can afford to improve shareholders' interests.

The problems begin when stocks buybacks act as subterfuges for dilutive activities such as mergers, options packages, or employee stock-ownership plans. Dozens of companies resorted to such financial trickery in the mid-1990s. They would announce major share repurchases, the intent of which was to cause an immediate boost in the stock, and then quietly reissue repurchased shares to finance a merger or satisfy employee stock options plans. The end result was added public relations mileage but little, if any, per-share benefit to existing shareholders.

Managed correctly, share repurchases can improve the value of a company and lift stocks prices. Indeed, when a company announces a share repurchase, it is best to hold your shares—not tender to the market—and reap the long-term windfall of owning a larger stake in the enterprise. Retiring shares automatically lifts your stake in future earnings. When a company repurchases one-fourth (25 percent) of its stock, it increases per-share earnings by one-third (33 percent). If it repurchases one-tenth (10 percent) of the stock, it increases per-share earnings by one-ninth (11.1 percent), and so on.

An increase in dividends when no other intelligent use of excess cash can be found.   When presented with excess cash, management in all cases must deploy that cash to best enhance the returns to shareholders. As pointed out in Chapters 9 and 10, management has three options in these situations: (1) retain all profits and reinvest them in the company, (2) retain some profits and return some to shareholders as dividends, or (3) return all profits to shareholders as dividends. As long as management can generate rates of return on equity and assets ahead of the market average, they should try to retain all of the excess cash and forgo dividends. As an example, I like to cite Callaway Golf, whose dividends are small relative to earnings and which has been generating 30 percent to 40 percent annual returns on equity. If Callaway distributed more of its earnings to investors, investors would be forced to find another outlet for their money, one with equally high returns. Since few companies generate returns on equity as high as Callaway, investors should logically reinvest their dividends in Callaway's stock. Considering the commissions and taxes on these transactions, Callaway would serve its shareholders better by retaining all of its earnings in the first place.

Yet there comes a time in a company's life cycle when returns begin falling and it no longer is wise to retain yearly profits at past rates. Rather, it is better to let shareholders decide for themselves where to place their money. Increasing the dividend is the prudent policy.

SECOND INTANGIBLE: JUDICIOUS USE OF LAYOFFS AND RESTRUCTURING CHARGES

Layoffs have proven beneficial to shareholders, as many industrial giants— AT&T, Lockheed Martin, Chemical Banking, Eastman Kodak, Procter & Gamble, General Motors, and Boeing included—have come to learn. But layoffs are a two-edged sword and certainly *not* an immediate guarantee of success. As a shareholder, you should never tolerate a company holding onto 5000 unnecessary employees. A payroll that bloated can add $200 million or more a year to the company's expenses. Yet you don't want the firm cutting workers as a quick fix, sacrificing potential growth in later years to boost the stock now. The bottom line is whether the company can improve future performance in the aftermath of a restructuring.

In assessing layoff news, individual investors should pay close attention first to the timing of the announcement, particularly as it relates to movements in the share price. Announcing a layoff is an easy way to boost the stock, since analysts rarely seem to question the action. Instead, they assume that such a step will increase future profits. Recognizing this, some companies will announce layoffs when the shares are starting to decline from a major rally or have sat at a low level for months. At the end of 1995, Kimberly-Clark announced it would cut 6000 jobs in the wake of its takeover of Scott Paper. On the surface, the job cuts seemed justifiable. Both companies manufactured the same paper products and didn't need duplicate factories and sales forces. But the layoffs also served to boost the share price, which likely was on the minds of Kimberly's executives as well. Wall Street believed that the company paid too much for Scott Paper and put pressure on Kimberly-Clark to cut costs. AT&T, in announcing a 40,000-employee layoff in 1996, all but acknowledged it was dressing up its divisions to enhance their appeal to investors.

Investors should be skeptical when companies toss out large round numbers—5000, 10,000, 15,000—when announcing job cuts. This usually means the company hasn't sufficiently evaluated its work force but is restructuring for the sake of image. What likely happened is the company set a financial goal, say, to cut expenses by $50 million, and determined how many workers it needed to ax to attain the goal. Only later did it sit down and determine which employees really were unnecessary. By contrast, one of the more honest layoffs was conducted by Wal-Mart in 1995 when it eliminated a few dozen workers whose jobs became obsolete when a new inventory system came on line. The layoff showed that Wal-Mart closely monitored the productivity of its resources.

Indeed, some job cuts are justifiable. As AT&T and the Baby Bells automated their operations, for example, they were able to eliminate more than 200,000 jobs between 1984 and 1995, this while improving their products, services, revenues, and cash flow. When banks merge, they no longer need two trust departments, two accounting and payroll departments, and two check-clearing centers. Merging also may allow banks to shutter dozens of local branch banks that competed with one another.

Another factor to consider when evaluating job cuts is time. No company could function properly if it eliminated its jobs all at once. In most cases, layoffs take place over years. A company trying to save $100 million a year through layoffs is not likely to attain those savings until it excuses all of the workers. Likewise, an investor should not expect immediate benefits to earnings. And in fact, you may not see a long-term improvement, either. A 1995 study by the American Management Association (AMA) found that only half of the large companies that laid off workers between 1989 and 1994 increased operating profits as a result. Twenty-nine percent saw no increase in earnings, while 20 percent actually experienced a decline. A 1992 study by Mitchell & Co. of large industrial companies that fired workers found that the companies' stocks had fallen an average of 26 percent three years after announcing the layoffs.

Investors simply can't assume that big job cuts benefit the company. Usually, the exact opposite is the case. Whether at established companies such as Procter & Gamble, or at companies on the decline such as Unisys, layoffs indicate that management faces problems maintaining the company's current profit levels. This is a pure and simple fact. A quick way to verify this is to look at the company's sales growth rate. Those that have been eliminating jobs—P&G, Eastman Kodak, DuPont, McDonnell Douglas, General Motors, and the big banks, for example—are companies whose sales are growing at glacial speeds. Some have been attempting to fabricate higher profits by doing away with jobs. The AMA study found that half of the companies studied cut employees because of a business downturn. Only one-fifth eliminated workers because of automation. The lesson here: *A company cannot downsize its way to prosperity.* Eventually, prosperity must be earned the old-fashioned way: by staking out new markets, developing new products, and attracting new customers to buy them.

Investors simply can't assume that big job cuts benefit the company. Usually, the exact opposite is the case.

Likewise, a company's chronic use of restructuring charges to obscure performance should have investors on constant alert. Nevertheless, one-third of all public companies take charges of one form or another during their fiscal years. The number and types of charges have reached worrisome proportions. Not all charges are meant to deceive, but serve legitimate financial purposes. Under traditional accounting, companies should recognize their costs as quickly as possible to get them off the books. If a company decides to lay off 5000 employees, it's only sensible—and recommended—that they record all possible costs associated with the layoff in one accounting period, even if the layoffs are stretched over several years. This rule applies whether the company decides to cut staff, consolidate regional offices, write down the value of assets, accept losses from the sale of a division, or pay legal judgments.

Companies often resort to accounting charges to streamline their business or carry out their future goals. Rarely do companies maintain the same business plan over years. And occasionally, lines of business fail to perform as expected. When faced with such failures, management has an obligation to shareholders to rid itself of poorly performing ventures before these ventures exact too high a toll on the financial statements. We live in an era when managers are feeling more heat than ever from stakeholders—most notably, mutual funds—to run the enterprise as efficiently as possible. Thus, companies are quicker to jettison assets and take charges lest they stand accused of tolerating substandard performance.

But since charges lead to adjustments to net income, investors cannot ignore their long-term effects. Those who ignore charges risk valuing the company at a higher price than its intrinsic value would recommend. And that's been a major problem in the 1990s; analysts and investors have toed the line, forgiven companies too easily, and, instead, applauded these often veiled attempts to cut costs.

Let's say that General Motors plans to shut three money-losing plants over the next five years to save $2 billion. Under existing accounting rules, GM can take a $2 billion charge against current-year earnings to cover those future costs. Thus, this year's earnings will drop considerably, but all subsequent years will look that much better because the losses from those plants won't be included anymore. I cite GM because it's precisely the type of company that tends to take charges: old, high-cost industrial concerns facing slow sales growth. These companies take advantage of accounting rules and sometimes use charges to manufacture earnings growth when there has been none. The 30 companies that make up the Dow Jones industrial average, for example, took charges totaling $49 billion between 1991 and mid-1996. These write-offs were instrumental to propelling the 30 stocks upward. Add back all the charges and the Dow Industrials companies earned 25 percent less money for investors than what they reported.

Most charges attempt to correct or gloss over problems such as rising costs or a sales slowdown. When companies write down assets, they are acknowledging they made a poor investment. When they close plants, they're revealing a sales slowdown or manufacturing inefficiencies. If a company reports so many charges that you can no longer grasp how well it's functioning, you should avoid the shares.

When charges are present, don't rely solely on the income statement to assess profitability. Instead, proceed directly to the statement of cash flows in the annual report. This will give you a better picture of the company's financial condition over the past year. The cash flow statement tells you just how much money really was earned and spent during the year. If the company is reporting a profit due to charges, but cash is draining away, suspect problems. Occasionally, a company takes a noncash charge, a charge that occurs on paper only and doesn't obstruct cash flow. Such noncash events included the huge write-offs for retirement benefits companies began taking in 1992. The charges caused most large industrial companies to post a decline in earnings that year. Some even reported losses, but they were fictitious, stated to satisfy accounting rules.

Thus, investors must exercise judgment in accepting charges. In 1996, accounting rules for reporting charges were tightened, but they still allow companies broad latitude to reclassify their costs. As such, you cannot accept this sort of managerial creativity on its face. In 1995, Intel took a $475 million charge for the recall of its faulty Pentium chips. The charge was dubious and should have been added back in when making earnings comparisons. This was an operating cost that resulted from poor execution. Companies constantly make these types of mistakes, though most won't try to write it off. In 1994, Borden tried to take a $642 million restructuring charge that covered everything from asset write-downs to marketing costs for a new Elsie the Cow ad campaign. Analysts were skeptical of what Borden attempted, as was the Securities and Exchange Commission, which eventually forced Borden to reverse more than $250 million of the charges.

As an acid test, go back and total up a company's previous charges, then add them back in to see how the company truly performed. You may be surprised by the results. Between 1984 and mid-1996, AT&T's total charges of $14.2 billion exceeded its total reported earnings. It didn't earn a dime for investors over that 12-year period. But by excluding the charges in their reports, AT&T and analysts were able to maintain that the company's earnings increased nearly every year. To evaluate the long-term effects of a charge, make mental adjustments to the company's future earnings. If Boeing takes a $400 million charge for future layoffs, there's a good chance those severance expenses will occur over the course of several years. Boeing merely loaded up all the expenses in one year to dress up future performance. Investors may wish to ignore the charge the first year and reduce pretax income, for example, by $100 million a year over the next four years.

THIRD INTANGIBLE: MANAGERS WHO ADD VALUE

The business world has been swept up in the value-added craze. If a product isn't made more valuable as it crosses an employee's desk, that employee is deemed ineffective. If a division isn't adding enough cash to headquarters, it is sold off. In this environment, it was only a matter of time before the investment world created ways to measure how company executives added value to share price.

Otherwise, an investor has no sacred method of determining whether a manager truly performed exceptionally. We can't tell, for example, whether Jack Welch is a genius at running General Electric or whether a convergence of factors—a good economy, a weak U.S. dollar, strong products, or an exceptional team of vice-presidents—helped to carry Welch toward his goals. We can, however, measure managers objectively by the returns they attain for shareholders, using either of two methods: EVA or the more simple *retained earnings* method.

If managers earn a rate of return on capital over and above the cost of that capital, they increase the value of the company for investors.

1. *The Economic Value Added (EVA) method.* Investors have always required that executives improve a company's worth. The traditional yardstick by which they have measured performance has been the company's growth in earnings or shareholder's equity—the "accounting value added." But a relatively new method called *economic value added* is getting serious attention as a means of measuring whether managers really benefit investors. The EVA method, developed by the consulting firm Stern Stewart & Co., measures managers' performance by holding them accountable for their use of the company's assets and cash. In basic terms, if managers earn a rate of return on capital over and above the cost of that capital, they increase the value of the company for investors. Theoretically, that should lead to increases in shareholders' equity and share price. The greater the rate of return, the more value managers have created, writes Thomas P. Jones of Stern Stewart:

> One of the jobs of corporate managers is to raise capital, and the only reason investors have to make that capital available is the belief that the managers can turn it into a return to the investors. The shareholders own the company, and to keep capital flowing into the company, the manager must provide them with an appropriate rate of return.[2]

For decades, the basic method of determining a reasonable share price has been to assign a multiple to the company's past and predicted future earnings. But the problem is that companies can manipulate earnings in any number of ways, and are doing it today more than ever. They can, for example, change accounting methods for inventories, revenue recognition, or depreciation. They can manipulate assets, sell off divisions, buy competitors, or take restructuring charges. Analysts have learned to avoid this trap by studying the company's cash flow, the sources and uses of cash to generate future earnings. The EVA approach takes the cash-flow method one step further. By assigning an opportunity cost to cash flow, EVA shows the real, after-costs return that managers attained on investors' dollars.

The basic calculation of EVA is straightforward. It's the rate of return on capital (after-tax operating profit divided by shareholders' equity) minus the *opportunity cost* of that capital, or the discount rate (as discussed in Chapter 8). If a company's operating profit was 25 percent of equity and the discount rate was 10 percent, management beat its hurdle rate by 15 percentage points and has contributed to the growth in the equity account.

The opportunity cost is the return investors expect on the company's mix of stocks and bonds. If a company has no debt and the market expects the stock to rise 9 percent a year, the discount rate used in EVA calculations is 9 percent. In the example above, if the operating profit was 25 percent of equity and the discount rate was 9 percent, management's contribution is 16 percent of equity. The table below shows how EVA would break out for a company with $2000 in sales and $1000 in equity.

---

[2] Thomas P. Jones, "The Economic Value Added Approach to Corporate Investment," Association for Investment Management and Research Proceedings, 1995, pp. 12–19.

Sales	$2,000
Operating Profit (*before depreciation*)	$400
Tax Rate	.375
After-Tax Operating Profit	$250 ($400 minus 37.5%)
Average Equity	$1,000
Return on Equity	25.0% ($250 divided by $1,000)
Discount Rate	9.0%
% Value Added	16.0% (25% − 9%)
Value Added	$160 (16% of $1,000 equity)

Thus, managers have added $160 to the company's value during the year on behalf of shareholders. The raw number doesn't mean as much as the *year-to-year change* in the number. If managers add $200 in value the following year, they truly will have increased net worth for investors. When management adds value to the firm, a higher share price should follow. EVA advocates argue that a company's stock price is merely the sum of shareholders' equity and the premium investors place on managers' ability to increase EVA. For example, the total market value of Wal-Mart's stock in early 1996 was $57.4 billion and Wal-Mart's shareholders' equity was $12.7 billion. One could argue that investors placed a premium of $44.7 billion on Wal-Mart's potential. The higher the premium, the more managers are expected to improve share value.

2. *Retained earnings method.* A simpler approach to assess management's progress is to view a company's growth in the context of retained earnings, the excess profits management has at its disposal each year after paying dividends. As I noted in Chapter 10, share-price increases, theoretically, should be linked to retained earnings. A stock should rise, *at minimum,* by the increase in retained earnings during the year. If DuPont earned $4 per share, paid $2.50 in dividends, and retained $1.50, we should expect DuPont's stock to rise by at least $1.50. The $1.50 became an asset and should have increased shareholders' equity, or book value, by at least $1.50. If DuPont was unable to raise the value of its net assets by at least $1.50 per share during the year, it made poor use of the money it retained and should have raised the dividend.

Over longer periods of 15 years or more, an investor can expect, at minimum, to see a linear relationship between growth in retained earnings and growth in share price. If the market moves in lockstep with the retained earnings account, we can conclude that the market has fairly valued the company during its growth phase. But such one-to-one growth ratios are not sufficient. When the market value of a company rises only as fast as retained earnings, investors are signaling that management has added no value. Investors have placed so little faith in the company's prospects that they assign an ever-lowering premium to the company's earnings. Consider a company that retains all of its earnings and whose retained earnings and market value grow by the same dollar value each year. We can show this using the example of a company earning $1 per share, trading at $12, and whose share price rises each year by the exact amount of the increase in retained earnings. Starting with a hypothetical P/E ratio of 12, we see how the market steadily lowers its perceived value of the company's earnings.

	EPS	Retained EPS	Share PRICE	P/E
1997	$1.00	$1.00	$12.00	12.0
1998	$1.15	$2.15	$13.15	11.4
1999	$1.32	$3.47	$14.47	11.0
2000	$1.52	$4.99	$15.99	10.5
2001	$1.75	$6.74	$17.74	10.1

When the market value of a company rises only as fast as retained earnings, investors are signaling that management has added no value.

By the fifth year, the market is willing to pay only 10 times earnings for a company whose earnings are growing at an exceptional rate of 15 percent a year. We can conclude from this exercise that either management is incapable of bringing the shares up to their full value or that the market has undervalued the enterprise. Investors should try to determine which scenario is true. Unless the market is truly mispricing the stock, it is best to avoid companies that have not grown their market value faster than retained earnings.

FOURTH INTANGIBLE: FRANCHISE VALUE
Wrigley chewing gum possesses an intangible property its competitors can't seem to match. So do Harley-Davidson, Tootsie Roll Industries,

Coca-Cola, NIKE, Walt Disney, and a number of other large American-based companies. Among overseas companies, Nestlé, and Mercedes-Benz come the closest to possessing that same brand magic. Sears once possessed such qualities, as did piano makers Kimball and Baldwin, Cadillac, Rawlings, and Topps trading cards, until demographic, distribution, and competitive forces undercut their markets. The onset of strip centers and the disintegration of the population into the suburbs allowed hundreds of retailers to open their doors and steal niches away from Sears. The appearance of rival trading card companies around 1980 eroded Topps' brand image virtually overnight. Today, it fights with more than one dozen card companies for shelf space.

Yet Disney, Harley-Davidson, and the others continue to operate unimpeded. They compete fiercely in their markets, to be sure, but their brand image is as strong as ever. More than 90 percent of Harley-Davidson owners say they would buy another motorcycle from Harley, rather than from Yamaha, Honda, or Suzuki. Disney has built one of the world's most recognized brands by diversifying beyond theme parks into an all-encompassing entertainment company with interests in television, movie studios, production, retailing, cruise ships, music, news production, cable, hotels, and leisure resorts. Its strategy has been to put the Disney name within reach of as many segments of the population as possible, which improves brand image further.

These companies all possess *franchise value,* an intangible asset that makes companies worth considerably more than their financial statements might imply. Franchise value is hard to quantify—though many business valuation experts and accounting firms have tried—but it is a very real component of stock analysis. Franchise value, in brief, exists when a company can extract more in sales volume from a market than could have been expected given its prices, production capabilities, marketing, advertising and distribution efforts, and cost structure. For example, if two companies produce and sell identical electric motors to the same manufacturers at the same price with the same sales efforts, one would expect each company to sell the same amount of motors. But if one company sells 20 percent more motors than the other, franchise value exists. An intangible factor is making the company's motors more appealing in the marketplace.

What might these factors be? The biggest and perhaps least quantifiable contributor is *brand name.* Why do some people automatically reach for a Hershey bar at the checkout counter rather than a generic chocolate bar next to it, though both may be priced similarly and may hold no perceivable taste difference? In all likelihood, brand and image captivated the buyer. Certain brands—Coke, NIKE, Lexus, McDonald's, Levi's, Wal-Mart, Citibank, and American Express, among others—are universally recognized, giving these companies a marketing edge competitors cannot hope to attain. Just how much an edge they possess is impossible to say. You can debate forever the dollar value of Coca-Cola's brand name, but there's no disputing that the word "Coke" possesses incredible value to the company. Coke and Pepsi could each penetrate a new market at the same time with the same resources, but Coke likely would win the largest market share.

Time is a major factor in establishing brand power. A product with a decades-old presence in the marketplace, such as NBC, Anheuser-Busch, Rawlings, or Chicago Cubs baseball, has built a level of buyer loyalty that will never show up on financial statements. But it's there, hidden in the earnings stream. Franchise value can also exist by legal fiat. When Eli Lilly obtained patent protection on *Prozac,* it guaranteed itself billions of dollars in future sales. No rival drug company can produce the equivalent of *Prozac* until Lilly loses patent protection. Trade barriers and tax breaks also can create franchise value, as can zoning restrictions, and licensing and franchise agreements.

To own a franchise is to have marketing power—in some cases, monopoly marketing power. Consider, for example, a local daily newspaper. Dozens of dailies exist in this country with little or no competition. Often, they print in midsized cities—Abilene, Huntington, Macon, Rockford, Lafayette, El Paso, Greenville, Kalamazoo, Wausau, etc.—too far apart to support television stations and too small to support two newspapers. In these towns, the local newspaper is the sole source of news for townsfolk and the only distribution channel for local advertising. If the butcher shop wants to run a sale, it must place an ad in the town newspaper. When the county government publishes legal notices, it buys space from the newspaper. If the local Wal-Mart has a back-to-school sale, it must spend thousands of dollars creating circulars inserted into the Sunday edition. That's the hidden franchise value of a local newspaper, its lock on demographics.

Today, few companies or institutions retain much franchise value. Hollywood at one time had a lock on movie making and could guarantee its own success year in and year out, but, alas, no longer. ABC, CBS, and NBC once had a lock on television audiences. But since the rise of cable-TV, the three networks' market shares have eroded year after year. The New York Stock Exchange was once considered the only place to trade respectable stocks, but no longer. Dozens of the world's most successful companies trade over the counter. For a 25-year period starting in the mid-1950s, Topps held a virtual monopoly on sports trading cards, allowing it to control prices, distribution, and profits. It created demand for its own products and spawned a collecting and trading black market for cards. But not long after competitors entered the field, specifically Fleer, Donruss, and Bowman, Topps found itself on the defensive. The perceived value of its cards dropped, as did market share, and the company no longer was the exalted brand in the minds of card buyers. Kmart once was the top brand for budget-conscious, middle-class shoppers. Now it fights an uphill battle trying to compete for customers against Target and Wal-Mart Stores, which today are stronger competitors.

These companies, along with thousands of others, lost their brand power because the barriers to competition have fallen drastically over the past 20 years. Capital is easy to raise and flows freely across borders. It is now as easy to build a manufacturing plant in sub-Saharan Africa as it is in Tennessee. And most new technologies and products are easy to replicate, capable of being copied by competitors within months, if not sooner. Because of the free flow of assets worldwide, competitors can catch up almost immediately. It was once the case that having a franchise meant you had a monopoly on prices and could raise them at will. Drug companies were free to charge top prices and keep their profit margins exceedingly high until generic manufacturers gathered enough financial strength to challenge them. For several years beginning in the mid-1980s, NIKE found it could raise prices of athlete-endorsed sneakers to more than $100 with no repercussions. Today, that luxury is gone. With the emergence of several competitors and near loss of pricing power, NIKE must periodically "discount" its shoes to revive sales.

Measuring Franchise Value

Just how should an investor value a brand? Admittedly, no ironclad methodology exists, but many consulting and marketing firms have developed models that attempt to capture the excess financial value created by a brand. One relatively easy method investors can use is to compare competing companies' profit margins and return on assets (ROA). If one company boasts higher profit margins selling essentially the same products as its competitors, brand power probably exists. Consider three equally capitalized companies that sell computer connectors, two with identical 15 percent profit margins and one with a 20 percent margin.

	Firm X	Firm Y	Firm Z
Sales	$5,000	$4,000	$8,000
Operating Profit	$750	$600	$1,600
Shares	500	500	500
EPS	$1.50	$1.20	$3.20
Assets	$7,500	$6,000	$8,000
Return on Assets	10%	10%	20%
Equity	$3,750	$3,750	$3,750
Return on Equity	20%	16%	43%

Clearly, Firm Z is the superior company and deserves a higher stock valuation than the other two companies. But how much of its success is owed to the brand? We can only venture an educated guess. Perhaps Firm Z owns more efficient plants, which creates higher profit margins. Perhaps, too, it attracts more customers as a low-cost producer. Or perhaps it has attained a critical mass of sales and can spread fixed costs over more units and raise the accounting profit on each unit.

Marketing experts who have attempted to quantify brand value believe the key lies in studying a company's *return on assets* (operating income divided by average assets deployed) or *return on capital* (operating income divided by the sum of shareholders' equity and debt). Firms possessing brand value tend to enjoy higher returns on assets and returns on capital than competitors and manufacturers in general. In the example above, Firm Z's returns are at least double those of its rivals. Some intangible factor must make this possible. Firm Z may have a better trained sales force, a more effective advertising strategy, or a better distribution network. Or customers may simply "like" the company's products and management better. If Firm Z's advantage derives simply from manufacturing efficiency, Firms X and Y might work feverishly to attain the same efficiency and close the gap as quickly as possible.

In quantifying brand value, investors should focus on return on capital (ROC), a measure of how well management utilizes the physical and financial resources with which it begins each year. An American company with a generic product line and no brand value should be able to obtain a return on capital of about 5 percent a year, more during cyclical boom times, less during recessions. Using a 5 percent ROC as a starting point, you can reasonably estimate brand value. If a company obtains a 15 percent ROC, assume that the extra 10 percent ROC derives from brand value. Convert that 10 percent into a dollar figure and then attach a multiple that takes into account the long-term discounted value of the brand. The formula is fairly straightforward:

Yearly brand value
$$= [(\text{after-tax operating income/capital}) - 5\%] * \text{capital}$$

Long-term brand value = yearly brand value * a premium

In the example above, Firm Z delivered a 43 percent return on equity, and since there is no debt, Z's return on capital also is 43 percent. Subtract 5 percent, and Firm Z's yearly brand value is 38 percent of capital, or $1425. To determine the long-term brand value, you must assign a multiple to $1425 to pick up the discounted future value of the brand. If you determine that Firm Z's long-term brand value is 15 times current brand value, the brand is worth $21,375. If you assign a multiple of 10, the brand is worth $14,250.

Obviously, brand value hinges on the accuracy of your premium. But using the same techniques discussed in Chapter 8 on estimating cash flow, you should be able to determine a reasonable multiple to attach to yearly brand value.

FIFTH INTANGIBLE: A LEGIBLE, CLEAR ANNUAL REPORT

Companies have scant opportunity to present facts to their owners. But when they do, the facts should be clear, complete, and provide enough information for meaningful analysis. An annual report that can't describe a company in basic terms raises doubts about the company's merits as an investment. And it raises doubts about management's candor. If executives do not wish to paint a clear picture, you must question why. Over the past 20 years, the trend has been to use annual reports increasingly as public relations packages, with every phrase, photo, caption, and chart carefully chosen to portray the company in the most positive light. Lost in the middle somewhere are a few obligatory financial statements.

It's easy for investors to become captivated by two dozen pages of glossy photos, followed by pages of the chairman's rambling and inane footnotes. Is all of this necessary? No. A basic, barebones explanation of the business along with the necessary financial statements is all that's required and should be expected. A good annual report provides all of the information needed to perform basic analysis of the past several years of performance. It also should exhibit the exact same financial information as in previous years, in the same format and page order. If the company's reporting is consistent, year-to-year comparisons can be made with confidence. Just as important, you'll be able to develop a systematic way of reading and interpreting the information.

Nucor's annual report is old-fashioned in the best sense of the word and a true pleasure to read. Investors won't find any fluff or glittery depiction of the company's facilities. The CEO's photo looks as if it was taken 20 years ago. In all probability it was; the company has been alternating the same two photos of Kenneth Iverson for years. Walt Disney's annual report, by contrast, contains nearly everything you don't need to know about the company, including gratuitous photos of employees, everyday Americans enjoying the theme parks, and racks of merchandise at Disney's retail stores. The 1996 annual report was among the worst ever produced. An investor couldn't find any meaningful financial information until page 55.

A good annual report need not be more than 16 to 20 pages in length. That includes four to six pages of financial statements, another two to four pages of footnotes, one to two pages for the chairman's letter, two pages dedicated to past financial performance, and the rest devoted to useful information about the company's markets and services. A company should not require more than five pages to describe its activities. But you should allow some latitude for overall length. Banks, insurers, and finance companies such as American Express are obligated to provide far more financial information than the typical company. Their reports may contain 10 to 20 pages of footnotes alone.

What to Look for in an Annual Report

1. *Are figures presented consistently?* Each year's report should contain the exact same financial tables and data in exactly the same places as the year before. Many companies change their format yearly and try to call investors' attention to different goals and figures. One year, they focus on return on equity; the next, backlog and order growth. A good report should contain enough information that an investor can compare several years of reports and spot trends in the marketplace, sales, expense, incomes, and cash flow.

2. *Are goals defined and consistent?* Read NIKE's annual report, or Microsoft's, and you quickly grasp the company's mission. But if you cannot deduce what the company is trying to be, you can conclude that (1) management has not set any goals in stone or (2) does not want to share those goals with you. Read past annual reports to gauge whether management has stuck to its past goals or abandoned them. If it abandoned previous plans, why?

3. *Is management frank about its accomplishments?* Or are the pages ruled by public relations spin and hype? A chairman who lacks specificity in his/her opening letter to shareholder's may be setting up investors for the kill inside. Does the report read like a personal, candid letter from the CEO—like Warren Buffett's do—or a public relations document crafted by the PR staff, reviewed by lawyers, and quickly signed by the CEO.

4. *Can you follow the money?* Some companies engage in so many acquisitions it's next to impossible to figure out if they are really making money. Using accounting adjustments, companies can smooth over most of the inefficiencies associated with a merger and cover up past mistakes. Mergers often lead to a restatement of past results, which all but invalidates figures from previous years' annual reports. When a company makes so many acquisitions that you cannot tell whether the company's continuing operations are profitable, walk away.

5. *Can you see this company's future?* Does the company have a vision for where its marketplace is headed? Does senior management intend to be aggressive or passive in exploiting new market opportunities? Will changes in the marketplace cause disruptions in future profitability? Investors should pay attention to any mention of future earnings. Has management issued so many options that future earnings targets cannot possibly be hit?

14

ASSEMBLING A PORTFOLIO: THE SUBSIDIARY APPROACH

"Once you attain competency, diversification is undesirable."

Gerald Loeb[1]

ONE OF THE MOST COMMON questions asked by investors has to do with portfolio diversification. Most investors rarely are comfortable with the size and mix of their stock holdings and seek academic answers to guide them. Regrettably, some have collected stocks like postage stamps and own shares in more than 100 companies. They have become, for all practical purposes, human mutual funds. Though such diversity makes them feel "safe," their portfolio's performance likely will never deviate much from the market's, though their net returns will suffer from high commissions. In addition, they have doomed themselves to countless frustrating days of paperwork and of tracking cost bases, stock splits, dividends, and spinoffs. What often gets lost like the proverbial needle in this haystack of responsibilities is *performance.* No investor can possibly monitor so many companies with any true degree of diligence. Sluggish stocks are likely to stay in their port-

[1] Gerald M. Loeb, *The Battle for Investment Survival,* New York, Simon & Schuster, 1965, p. 42.

folios for years, overvalued stocks aren't sold at appropriate times, and these investors lose control over the ability to measure results.

DIVERSIFICATION IS NOT NECESSARY

The cause of this dilemma—modern portfolio theory—is not new; it dates to research conducted in the 1950s and 1960s that tested the possible returns investors could expect from holding various baskets of stocks. In attempting to "minimize risk," researchers tested how individual stocks reacted to movements in the market and used mathematical principles to show that a portfolio's volatility, its up and down fluctuations, could be controlled by carefully selecting stocks that moved counter to one another.

These mathematical quests led to the general theory of diversification: Buy stocks in different industries to ensure against their all declining at the same time. Eventually, researchers concluded that while an investor could never eliminate a portfolio's volatility, she can minimize it by owning about 20 stocks. Buying more than 30 stocks provides negligible benefits. But with 20 stocks, academics argued most individuals were "practically" diversified.

What does it mean to be diversified? A properly diversified portfolio, in academic parlance, is one that eliminates *nonsystematic risk,* that is, the risk that a single stock can cause material disruptions to your portfolio's returns. The theory held that if you combine 20, 30, 40—even more— stocks in a portfolio, you could eliminate the risk that one stock imploded and caused your entire portfolio to suffer. For every stock that unexpectedly declined, you could expect one to rise and offset the loss.

But being well diversified never protects your portfolio from losses. Even the most well managed mutual funds that own 200 stocks or more lose money periodically. Having so many stocks merely *lessens the probability of loss,* a distinction that is important for all investors to understand. An investor always is vulnerable to *systematic risk,* the risk that an unforeseen event can cause the entire stock market to drop. No amount of stock buying can reduce all systematic risk. The best you can do is to spread your money into different instruments such as bonds and foreign stocks to insulate yourself from a stock market meltdown.

Indeed, many investors have learned the hard way that owning 20 stocks alone won't necessarily reduce their risks. Many investors believed they were diversified in 1994 because they owned one dozen or more utilities and all the "Baby Bell" stocks. They learned the hard way the herd rule: Like stocks fall together. Indeed, when the stock market plunged on

October 19, 1987, nearly every stock listed on the New York Stock Exchange, American Stock Exchange, and Nasdaq dropped in price. On the surface, it seems improbable that nearly every public company could fall in one day or that they were suddenly worth less intrinsically, but decline they did.

In fact, later research has found that even 20 stocks are insufficient to achieve diversification. If you want to ensure that your portfolio returns do not deviate much from the market, you might have to own 60 to 100 stocks, a financially impossible task for most investors.

> # Risk cannot be defined by mathematics or share-price movements. Rather, investors create risk by chasing stocks indiscriminately, by failing to do their homework.

But to a value investor, blanket statements about risk and return, which may have meaning at the billion-dollar money management level, are inert. Risk cannot be defined by mathematics or share-price movements. Rather, investors create risk by chasing stocks indiscriminately, by failing to do their homework. You encounter the biggest risks when you fail to evaluate a company properly and as a result, pay more per share than the company is truly worth. A company purchased at $60 per share offers a compelling value and little business risk if the shares actually are worth $90. The same shares offer tremendous potential risk if the company's intrinsic value is only $30. To quote Warren Buffett:

> I put heavy weight on certainty . . . If you do that, the whole idea of a risk factor doesn't make any sense to me. You don't [invest] where you take a significant risk. But it's not risky to buy securities at a fraction of what they're worth.[2]

Mathematical diversification should not be an end or the means. To many, it has become an excuse, one that necessarily leads to mediocre stock pick-

---

[2] Jim Rasmussen, "Buffett Talks Strategy with Students," *Omaha World-Herald,* January 2, 1996, p. 17.

ing. One clear advantage to value investing is that investors need not hoard stocks like souvenir spoons or Beenie Babies. A well-rounded portfolio of eight to a dozen companies, each bought at favorable prices, possessing solid fundamentals, and offering suitable upside potential, is sufficient for most investors to achieve their goals.

> ## Mathematical diversification should not be an end or the means. To many, it has become an excuse, one that necessarily leads to mediocre stock picking.

THE FIVE KEYS TO PROPER DIVERSIFICATION

1. *Avoid viewing diversification as a purely mathematical task.* The mathematics required to create to perfectly risk-neutralized portfolio is potent and beyond the scope of most individual investors. While diversification remains a worthy goal, applying its principles in practice is time-consuming and may not enhance your portfolio's performance.

2. *Avoid getting so caught up diversifying that you lose sight of what you own.* Holding 30 to 40 stocks won't guarantee that you've removed risk, especially if you've chosen the wrong stocks. The general theories of diversification provide much latitude when it comes to actually tailoring a portfolio. You may decide, for example, to hold 10 percent of your portfolio in retailers, but then you are left with the choice of whether to buy the Wal-Marts of the world or the Kmarts.

3. *Define risk based on company performance, not stock gyrations.* If you want to diversify risk of loss, buy companies whose performance has been predictable. Nothing negates stock risk more than steadiness. A company whose earnings tend to rise 10 percent a year is not likely to experience nearly the same up-and-down stock fluctuations as a company whose quarterly or annual earnings performance is erratic. Furthermore, you should try to purchase companies as cheaply as possible to minimize the risk of stock volatility and the chances that the company disappoints you in the future. If a stock trades for $50 and the company is worth, say, $25 per share, you are buying into a potential 50 percent decline in price should investors tire of holding their shares. But if you bought the company at $20 per share, the stock price already discounts some potentially disappointing performance down the road.

4. *Keep your portfolio fairly small and understandable.* Many investment clubs have attained spectacular returns this decade holding just 12 to 15 stocks, many of them name-brand consumer-products companies. Their success relies on careful stock screening and having manageable portfolios. It's more prudent to own 10 companies you understand intimately than 50 randomly chosen companies whose performance you can't follow.

5. *Use a king-of-the-hill approach.* Many successful money managers may intentionally limit their portfolio to 20 to 25 stocks, but continue to replace underperforming issues. They might spread their stocks over several industries—for example, oil, banking, drugs, heavy equipment, and retail—but buy the best two to three stocks within those industries. When one company experiences disappointing performance, they seek to replace it with another company in the same industry that exhibits better prospects. Over time, their portfolio graduates to an assemblage of high-quality issues.

DOLLAR-COST AVERAGING

So much has been written about dollar-cost averaging the past few years that I felt it necessary to address the advantages and disadvantages of this popular investment philosophy. Dollar-cost averaging, the practice of making regular contributions to your stock portfolio regardless of price, has become one of the most steadfast tenets of the "buy-and-hold" crowd. In the 1990s, it evolved into a *rational methodology* that has been exploited endlessly to lure investors, experienced and otherwise, into the market. Millions of investors now deploy dollar-cost averaging to manage their entire stock, mutual fund, or 401(k) portfolio.

The strategy, on the surface, seems too simple and too good to be true. Dollar-cost averaging is a forced savings plan. An individual decides to invest, say, $200 a month from his savings into the stock market without regard to the market's condition or his personal financial situation. Its underlying premise is that the more money you can sock away in the market today, the greater your wealth at retirement. It advocates buying small amounts of shares periodically but letting the market determine how many shares you buy and at what price. It's touted as a "can't-lose" way to invest because it forces you to buy fewer shares as the price rises and more shares as the price falls. In other words, it ignores market timing altogether. Here's an example of how an individual might fare investing $200 a month in one stock.

Month	Investment	Price	Shares Bought	Total Value
January	$200	$15	13	$200
February	$200	$18	11	$432
March	$200	$21	9	$693
April	$200	$16	13	$736
May	$200	$12	16	$744
Total	$1,000	$16	62	$744

In this example, the investor added $200 a month to her portfolio buying a stock that ranged in price from $12 to $21. At the end of five months, her $1000 bought her 62 shares, with some money left over each month, for an average purchase price of $16.12 per share. When the stock peaked at $21, her $200 bought only nine shares. When the price declined to $12, she was able to purchase 16 shares.

Dollar-cost averaging is anathema to value investing and has no place in a value portfolio.

After reading the previous chapters, you can probably see the logical problems with this strategy. Indeed, dollar-cost averaging is anathema to value investing and has no place in a value portfolio. Dollar-cost averaging inhibits your returns, making it more difficult to beat the market. Further, it induces poor performance during extended bull markets, a time when investors are wont to add to their positions at ever-higher price levels. Since the purpose of value investing is to select companies at prices that are as reasonable as possible, it is senseless to diffuse such a strategy by remaining oblivious to price and spreading purchases over a period of months. Successful value investors never should base their portfolio decisions on trial and error, the emblem of dollar-cost averaging. *Price is paramount.* No purchase should ever occur at a price that cannot be justified by business fundamentals. Those who have used dollar-cost averaging in the 1990s and paid higher and higher prices for stocks such as Walgreen, Merck, Microsoft, Boston Scientific, or Procter & Gamble, have taken on significant risk and may one day come to loathe the very strategy they embraced.

Dollar-cost averaging owes its popularity solely to the bull market and a tireless marketing campaign by the brokerage industry. The premise that stock prices will rise perpetually is merely a ploy by the industry to keep you buying—and paying commissions—in good times and bad. The key difference between a value investor and a dollar-cost averaging strategy can be summed up as follows:

> A dollar-cost averaging strategy allows the market to determine your portfolio allocation, your gains and losses, and removes valuation and risk assessment from the purchase decision. Value investors, by contrast, are not price takers; they should focus on risk and price at all times. They should wait until the stocks of their favorite companies fall to a suitably undervalued level and then buy as many shares as they can afford—all at once.

BUILDING A VALUE PORTFOLIO

Let's develop some of principles outlined in earlier chapters, starting with a one-stock portfolio, Merck & Co., and using these parameters:

Holding period: 6 years

Shares purchased: 200

Purchase price: $90

Total investment: $18,000

P/E at time of purchase: 29

1996 EPS: $3.07

Before buying shares of Merck, you should develop a reasonable estimate of the earnings Merck could generate for you over your holding period—in this case, six years. You might estimate Merck's earnings based on its average earnings over the past several years. Or you could try to project its cash flow over your six-year holding period, a more daunting task. In this case, given Merck's nearly constant growth record, it would be more appropriate to estimate future earnings by applying Merck's historical earnings growth rate. Let's assume that earnings grow at 14 percent rates, starting with a 1996 earnings base of $3.07. By the year 2001, Merck will have generated $5922 in earnings on your behalf. Next, adjust for possible dividends. Merck traditionally has paid out about 45 percent of its earnings in dividends. So it's reasonable to assume the following stream of earnings and dividends from a 200-share investment:

	1997	1998	1999	2000	2000	2001	Total
Merck's Earnings	$3.50	$3.95	$4.50	$5.14	$5.85	$6.67	$29.61
Merck Dividends	$1.58	$1.78	$2.03	$2.31	$2.63	$3.00	$13.33
Earnings × 200 Shares	$700	$790	$900	$1,028	$1,170	$1,334	$5,922
Dividends × 200 Shares	$316	$356	$406	$462	$526	$600	$2,666
Retained EPS × 200	$384	$434	$494	$566	$644	$734	$3,256

What returns can an investor anticipate from this performance? *At minimum,* you should expect your total return to be at least $5,922, or $29.61 per share. Of that $29.61, retained earnings constitute $16.28; dividends the remaining $13.33. If Merck paid no dividend, you would expect the stock to rise the full $29.61 over six years. The dividend, since it reflects a return of capital, reduces the potential price appreciation, a price you pay for getting some of your earnings back more quickly.

Is this return suitable? Over six years, you can expect $5,922 in gains on a total investment of $18,000. That's a *minimum* total return of 32.9 percent—or just 4.85 percent annualized. That compares poorly to historical market averages, averages for drug stocks, and Merck's growth rate.

P/E INFLUENCES THE RETURN ON OWNER EARNINGS
So the question arises: Why are Merck's expected returns so low? It's because you bought shares at an inflated P/E ratio. You paid such a huge premium to earnings to acquire Merck—the P/E of 29 was more than double Merck's growth rate—that you extended the payback period several more years. Thus, you must expect substandard increases in the value of the common stock. The only way Merck's stock could generate a higher return for you is if (1) Merck's growth rate increased or (2) investors piled into the stock after you and kept the shares trading at a P/E ratio higher than the earnings growth rate.

Neither scenario is particularly desirable, since you must place your faith in forecasts or the whims of the market and fickle investors. But what would happen to your returns if Merck had been purchased at a P/E of only 20, or $61.40 per share? First, your $18,000 investment could have bought you more shares—293 instead of 200. Starting with 293 shares, here's how your owner earnings would accumulate.

	1997	1998	1999	2000	2000	2001	Total
Merck's Earnings	$3.50	$3.95	$4.50	$5.14	$5.85	$6.67	$29.61
Earnings × 293 Shares	$1,026	$1,157	$1,319	$1,506	$1,714	$1,954	$8,676

Notice, the $8,676 still translates into $29.61 per share over six years, only now it is compared to a purchase price of only $61.40 ($3.07 × 20), rather than $90. The expected total return increases to 48.2 percent. That's a more respectable annualized return of 6.78 percent. But it's still not quite up to historical averages and badly lags Merck's growth rate. And you must still rely on fickle market forces to keep the shares overvalued. Thus, *to improve your owner earnings, you must buy shares at the lowest possible P/E ratio.*

If the market happened to price Merck at just 10 times earnings, your returns on owner earnings would increase dramatically. The owner earnings generated would nearly equal the $30.70 average buying price. And your minimum annualized return would jump to 11.9 percent, as shown below.

	1997	1998	1999	2000	2000	2001	Total
Merck Earnings	$3.50	$3.95	$4.50	$5.14	$5.85	$6.67	$29.61
Earnings × 586 Shares	$2,052	$2,314	$2,638	$3,012	$3,428	$3,908	$17,352

Refer to the payback chart in Chapter 7. If you bought Merck at a P/E of 10 and earnings grew at 14 percent, payback comes in roughly six years. If you bought Merck at a P/E equal to its growth rate, payback comes in roughly seven to eight years. But if you bought the stock at a P/E of 29, as in our first example, it takes 12 years for Merck to return your investment. Again, by example, we have proved the supposition that buying a company with a sufficient cushion against downside risk—in this case, a lower P/E ratio—generates better returns.

ROUNDING OUT THE PORTFOLIO: THE "SUBSIDIARY" APPROACH

Constructing a perfectly hedged portfolio is exceedingly difficult for an investor without the assistance of sophisticated software. Practically speaking, hedging models become impossible for a lay investor to maintain beyond five stocks and require nothing short of expensive software and hundreds of data inputs. Not long after learning portfolio allocation systems in graduate school, I rejected them outright because of their complexity and seemingly messianic reliance on statistics and expectations. One glitch in the economy, one hiccup in the market, or one outlandish price decline throws the entire model off and requires ever-more fine tuning. Such a system is never complete but requires constant balancing based on new information. It's no wonder why so many in this field believe stock prices are efficient; model makers have stuffed every possible piece of data into their systems. They truly believe that no event can occur outside of what has already been studied and predicted.

Here, I offer a portfolio modeling system as simple as any you will encounter. I call it the *subsidiary approach,* which is an expanded form of the owner-earnings model we studied with Merck. Throughout this book, I've tried to teach you to think like an owner, not a trader of paper certificates. If you are willing to buy shares of a company, whether 100 or 50,000, you ought to have made some assumptions about the company's performance. And you should expect the company to generate satisfactory earnings on your behalf that are either returned to you or retained to benefit the company further. The subsidiary approach allows you to forecast, screen stocks, and mold an optimum portfolio based on wonderfully simple calculations.

Since companies exist to return profits to shareholders, they are beholden to you. They become your entourage, a collection of *personal subsidiaries* that operate for your benefit. One of the reasons Warren Buffett bought so many disparate companies outright under the umbrella of Berkshire Hathaway was to collect subsidiaries that sent cash back to the parent. To further his investment success, Buffett has needed a constant supply of cash to invest in the market. His acquisition of profitable enterprises such as GEICO, World Book Encyclopedia, Dairy Queen, Buffalo News, Kirby, See's Candies, Nebraska Furniture Mart, and others provided him a steady source of money—quarterly cash flow—to reinvest. Since Berkshire owns these subsidiaries, it owns their earnings. Buffett requires that these companies' managers send a quarterly check, or dividend, to Berkshire based on their net income or cash flow.

Your stock portfolio is no different. Whether you own one company or 50, treat them as *your subsidiaries,* whose primary function is to send cash your way. Whether you own 100 shares of stock or thousands of shares, you possess the right to demand that these companies generate a return sufficient to meet your needs. In constructing a portfolio using the subsidiary approach, first we must build upon the following five principles introduced in earlier chapters.

- The size of the portfolio is inconsequential as long as risk has been minimized in each stock. You should not automatically accumulate stocks for the purpose of diversifying.

- The sector composition of the portfolio is immaterial. Diversifying across several industries isn't necessary as long as each individual stock already carries reduced risk.

- Companies offering a lower payback period should be purchased over higher payback companies, holding other factors equal.

- Companies should possess solid fundamentals.
- Expected stock price movements are irrelevant when choosing companies.

Using these principles, we'll construct a hypothetical portfolio of five companies, starting with 200 shares of Merck and adding 100 shares of General Electric, 150 of Cisco Systems, 100 of The Limited, and 100 of Norfolk Southern. Let's make the following assumptions about their six-year per-share earnings.

Earnings

	1997	1998	1999	2000	2001	2002	Total
Merck	3.50	3.95	4.50	5.14	5.85	6.67	29.61
General Electric	3.10	3.41	3.75	4.13	4.54	4.99	23.92
Cisco Systems	2.05	2.56	3.20	4.00	5.00	6.26	23.07
The Limited	1.15	1.15	1.15	1.15	1.20	1.20	7.00
Norfolk Southern	2.25	2.90	1.35	−.95	1.80	2.35	9.70
Total	12.05	13.97	13.95	13.47	18.39	21.47	93.30

Because these are your personal subsidiaries, you are entitled to the following earnings:

Earnings You Own

Shares		1997	1998	1999	2000	2001	2002	Total
200	Merck	700	790	900	1,028	1,170	1,334	$5,922
100	General Electric	310	341	375	413	454	499	$2,392
150	Cisco Systems	308	384	480	600	750	939	$3,461
100	The Limited	115	115	115	115	120	120	$700
100	Norfolk Southern	225	290	135	−95	180	235	$970
	Total	1,658	1,920	2,005	2,061	2,674	3,127	$13,445

After a six-year holding period, the five companies will have earned $13,445 on your behalf. Each will distribute those earnings differently. Merck, as mentioned above, may retain $3256 of its earnings and pay you $2666 in dividends. Norfolk Southern might decide to pay $500 in dividends and retain the other $470. Cisco, which has never paid a dividend, likely will retain all $3461.

But it's reasonable to expect that your initial investment increases by at least the amount of earnings retained by these five companies over your holding period. If the companies paid a combined $3000 in dividends over the six-year period, the value of all your shares should rise by at least $10,445. The same principle applies to the individual companies. If Norfolk Southern paid out all $970 in earnings as dividends, you shouldn't expect much capital appreciation in the shares unless the market suddenly believed that Norfolk's earnings growth would accelerate. In that case, it might attach a higher P/E ratio to the stock. Absent a revaluation by investors, you will receive most if not all of your return from dividends.

Whether $13,445 constitutes a suitable return depends, as it did with Merck, on the purchase price and beginning P/E ratio. Let's say that you bought the five stocks at the following prices and P/E ratios. Using the owner earnings table above, we can project the total minimum return you can expect (see final column) based on the owner earnings retained.

Shares		Price	P/E	Investment	Owner Earnings	Total Return
200	Merck	$90	29	$18,000	$5,922	32.9%
100	General Electric	$100	24	$10,000	$2,392	23.9%
150	Cisco Systems	$75	35	$11,250	$3,461	30.8%
100	The Limited	$19	16	$1,900	$700	26.8%
100	Norfolk Southern	$45	20	$4,500	$970	21.6%
	Total			$45,650	$13,445	29.4%

With the market returning an average of 10 percent a year this century, a 29.4 percent return over a six-year period looks measly. This can be attributed to the high premium you paid for earnings. You paid 35 times earnings for Cisco, though Cisco's earnings are growing at 25 percent rates. Merck, as we showed earlier, is priced at twice its growth rate, as is General Electric. Norfolk Southern was unrealistically priced given its uneven earnings stream. An investor should not have been willing to pay $45 for the shares.

To build a successful value portfolio, you must maximize the owner earnings you expect to attain from your initial investment over your holding period. It's only logical to demand that your portfolio of subsidiaries deliver as much money to you as possible and as quickly as possible. In our example above, the task is to develop the right mix of stocks to maximize the return on a $45,460 initial investment. Using only the five stocks listed, you can increase your owner earnings in three ways. Each will reduce the payback period.

1. *Obtain each of the five stocks at cheaper prices and P/E.* As we showed with Merck, you can double the return on your investment simply by waiting for the stocks' P/E to drop 50 percent. A combination of a price decline and earnings increase can make that happen.
2. *Buy one stock capable of generating higher owner earnings than the rest.*
3. *Buy one stock trading at a P/E beneath its growth rate.*

To build a successful value portfolio, you must maximize the owner earnings you expect to attain from your initial investment over your holding period.

It's possible to construct a perfect earnings-maximized portfolio containing these five stocks based on projected earnings streams and P/E ratios. But the mathematics involved are far too complex to attempt. It involves a method called *linear programming.* But to see what is possible, I offer two variations on our sample portfolio that would have provided superior returns: (1) a one-stock portfolio, Cisco Systems, bought at $50 per share; and (2) a three-stock portfolio—Limited, Norfolk, and GE—bought at prices 25 percent below prevailing levels. In both examples, we will keep the $45,650 initial investment the same, meaning that different allotments of shares were needed.

Earnings You Own

Shares		1997	1998	1999	2000	2001	2002	Total	Return
913	Cisco Systems	1,872	2,337	2,922	3,652	4,565	5,715	$21,063	46.1%

Earnings You Own

Shares		1997	1998	1999	2000	2001	2002	Tota	Return
371	General Electric	1,150	1,265	1,391	1,532	1,684	1,851	$8,873	31.9%
371	The Limited	427	427	427	427	445	445	$2,598	49.1%
371	Norfolk So.		835	1076	501	−352	668	872	$3,600	28.8%
		2,412	2,768	2,319	1,607	2,797	3,168	$15,071	33.0%

Intuitively, we can see how the concept of payback plays a big role in developing a portfolio. Since investors can enhance returns and reduce risk by buying low payback stocks, it makes sense that they can improve the returns of their entire portfolio by accumulating stocks that offer low paybacks. Let's look at our five-stock portfolio again, this time assessing each issue in terms of payback.

Shares		P/E	Growth Rate	Payback	Investment	Percentage of Portfolio
200	Merck	29	14	12	$18,000	39.4
100	General Electric	24	10	12	$10,000	21.9
150	Cisco Systems	35	25	10	$11,250	24.6
100	The Limited	16	1	14	$1,900	4.2
100	Norfolk Southern	20	1	18	$4,500	9.9
	Weighted Average	27.9	14	12	$45,650	100.0

Looking at these figures, the obvious solution to enhancing the portfolio's return is to lower the weighted average payback period, currently at 12 years. One way would be to load up on Cisco with its optimal 10-year payback. However, that would make you vulnerable to the risk that Cisco wouldn't perform as anticipated and your portfolio's value would decline sharply. Furthermore, it assumes no change in market dynamics. If The Limited's growth rate improved just a few percentage points, it might offer a better payback than Cisco. Or if GE's share price fell 20 percent, its payback would equal Cisco's. Merck's payback could improve to eight years if earnings picked up and the stock dropped. Any of a number of events could potentially lower your portfolio payback.

In constructing these hypothetical returns, we isolated five companies out of thousands available for purchase. Through due diligence, an investor could easily venture outside this list and find suitable companies offering a lower payback. But the basic principles still would apply: to view your stocks as subsidiaries and maximize owner earnings per dollar of investment.

THE VALUE OF GROWTH

We showed in Chapter 5 that paying a higher P/E ratio for a company is justified if the company bears an attractive "earnings yield." A company capable of producing ever-higher earnings for you over time gives you more flexibility when buying shares. In the example above, Merck was bought at

$90, or 29 times earnings. In the first five years, we estimated that Merck would generate $29.61 in per-share earnings on your behalf, or a 32.9 percent return on your investment. Don't assume, however, that this means Merck's stock will rise a total of only 32.9 percent in five years. That is the *minimum* we should expect the shares to climb (recall the Chapter 10 discussion of retained earnings). By the fifth year, when Merck is earning $6.67 per share, its earnings "yield" should be a respectable 7.4 percent. As long as Merck's earnings continue to grow, yearly earnings will provide an ever-larger return on your $90 investment. So you cannot take the 32.9 percent figure literally; otherwise, you will become unnecessarily discouraged and avoid most companies. Instead, use the 32.9 percent return as a benchmark to beat. Different combinations of earnings and purchase prices will yield you a five-year return in Merck that is higher than 32.9 percent.

"WAREHOUSING" YOUR STOCK PICKS

Successful investors are discriminating; they avoid buying anything and everything. Any stock can potentially be a value pick at the right price. But don't fool yourself into thinking that the entire market is fair game for your portfolio. Of the 10,000 publicly listed companies in America, only a small fraction offer compelling enough long-term prospects. Hundreds of companies should be sidestepped altogether because of their poor fundamentals. Most of the rest offer good returns only periodically, perhaps for a year or less. Once you settle on a methodology for choosing companies, you should, by process of elimination, reduce the number of possible purchase candidates from 10,000 to a few dozen.

Ironically, having cash on hand, particularly in a bull market, can be the downfall of many investors, for it leads them to buy stocks that, frankly, they should not own. Why do they do this? Sometimes their favorite stocks are temporarily overvalued and outside the range of purchasing. Rather than patiently wait for their stocks to decline, investors purchase shares of lesser companies whose fundamentals they have not studied. You can avoid this trap by adopting what I call the *warehouse method*. With this approach, you identify all the stocks you wish to own over the next several years and buy them one at a time—when they fall to an attractive price. If the stocks do not fall to your desired level immediately, take no action—and don't worry. They will fall to an attractive price sooner or later. In the meantime, focus on other desirable companies that may have fallen to attractive levels. Maintaining a checklist of stocks to buy will keep you focused on value and price. Your checklist may be elaborate or as simple as the one in Figure 14-1.

FIGURE 14-1   Buying checklist.

Name	Price	Will Buy At	Comments
American Express	$100	$80	*Not cheap enough yet*
Amgen	$50	$38	*Too pricey*
Cisco Systems	$60	Under $49	*Too pricey; be patient*
Federal Express	$64	$65	*Prepare to buy*
General Electric	$80	$82	*Can buy now!*
Intel	$75	$65	*Too much price volatility*
NIKE	$55	Under $44	*Near-term earnings falling*
Nucor	$48	Under $50	*Buy!*
Procter & Gamble	$90	Under $85	*Prepare to buy*
Walgreen	$32	$24	*Way overvalued*
Walt Disney	$100	$75	*Earnings prospects questionable*

The obvious advantage to warehousing stocks is that it forces you to be vigilant. Before buying, you must determine a reasonable value for the company, which means studying the enterprise. Putting some time into the valuation process will greatly lessen your chances of buying prematurely. Buying companies in this manner also allows you to build the portfolio you really want and prevents you from adding undesirable stocks simply because you have idle money. In addition, the method harnesses your impatience and most important, ensures top performance, since you will not overpay for any company.

You should update your checklist periodically to make sure your target prices are reasonable. If a company's growth prospects dwindle, the original buying price you set may be too high. Conversely, if the company's fundamentals improve, the stock may not retreat to your buying level again. In such cases, you must reappraise the company to determine whether it is truly worth a higher share price.

WHEN TO SELL

No book on value investing would be complete without a discussion on exit strategy. Through experience, I have found the question of when to sell to be among the most common. It also is among the most vexing, as it combines the ironclad rules of finance with human emotion. The most successful investors all take different approaches to answering this question, and not one of their methods has been proven to be the best. Some value investors follow Benjamin Graham's method to the letter and sell a company as soon as a stock rises above the company's book value. On the other end of the spectrum, Warren Buffett buys a piece of a company on the assumption he will hold it indefinitely. As long as the company's performance remains on an upward path, Buffett will continue to hold his shares. On occasion, however, he has sold shares within one to two years of buying them, as he did with Walt Disney in the mid-1960s and McDonald's in 1997, when the company's earnings prospects deteriorated. Occasionally, he sells shares that have risen to unsustainable levels, as he did when he sold a portion of his Walt Disney stock in 1997.

In general, you do not sell until *it is apparent you have misjudged the company* or *the market price fully reflects the value of the company.*

There is one condition under which most value investors would sell, i.e., when the market has bid the company's stock up to frothy levels and there is little chance the stock can retain its value in the near future. The clearest warning signs are P/E ratios that far exceed the company's growth rate. Companies that generate 12 percent earnings growth cannot justify a P/E of 30, even in the most favorable economic environment. An acceptable price may be 18 to 20 times earnings. Beyond that level, you must conclude that the stock has been bid up solely on speculation rather than fundamentals. Sooner or later, the stock will decline, perhaps back to 12 times earnings. In Chapter 7 we showed how buying at P/E ratios that exceed the company's earnings growth rate increases the "payback" period and increases risk. Using my payback chart, you can determine just how far payback has been extended and risk increased. Otherwise, there's no magic formula for determining when a stock has traded at unrealistic prices and should be sold. Overvalued conditions have been known to persist for years—in the stock market in the 1960s and 1990s, for example.

Recall from Chapter 7 the example of PepsiCo, whose stock price has grown at approximately the rate of earnings since the mid-1960s (see Figure 14-2). Note how the stock price always regressed to the mean; it rose or fell until it coincided again with the trendline of earnings. Periods of high valuation always were followed by periods of decline, and vice versa. You can see how PepsiCo's P/E ratio bobbed around the earnings line. The conclusion to be drawn is that the rate of growth of earnings closely approximates a fair P/E ratio. A company whose earnings increase 10 percent a year consistently will be priced at an average of 10 times earnings over longer periods. If the P/E lies below the company's growth rate, the stock will rise at least to its fair level. If the P/E already has risen far above presumed earnings, you invite disaster. PepsiCo was so overvalued by 1972

FIGURE 14-2   PepsiCo, 1960–1994.

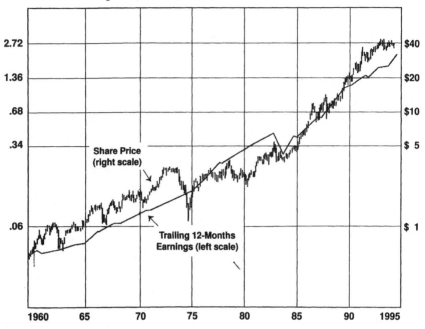

that steadily rising earnings could no longer provide a prop. Between 1972 and 1974, PepsiCo's stock fell 65 percent. The stock did not break above its 1972 peak until 1981, nine years later.

The criteria you use in buying the company should be those that drive the sale.

THE FINAL RULES FOR SELLING

1. *Tie the decision to sell to the purchase.* The criteria you use in buying the company should be those that drive the sale. Never mix standards. My selling criteria, which I exhort in my newsletter, *Today's Value Investor,* are linked to fundamentals and the very criteria on which I base a purchase. I never sell a stock simply because it has fallen in price or because it has risen too fast. If I recommend a company because of its high returns on equity, I will recommend the sale of the shares if return on equity falls below my hurdle rate. If I buy a company based on its earnings yield, I will sell the stock if the yield falls to unattractive levels relative to bonds. If I buy a company because its profit margins show signs of improvement, I will sell if margins begin to deteriorate again.

2. *Don't tie the sale to Wall Street's capricious pricing.* Never sell simply because the stock price fell after you bought it. Without a doubt, this is one of the most egregious mistakes investors can make. To quote Peter Lynch:

> Some people automatically sell the "winners"—stocks that go up—and hold onto their "losers"—stocks that go down—which is about as sensible as pulling out the flowers and watering the weeds. Others automatically sell their losers and hold onto their winners, which doesn't work out any better. Both strategies fail because they're tied to the current movement of the stock price as an indicator of the company's fundamental value.[3]

To sell without fundamental justification is to hold yourself hostage to fickle investors, and it exposes the fact that you were gambling on a short-term price movement rather than investing. Selling after the price has dropped is a nice way of acknowledging that the market is efficient and that you made a mistake in buying at a higher price. Sometimes, the reverse is true; the public wrongly dumped the stock. First and foremost, you must stick to your initial instincts about the company, unless new information leads you to question your original valuation. *If you still like the company after the stock falls, you should like it more at a lower price and add to your position.* No one has ever been able to time the exact bottoms and tops of stocks. Most great value investors acknowledge this. It is of little concern to them if the stock they bought immediately falls 20 percent, which has happened to everyone in this industry. What matters most is your long-term rate of return, which is determined by the price paid. If you bought the stock at a price low enough to allow significant upside potential, then short-term dips in the price are of little consequence. Successful investors step to the plate and buy more.

3. *Don't sell because of market forecasts.* A common mistake is to take short-term profits and run out of fear of a market correction. If you are buying a company at a price far below its intrinsic worth, take solace in the fact that the stock won't drop as much as the market. Value investing, by definition, means finding attractively priced companies within a market that often is unattractively priced. It should be of little consequence where general price levels stand. If you bought cheaply, you don't have to worry. If

[3] Peter Lynch, *One Up on Wall Street,* New York, Penguin Books, 1989, p. 245.

the average stock trades at 22 times earnings and your stocks trade at 14 times earnings, you have bought yourself plenty of downside protection in a poor market. You won't be completely immune from market declines—few stocks are—but you will be much better protected.

4. *Don't let tax consequences dictate selling.* There are many reasons to sell a stock, among them poor company performance, the need to raise cash, and the need to shift investments, but taxes should not be the main reason. Rather, taxes should take a back seat to all other decisions or serve as a tie-breaker if you are otherwise indifferent. Capital gains taxes are the product of successful investing and are avoidable only if you hold a stock indefinitely. Good stocks should be held for years, if not decades, to allow you to maximize your after-tax returns. However, there will be times when the stock's price is so unrealistically high or the company's performance so sluggish that you must sell. So sell, no matter what your capital gains are to date.

Some investors, in an effort to avoid taxes, refuse to part with stocks even in the face of deteriorating fundamentals. They fail to realize that they can lose more in net worth clinging to a weakening stock than they would have lost in taxes by selling it. Admittedly, the threat of a huge tax bill can be depressing. Someone who bought 1000 shares of Walt Disney in 1966 at $32, for example, wound up holding 128,000 shares at $100 by early 1998 because of splits. Selling all of their shares at $100 would have created a capital gains liability of $12,768,000. Assuming a 31 percent tax bracket, capital gains taxes would be $3,958,080. But what if Disney's stock fell to $80? First, the investors' net worth would fall by $2,560,000. Then, if he or she sold the shares, there still would be a loss of $3,164,480 in taxes. Holding on in a futile effort to avoid taxes increases the total liability, the decline in net worth plus taxes, to $5,724,480.

15

ADOPTING THE WARREN BUFFETT WAY

"The more you enter into a dialogue on price and value, the more you will begin to understand and appreciate the Warren Buffett Way."

Robert Hagstrom Jr.[1]

TO INDIVIDUAL INVESTORS THE WORLD OVER, Warren Buffett has become the patron saint of due diligence, a man who wrested control of the stock market and proved most known and widely taught financial theories to be ineffectual. Armed with the teachings of Benjamin Graham, he took $100 of his own money, pooled it with $105,000 from family and friends, and over the next 40 years, turned it into a personal fortune of more than $30 billion. Buffett created additional billions in profits for hundreds of investors who entrusted him with their savings. Indeed, no capitalist in this century has figured so prominently in American history as a result of merely trading paper stock certificates. Other great capitalists such as Bill Gates, Sam Walton, and Henry Ford created wealth for society building factories and marketing consumer products. Buffett took what was, for him, the logical next step: He turned the act of passive business ownership into a profit-making endeavor and an end unto itself.

[1] Robert G. Hagstrom, Jr., *The Warren Buffett Way,* New York, John Wiley & Sons, Inc., 1994, p. 236.

The enigma that surrounds Buffett he in part has brought on himself, for he shuns publicity and rarely reveals what he buys or sells. But it also partly reflects the public's misunderstanding of his methods and motives. Lesser people have craved more and attained a lot less on Wall Street. Buffett seemed to attain more for the sake of showing it was possible. Along the way, his unbelievable track record exploded the popular myth that investing was for crapshooters whose odds of winning were fortuitous at best. Buffett's life story, eccentricities, and string of successes serve as one long mockery of the ticker tape. Yet he has brought integrity to stock picking as no one has. Buffett is among the world's richest people, yet he pays himself a modest $100,000 a year in salary and plans to pass his wealth to charitable trusts after his death. He inhabits the same middle-class home in Omaha, Nebraska, has been known to eat at McDonald's or a local steakhouse, plays bridge incessantly, drinks gallons of Cherry Coke each month, and won't waste a shred of paper at his Spartan, understaffed office.

> Buffett's life story, eccentricities, and string of successes serve as one long mockery of the ticker tape. Yet he has brought integrity to stock picking as no one has.

In more than four decades of managing money, he's never had a losing year and has defeated the market's returns in all but a handful of years. During the 1960s, his investing partnership attained perhaps the best 10-year scorecard of any money manager. He not only beat the returns of major stock indices for 10 consecutive years but by a wide margin (see Chapter 2). From 1960 to 1969, Buffett posted an annualized return of 28.9 percent for his investors, while the Dow Jones industrial average returned a modest 5.2 percent. An investor who deposited $10,000 in Buffett's limited partnership in 1960 walked away with $126,000 in 1969, when Buffett folded his tent because he could find few stocks trading at reasonable values.

Buffett's longevity and tremendous success stems from four guiding principles: (1) a disdain for losses, (2) his keen ability to keep his trading objective (that is, based on mathematics, not emotion), (3) a honed instinct to recognize undervalued securities, and (4) the recognition that internal growth drives long-term returns. Volumes have been written on Buffett's methods, and hundreds of articles have tried to untangle his synaptic power from infrequent public quotes. He has left behind, however, a large enough body of material, including two decades of annual reports that he himself wrote, that any investor could pick up his trail and profit handsomely in the market. Buffett's variation on Graham can be neatly summed up in 10 points.

1. THE "TAKING STRIKES" CONCEPT

As his legacy to the game of baseball, the Splendid Splinter, Ted Williams, left the world one of the best books ever written by an athlete, *The Science of Hitting*. Williams's basic thesis was that the strike zone could be carved into minizones that tested, to various degrees, the abilities of both hitter and pitcher. A high and inside strike, for example, tested the batter's weakness against the pitcher's strength. A low and inside pitch might test the batter's strength and the pitcher's weakness. Williams outlined a plan of patience for hitters. They should understand their strengths and limitations and look to drive only those pitches that crossed their strength zones.

Buffett often applies a similar analogy to investing. Following the stock market, he believes, is like standing at the plate and watching thousands of pitches whiz by. Each pitch represents one stock offered at one price at one moment in time. But unlike the batter in the stadium, you are under no obligation to lift the bat off your shoulder and swing, for there is no one to judge your trip to the plate. In a 1995 lecture to business students at the University of North Carolina, Buffett briefly outlined this balls-and-strikes concept:

> In investments, there's no such thing as a called strike. You can stand there at the plate and the pitcher can throw the ball right down the middle, and if it's General Motors at $47 and you don't know enough to decide on General Motors at $47, you let it go right on by and no one's going to call a strike. The only way you can have a strike is to swing and miss.

Indeed, one of the obvious advantages that you, the individual investor, have over professional money managers is that you are not forced into errors. You are not obligated to beat the S&P 500 this quarter or flip the next hot initial public offering for a profit. You are not responsible for earning a suitable return for thousands of clients, nor is anyone forcing you to dress up your portfolio in advance of an annual report. You don't have to worry about sector rotation, asset allocation, whether Motorola will meet its quarterly earnings targets, or whether you are lagging the performance of competing money managers. Your sole responsibility is to generate a satisfactory, long-term return for yourself. Thus, you have the luxury of study-

ing 100-plus stocks a month and choosing only one. You can bask in reject-
ing Sun Microsystems at $50 and waiting until the shares fall to a reason-
able price level before buying. If Sun's stock stays overvalued, you can
smile and walk away and focus on any of 10,000 other publicly traded companies. You can hang up on brokers month after month until they finally
offer a stock you have studied at a decent price. You have the luxury of
putting all of your money into bonds—or cash, gold coins, or real estate—
if you cannot find a stock that is attractively priced. Buffett did just that in
1969; he closed his partnership and stayed away from stocks until the market bottomed in 1974.

The stock market doesn't force you to buy. It just seduces you, as Buffett has said. You can walk away from any stock at any price and take comfort in the fact that you have not risked any cash. But once you discover a
stock to your liking, one the market has offered up at a ridiculously low
price, swing for the fence. Such opportunities do not come along often and
investors should not assume they do. You might be lucky to find 20 golden
opportunities throughout your investing lifetime, quality stocks so undervalued they harbor no business risk at all. But dozens of other, slightly less-
attractive opportunities will present themselves, and you should be ready to
swing when they arrive.

2. AVOID LOSSES

If you invested all of your assets in fixed-income securities and held them
to maturity, you would never suffer a loss. Losses occur when investors take
bigger risks hoping for bigger gains. To reduce the chance of losses, you
must minimize mistakes. The fewer errors made over your investing career,
the better your long-term returns. Recall from Chapter 2 the advantages
you derive from beating the market by a few percentage points a year. Over
time, the effects of your success grow immensely due to the power of compounding. The same holds true if you can avoid any yearly loss.

When you lose money, even if for as short a time as a year, you greatly
erode the terminal value of your portfolio. You consume precious resources
that must be replaced. In addition, you waste precious time trying to make
up lost ground. Losses also reduce the positive effects of compounding.
Consider two portfolios, A and B, both which gain 10 percent a year for 30
years. Portfolio B, however, suffers a 10 percent loss in the fifth year. A
$10,000 investment in Portfolio A would return $174,490 by the 30th year.
Portfolio B's would return considerably less—only $142,760—because of
one poor year (see Figure 15-1). If Portfolio B sustained two 10 percent
losses, say, in the fifth and 15th years, the investor would be left with just

FIGURE 15-1   **The value of avoiding losses.**

	Investor A*		Investor B**	
Year	Yearly Gain	Portfolio	Yearly Gain	Portfolio
0		$10,000		$10,000
1	10%	$11,000	10%	$11,000
2	10%	$12,100	10%	$12,100
3	10%	$13,310	10%	$13,310
4	10%	$14,641	10%	$14,641
5	10%	$16,105	−10%	$13,177
10	10%	$25,937	10%	$21,222
15	10%	$41,772	−10%	$27,963
20	10%	$67,275	10%	$45,035
25	10%	$108,347	10%	$72,530
30	10%	$174,494	10%	$116,810

Investor A attains constant 10% gains for 30 years.
**Investor B has 10% losses in years 5 and 15 and attains 10% gains all other years.*

$116,810. Avoiding losses, as Buffett strives to do, is paramount to good investing.

How can investors avoid losses? Certainly they can stay above water by selling shares every time a stock threatens to fall below its break-even point. In the long run, however, such a strategy will lead to inferior returns because of excessive trading and high commissions. Another way is simply to hold onto the stock until it rallies above your original cost. Such strategies are recommended only when you possess confidence in the underlying company. The method I espouse is Benjamin Graham's *margin of safety* principle (see Chapter 1): Buy inexpensively to minimize your risk of loss.

3. HOLD A FEW EGGS YOU KNOW WILL HATCH

Collecting stocks for the sake of diversification is foolish to someone like Buffett, who typically owns large stakes in no more than one dozen stocks at any one time. Investors who keep adding stocks to their portfolios for the sake of protection are in essence practicing a trial-and-error, "Noah's Ark" approach. They may not derive any added benefits beyond having two of everything. Buffett, like many value investors, defines "risk" unlike the textbooks. Academics define risk mathematically, by stock volatility. To

them, the sheer act of buying many stocks controls excessive price fluctuations. Store up enough stocks from different industries, they argue, and you
minimize the possibility that a dreadful decline in one stock will harm your
returns. Of course, this method also reduces the effect that a few great stocks
have on your returns. The reality is that by holding good, bad, and downright
ugly stocks in one nest, what hatches can only be mediocre at best.

Buffett's approach is to concentrate as much money as possible on a
handful of undervalued securities and hold them. Figure 15-2 shows Buffett's major holdings since 1977, as revealed by Berkshire Hathaway's
annual reports. We can see that over 20 years, Buffett has owned large
stakes in several dozen companies, not merely the eight favorite stocks he
owned in 1997. On average, he holds each stock for several years, though
there have been times when Buffett has sold a large portion, if not all, of his
holdings in relatively short order. We can see, too, that Buffett favors certain industries and by inference, shuns others. Consumer products companies have figured prominently in Buffett's portfolio, as have media and
publishing companies and ad agencies. From time to time, Buffett has
bought large stakes in financial companies—Federal Home Loan Mortgage, GEICO Insurance, National Student Marketing, PNC Banks, and
Wells Fargo—and heavy industries—ALCOA, GATX, Cleveland Cliffs,
Exxon, Handy & Harman, Kaiser Aluminum, and R.J. Reynolds. In these
instances, Buffett was trying to capitalize on shorter-term industry trends,
such as a bottoming of commodities prices or a decline in interest rates.

From Figure 15-2, we can infer how Buffett diversifies. He focuses
Berkshire's portfolio around a small handful of buy-and-hold companies
and devotes the rest of the portfolio to companies able to provide shorter-
term (three- to five-year) cyclical gains. To say that Buffett always practices
buy-and-hold principles is misleading. While he often may plan to hold a
stock forever, circumstances occasionally have prompted Buffett to dump
positions, at times more frequently than biographers have portrayed. Take,
for example, McDonald's, which Buffett bought in 1996 but sold a year
later, or Exxon, purchased in 1984 at around seven times earnings but presumably sold before crude oil prices crashed in early 1986. Buffett purchased 772,000 shares of Woolworth in 1979 at a price around six times
earnings. He sold the stock before the 1981–1982 recession hit. Later, he
publicly swore off retailers. We also can infer that Buffett engages in market timing. He is most ravenous in poor stock markets, when he loads up on
cheap stocks. He listed no fewer than 17 different stock holdings in his
1980 annual report. By 1987, when the market reached a state of excessive
valuation and subsequently crashed, he listed only three—GEICO, *The*

Washington Post, and Capital Cities/ABC. Rather than plow more money into overvalued stocks, Buffett bought a corporate jet for Berkshire, remarking, "I'd rather buy a good stock than a good jet, but there's nothing that we can see buying even if it went down 10 percent."[2]

4. LOOK FOR "SURE THINGS" TO KEEP YOUR RETURNS POSITIVE

Buffett has made wide use of takeover arbitrage to deliver nearly risk-free returns. In uncertain markets, takeover trades have cushioned him against losses and kept his yearly returns positive. In a takeover arbitrage, an investor buys shares of a company after it has agreed to be acquired and profits from the spread between the market price and the tender-offer price. For example, a company may receive a tender offer for $50 per share, but until the deal settles, its shares may trade for only $46, an 8 percent discount. If the deal goes through, you lock in a $4, 8 percent gain. While 8 percent may not sound so hot, the annualized return may be two to three times that, depending on how quickly the companies consummate the transaction. An 8 percent discount, for example, turns into a 36 percent annualized gain if the deal closes in one quarter. String a few of these deals back-to-back and you can counter an otherwise poor year in the market. When playing takeovers, Buffett searches for deals that are almost certain to transpire. If both parties call off their merger or the federal government intervenes to block the transaction, the target company's stock may drop sharply, the major risk an arbitrageur assumes. On occasion, Buffett has scored spectacular success when the stock of the target company soared following the announcement.

5. DON'T LOOK FOR ABSOLUTE VALUES, FOR THEY ARE TOO RARE

The Depression era that profoundly influenced Graham was a faint memory to millions of Americans by the time Buffett was investing full swing. So, too, was World War II. Stability had returned to the American economy and the markets, and the era of the super bargain stocks, ones selling for a P/E of two or for a fraction of their balance sheet cash, had dissolved. Not having seen the full effects of Depression-era market prices, Buffett clung less and less to Graham's rigid balance-sheet appraisal of companies and leaned more on the writings of Philip Fisher, one of the first to explore the merits of investing in growth companies. After several years of practicing Graham's methods, Buffett rejected what he called Graham's "cigar-butt" approach to investing—picking cheap companies that had one good puff

---

[2] From the 1986 annual report of Berkshire Hathaway.

FIGURE 15-2 Warren Buffett's major holdings, 1977–1997 [shares held (000s), unadjusted for splits].

Source: Berkshire Hathaway annual reports.

	1977	1978	1979	1980	1981	1982	1983	1984	1985	1986	1987	1988	1989	1990	1991	1992	1993	1994	1995	1996	1997
Affiliated Publications			290	435	452	461	691	691	691	1,036											
ALCOA				464	704																
Amerada Hess		113																			
American Express																		27,760	49,457	49,457	49,457
Arcata					420																
Beatrice Cos.									2351												
Capital Cities/ABC[1]	220	247	246					740	901	2,990	3,000	3,000	3,000	3,000	3,000	3,000	2,000	20,000	20,000		
Cleveland Cliffs Iron				475	475																
Coca-Cola												14,173	23,350	46,700	46,700	93,400	93,400	100,000	100,000	200,000	200,000
Crum & Forster						909															
Exxon								3896													
Federal Home Loan Mtg.												2,400	2,400	2,400	2,495	16,197	13,655	12,761	12,503	64,246	63,978
Gannett																		6,854			
GATX					442																
GEICO[3]	1,294	1,294	5,730	7,200	7,200	7,200	6,850	6,850	6,850	6,850	6,850	6,850	6,850	6,850	6,850	6,850	34,250	34,250	34,250	34,250	
General Dynamics																4,350	4,350				
General Foods			329	1984	2101	2101	4452	4047													
Gillette															24,000	24,000	24,000	24,000	48,000	48,000	48,000
Guiness PLC															31,247	38,335	38,335				
Handy & Harman			1008	2015	2015	2379	2379	2379	2379	2379	2379										
Interpublic Group	593	593	711	711	711	711	636	819													

Company																	
Kaiser Aluminum	325	1,066	1,212	1,212													
Kaiser Industries	1,306																
Knight-Ridder	227	454															
Lear Siegler																	
McDonald's										489					30,157		
Media General	283	283	283	283	197												
National Detroit Corp.	247																
National Student Mkt.	882																
Northwest Industries					556												
Ogilvy & Mather	171	391	391	391	391	250											
Pinkerton's	370	370	370														
PNC Bank															19,453		
R.J. Reynolds	246	1765	3108	5619													
SAFECO	954	1251	785														
Time			1531	901	2553	848											
Times Mirror Co.	151																
Travelers Group[2]															24,614	23,733	
Walt Disney	934	1,868	934	1,869	1,869	1,869	1,728	1,728	1,728	1,728	1,728	1,728	1,728	1,728			
Washington Post	5,000	5,000	6,358	6,791	6,791	6,791											
Wells Fargo	7,291	6,690															
Woolworth (F.W.)	772	667															

[1] Purchased by Walt Disney.
[2] Attained from the takeover of Salomon Brothers.
[3] Taken private by Buffett in 1996.

left in them. Buffett never accepted growth methodologies outright, however; too much Graham remained in him. He never let his valuations fall prey to forecasts, nor did he ever rely on a drunken market to validate his investing decisions. To Buffett's great credit, he correctly recognized that growth and value styles were interlocked. "Ben Graham wanted everything to be a quantitative bargain. I want it to be a quantitative bargain in terms of future streams of cash," Buffett said in 1993.[3] If a company cannot grow or increase its retained earnings at sufficient rates (see Chapter 10), it is an unworthy investment to Buffett, no matter how cut-rate the price. It is imperative that companies keep growing to increase intrinsic value. It is equally essential that earnings grow at a rate sufficient to compensate Buffett for inflation. This marrying of value and growth investing, premised on a desire to beat inflation and bond returns, is perhaps Buffett's greatest contribution to the world of finance.

> ## To Buffett's great credit, he correctly recognized that growth and value styles were interlocked.

Buffett's style continues to blend growth with value, as evident by his purchases in recent years of American Express, Gillette, Wells Fargo Bank, and Coca-Cola. These four buys show he is not afraid to pay a higher P/E ratio for a growth company, as long as the company's long-term earnings offer a degree of certainty. An investor can fall asleep for 15 years, Buffett is wont to say, and awake to find Coca-Cola and Gillette operating in the same lines of business they were before, selling syrup and toiletries. That's how Buffett measures certainty.

6. BUY COMPANIES YOU CAN UNDERSTAND

If you don't know the difference between a router made by Black & Decker and one made by Cisco Systems, sidestep both stocks. When you buy a company whose operations are abstruse, you may as well be sitting in the cockpit of a DC-10: You'll land on your feet only if the plane's on autopilot or you're lucky enough to flip the right switches. You may always be

---

[3] Robert Lenzner, "Warren Buffett's Idea of Heaven: I don't have to work with people I don't like," *Forbes 400,* October 18, 1993, p. 40.

tempted to play an exotic, rapidly rising stock in a fast-growing industry, but if you lack even a rudimentary understanding of the company's products or services, avoid it, Buffett believes. Your portfolio will not suffer as a result. The sin of regret is never as painful as the sin of investing beyond your ability. Some of the strongest-performing companies in the 1990s were unexciting enterprises in equally ho-hum industries that virtually anyone could have grasped: funeral home operator Service Corp. International, drugstore chain Walgreen, discount retailer Home Depot, and motorcycle king Harley-Davidson, to name a few.

I often counsel clients to steer clear of most foreign stocks for this same reason. You should avoid investing overseas unless you understand the economic, tax, accounting, and political landscapes under which foreign companies operate. The less you know about an investment before you buy, the more you are venturing into that perilous territory called gambling. With more than 10,000 publicly traded companies headquartered in the United States, there are few reasons to look past the continental shelf. The United States offers the most diversified roster of companies and industries of anywhere, with dozens of niche industries and companies for the picking. Rarely will you find an exceptional foreign stock that offers better appreciation potential than a comparable American stock.

Buffett intentionally shuns many U.S. and foreign companies, namely, those in the technology sector, because of his limited knowledge of the industry. But he has never regretted ignoring the likes of Oracle, Intel, Hewlett-Packard, or Texas Instruments. Asked why he won't buy technology companies, Buffett told Berkshire Hathaway shareholders in 1998 that he will not try to compete in a field dominated by experts.

> The truth is, I don't know [what] Microsoft or Intel will look like in 10 years. And I don't want to play that game where I think the other guy's got an advantage over me. I could spend all my time thinking about technology for the next year and I'd be the hundredth-of-thousandth-of-the-ten-thousandth smartest guy in the country looking at these businesses. So that is a seven- or eight-foot bar that I can't clear.[4]

7. LOOK FOR HIGH RETURNS ON EQUITY

In Chapter 10, I discussed the importance of return on equity (ROE) to a value investor. Buffett obsesses on this standard of performance. On many occasions over the past 20 years, Buffett has stated his preference for com-

---

[4] From the transcript of the 1998 annual meeting of Berkshire Hathaway, released on the website of Morningstar, Inc.

panies that can generate a minimum 15 percent annual return on equity. By setting such a high hurdle rate, Buffett intentionally limits himself to companies experiencing strong and steady earnings growth (recall the link between ROE and earnings growth in Chapter 8). A company that pays no dividend and posts consistent ROEs above 15 percent will attain yearly earnings growth in excess of 15 percent. That should translate into long-term stock-price growth of at least 15 percent a year as well, a rate that far exceeds inflation and bond yields. In calculating ROE, Buffett makes a simple adjustment: He divides yearly *operating income* (not net income) by shareholder equity. Let's say a company reported $10 million in net income and $15 million in operating income off an equity base of $30 million. Using net income as the numerator, ROE would be 33.3 percent. Using operating income, ROE would be 50 percent. Taking the operating return on equity results in a truer picture of how well management used the capital stock and bond investors provided. Companies can manipulate net income any number of ways by reporting nonrecurring gains or losses.

8. LOOK FOR A MOAT

A business whose products are proprietary, novel, or difficult to replicate by competitors has an impenetrable shield, a "moat" that can allow it to grow unimpeded for years. FlightSafety International, the maker of cockpit simulators, operated without serious competitors for years before Buffett bought the company in 1996. Dairy Queen International, which Buffett bought in 1997, has no coast-to-coast rivals in the soft-serve ice cream business. Walt Disney has no comparable competitors anywhere on earth.

Buffett looks for stocks with defensible franchises, such as Coca-Cola, whose brand name is among the world's most recognized. Coke holds leading market shares in nearly every country in which it sells soft drinks. That the company can increase sales 10 percent to 12 percent a year after 110 years in business is testament to its incredible franchise. Another moat stock Buffett owns is Gillette, whose razor blades and cartridges also hold dominant market shares in most countries. "I sleep well knowing that 2 billion men wake up every morning needing to shave," Buffett is fond of saying.

Moats can exist worldwide, like Coca-Cola's, or locally, like your neighborhood savings bank or grocery chain. Some of Buffett's best-performing investments have been private businesses, among them See's Candies and the Nebraska Furniture Mart, which hold virtual monopolies in their communities. When a business possesses a moat, it has the ability to raise prices without fear of losing market share, a luxury few American businesses have anymore. By contrast, Buffett avoids companies offering commoditylike products or services, such as steel manufacturers, automakers, airlines, and retailers. These companies must spend large amounts of their yearly earnings upgrading assets or innovating their product lines just to keep pace with other more nimble competitors.

9. DON'T SELL TOO EARLY IF THE COMPANY IS STRONG

If you can picture where a company will be in 15 to 20 years, you can safely count on the enterprise to deliver consistent returns. Because these types of companies are relatively rare, it makes sense to hold onto them once you've bought shares at an attractive price. Buffett made some of his biggest mistakes when he rushed to take profits and lost sight of the company's longer-term potential. One of Buffett's first investments was City Service Preferred, which he bought at the tender age of 11 for $38. The stock eventually rose to $200, but Buffett sold his shares at $40, pocketing what to a child must have seemed like a good profit. In the mid-1960s, Buffett bought 6 percent of Walt Disney's stock for the ridiculously low price of $5 million but sold the entire stake a year later for $6 million. Had he held on, his original investment would have been worth close to $2 billion in 1998.

Virtually every stock you sell will likely trade one day for a lot more money. If you think a company has the potential to sell for much greater values in the future, hoard it like the king's gold. If you are not confident the stock will continue rallying, you should have run from the stock to begin with. Don't own a stock for five minutes if you are not willing to hold it for at least five years.

> Virtually every stock you sell will likely trade one day for a lot more money. If you think a company has the potential to sell for much greater values in the future, hoard it like the king's gold.

10. PUT BLINDERS ON AND IGNORE THE MARKET

Here's where Buffett's strategy becomes a hard pill to swallow, because he advocates ignoring daily market movements. He doesn't care whether the Dow Industrials are rallying or declining, or what the latest economic data suggests. He ignores short-term "noise" and assumes that a stock price, over time, will track the company's growth rates. It wouldn't bother Buffett one bit if the stock market closed for two years and he was unable to obtain a quote on any of his businesses. With or without Wall Street, these enterprises would continue to operate as usual and generate profits that increase their intrinsic value and the value of Buffett's stake. Imagine for a moment that the stock market closed tomorrow. What would be the result? The brokerage industry would surely crumble, but not companies. Would General Electric cease to function if no one could trade its shares? Would orders for Intel's microprocessors dry up? Would consumers stop buying Procter & Gamble's detergent? Would Ford have to recall all of its new cars? Of course not. These enterprises probably would go about their business as usual. Rather than operate with an eye toward next quarter's earnings, they could run their plants happily, finally relieved of the pressure to satisfy fund managers, arbitrageurs, analysts, and day traders. General Electric, Intel, P&G, and Ford, of course, would still have value. But their value would be based, as it should be, on earnings and cash flow revealed in financial statements, not on whims, rumors, chart patterns, or analysts' mutterings.

SUMMING IT UP IN MR. BUFFETT'S WORDS

Writing in 1987, Warren Buffett said that investors would greatly improve their stock picking if they realized one fact about Wall Street: It exists to serve you, not guide you. Never assume that the prevailing price offered on a company represents a fair price. You are free to ignore every stock that isn't priced to your liking. The passage below, taken from Buffett's annual letter to shareholders, is one of the greatest investing primers ever written.

> Whenever Charlie [Berkshire Hathaway director Charlie Munger] and I buy common stocks for Berkshire's insurance companies, we approach the transaction as if we were buying into a private business. We look at the economic prospects of the business, the people in charge of running it, and the price we must pay. We do not have any time or price of sale. Indeed, we are willing to hold a stock indefinitely so long as we expect the business to increase in intrinsic value at a satisfactory rate. When investing, we view ourselves as business analysts—not as market analysts, not as macroeconomic analysts, and not even as security analysts.
>
> Our approach makes an active trading market useful, since it periodically presents us with mouth-watering opportunities. But by no means is it essential: a prolonged suspension of trading in the securities we hold would not bother us any more than does the lack of daily quotations on World Book or Fechheimer [two companies that Berkshire Hathaway

owns]. Eventually, our economic fate will be determined by the economic fate of the business we own, whether our ownership is partial or total.

Ben Graham, my friend and teacher, long ago described the mental attitude toward market fluctuations that I believe to be most conducive to investment success. He said that you should imagine market quotations as coming from a remarkably accommodating fellow named Mr. Market who is your partner in a private business. Without fail, Mr. Market appears daily and names a price at which he will either buy your interest or sell you his.

Even though the business that the two of you own may have economic characteristics that are stable, Mr. Market's quotations will be anything but. For, sad to say, the poor fellow has incurable emotional problems. At times he feels euphoric and can see only the favorable factors affecting the business. When in that mood, he names a very high buy-sell price because he fears that you will snap up his interest and rob him of imminent gains. At other times he is depressed and can see nothing but trouble ahead for both the business and the world. On these occasions he will name a very low price, since he is terrified that you will unload his interest on him.

Mr. Market has another endearing characteristic: He doesn't mind being ignored. If his quotation is uninteresting to you today, he will be back with a new one tomorrow. Transactions are strictly at your option. Under these conditions, the more manic-depressive his behavior, the better for you.

But, like Cinderella at the ball, you must heed one warning or everything will turn into pumpkins and mice: Mr. Market is there to serve you, not to guide you. It is his pocketbook, not his wisdom, that you will find useful. If he shows up some day in a particularly foolish mood, you are free to either ignore him or to take advantage of him, but it will be disastrous if you fall under his influence. Indeed, if you aren't certain that you understand and can value your business far better than Mr. Market, you don't belong in the game. As they say in poker, "If you've been in the game 30 minutes and you don't know who the patsy is, you're the patsy."

Ben's Mr. Market allegory may seem out of date in today's investment world, in which most professionals and academicians talk of efficient markets, dynamic hedging and betas. Their interest in such matters is understandable, since techniques shrouded in mystery clearly have value to the purveyor of investment advice. After all, what witch doctor has ever achieved fame and fortune by simply advising "take two aspirins?"

The value of market esoterica to the consumer of investment advice is a different story. In my opinion, investment success will not be produced by arcane formulae, computer programs or signals flashed by the price behavior of stocks and markets. Rather an investor will succeed by coupling good business judgment with an ability to insulate his thoughts and behavior from the super-contagious emotions that swirl about the marketplace. In my own efforts to stay insulated, I have found it highly useful to keep Ben's Mr. Market concept firmly in mind.

Following Ben's teachings, Charlie and I let our marketable equities tell us by their operating results—not by their daily or even yearly, price quotations—whether our investments are successful. That market may ignore business success for a while, but eventually will confirm it. As Ben said: "In the short run, the market is a voting machine but in the long run it is a weighing machine." The speed at which a business's success is recognized, furthermore, is not that important as long as the company's intrinsic value is increasing at a satisfactory rate. In fact, delayed recognition can be an advantage: It may give us the chance to buy more of a good thing at a bargain price.

Sometimes, of course, the market may judge a business to be more valuable than the underlying facts would indicate it is. In such a case, we will sell our holdings. Sometimes, also, we will sell a security that is fairly valued or even undervalued because we require funds for a still more undervalued investment or one we believe we understand better.

We need to emphasize, however, that we do not sell holdings just because they have appreciated or because we have held them for a long time. (Of Wall Street maxims the most foolish may be "You can't go broke taking a profit.") We are quite content to hold any security indefinitely, so long as the prospective return on equity capital of the underlying business is satisfactory, management is competent and honest, and the market does not over value the business.[5]

In 11 simple paragraphs, Buffett summarized the key elements of successful value investing. He boiled down everything that has ever been written about finance and stock-picking—the good, bad, and the downright chicanery—and condensed it into a few key themes that should lead any investor to success. To briefly restate them:

1. *View yourself as a "business analyst," not as a stock market prognosticator.* No one has ever foretold the direction of the economy or the stock market with any consistency. Neither will you. If you accept this limitation, you already are well ahead of the game. Hence, any investment decision you make premised on movements in the market or the economy has a higher probability of failure. However, if you narrow your task to that of evaluating businesses, you can't help but score successes in the long run.

---

[5] From the Chairman's Letter in the 1987 annual report of Berkshire Hathaway. Reprinted with permission of Warren E. Buffett.

2.   *Don't be swayed by share-price movements, for they often reflect irrational responses to events.* The true measure of success is the rate at which your companies continue to grow. Over the long term, share price follows the growth of the company.

3.   *Don't be a price-taker in the stock market.* Just because your favorite stock trades for $30 per share doesn't mean the business is worth $30. It may be worth $20; it may be worth $50. You alone must decide whether the offering price is a fair one.

4.   *Market participants, on occasion, are patently wrong in assessing the true value of businesses.* The prudent investor stands ready to snap up companies thrown out at bargain prices and sell when their value has been grossly overestimated.

5.   *Wall Street's mission is to sell you something and to create quantitative justifications to induce you to trade.* It thrives on maintaining a shroud of secrecy. By positioning investing as a rigorous academic endeavor, the industry tries to hold you hostage to its arcane methodologies and build a cult of awe around its leading personalities.

6.   *No amount of technical or mathematical know-how can substitute for old-fashioned financial-statement analysis.* Successful stock investing requires no more than a moderate grounding in mathematics, a working knowledge of basic business principles, a little intuition that can be acquired through experience, and the ability to read financial statements—nothing more, nothing less.

7.   *Being a value investor sets you apart from, but ahead of, the crowd.* If everyone subscribed to value investing, few values would exist anymore in the market. The fact that most investors respond irrationally to information or fail to value a company before purchasing works to your advantage. From their fickleness, you shall prosper.

Finding Stock Information on the Internet

I N THE 1980s, MOST INVESTORS based their investment decisions on the annual reports they received in the mail. They likely tracked their favorite stocks through the local newspaper and charted the stock's progress with graph paper and pencil. By the early 1990s, investors turned to the computer. Those that could use spreadsheets wrote their own portfolio tracking programs and used expensive charting software and quote services to keep abreast of their winnings.

How the game has changed. Millions more investors today are computer literate and rely almost exclusively on software packages and applications programs to manage their investments. For the cost of a computer modem and a modest monthly phone fee, investors can hook up to the Internet and access data that once cost Wall Street's investment houses tens of thousands of dollars a year, if it was available at all.

Investors should exploit fully the opportunities available on the Internet, but don't lose sight of your goals and the principles of prudent investing in the process. The temptations of the Internet—nearly commissionless trading and instant access to information—have already turned many investors into gunslingers. Middle America is speculating in stocks at a frequency never before seen, thanks to the availability of up-to-the-minute charts, earnings estimates, and news services.

Use the Internet to gather information, but don't rely on it to evaluate that information. Decision making must rest with you. Rightly or wrongly, the Internet has provided a forum for anyone in the world to offer his or her opinion on the stock market. Avoid being swayed by their abundant commentaries and puffery and stick to the facts.

For investors wanting to take advantage of the information on the Internet, I list the most useful websites. This list, though not comprehensive, will give you access to all the great sources of information the Internet offers. The website addresses listed below are subject to change and were current as of August 1998.

COMPANY WEBSITES

Hundreds of companies have created their own websites, including most of the popular large-cap companies trading on the New York Stock Exchange, American Stock Exchange, or Nasdaq. These sites run the gamut for their usefulness. Some, like Microsoft's, are snazzy and interactive. Some offer basic product information for business clients or consumers. Others maintain extensive archives of their financial reports, which makes them a one-stop shop for stock pickers. It's recommended that investors visit a company's website before buying shares. There, you're likely to find detailed descriptions of the company's products, the location of its plants or sales offices, and sometimes links to industry sources such as suppliers and distributors.

Both *ValueLine* and *S&P Stock Reports,* found in many local libraries, list web addresses for companies their analysts follow. A more complete directory may be found on the website *Invest-O-Rama* (*www.investorama.com*), which boasts more than 8000 financial links, including an alphabetical listing of hundreds of company websites.

GOVERNMENT AGENCIES

The best raw information you need to value companies will come from the federal government. Various agencies release economic statistics that will help you follow industry and consumer trends. The government also serves as the warehouse for all financial reports filed by public companies. The most important website for investors is the EDGAR database of the Securities and Exchange Commission. EDGAR holds all relevant financial reports companies must file, including 10Ks, 10Qs, merger documents, and prospectuses for mutual funds and public offerings. Today, most financial reports are delivered electronically to Washington, meaning an investor can retrieve them via the Internet without having to call the company and wait weeks to receive reports in the mail. Many analysts rely almost exclusively on EDGAR nowadays for their financial information. Other handy sites include the U.S. Census Bureau, which archives most of the data it publishes in book form, and the Federal Reserve Board, which publishes speeches of its governors and releases "Beige Book" reports on the state of the economy. Among the most useful government websites are:

Bureau of Labor Statistics—*www.bls.gov*

Comptroller of the Currency—*www.occ.treas.gov*

Conference Board (The)—*www.crc-conquest.org*

Department of Commerce—STAT database—*www.stat-usa.gov*

Economic Statistics Briefing Room—*www.whitehouse.gov/fsbr/ esbr.html*

Federal Deposit Insurance Corp.—*www.fdic.gov*

Federal Reserve Board—*www.bog.frb.fed.us*

Federal Reserve Bank of St. Louis—*www.stls.frb.org*

Government Accounting Office—*www.gao.gov*

Securities and Exchange Commission—*www.sec.gov*

SEC—EDGAR database—*www.sec.gov./cgi-bin/srch-edgar*

Treasury Department—*www.ustreas.gov*

U.S. Census Bureau—*www.census.gov*

U.S. House of Representatives—*www.house.gov*

U.S. Senate—*www.senate.gov*

White House—*www.whitehouse.gov*

Another great source of information comes from state governments, which have built extensive websites giving you access to their departments, reports, and statistics. I have used state websites, for example, to obtain economic reports and forecasts about a region, as well as housing, construction, retail sales, and demographic data. Many local governments have also created websites and are excellent sources for demographic, real estate, and commercial information.

NEWSPAPERS AND MAGAZINES

Most regional and national newspapers have websites today that allow investors access to their top business stories and archives of past articles. More local newspapers are beginning to offer their articles on the Internet too. Local newspapers can be invaluable sources for information on a company. Sometimes it's not enough to screen *The Wall Street Journal* for stories on, say, Anheuser Busch. The archives of the *St. Louis Post Dispatch* might yield more coverage since their reporters have covered the company for decades and likely have better relations with company officials and civic and union leaders.

For immediate links to some of the nation's top newspapers, click on News Online at *www.fundlinks.com/news-b.htm.* Most major financial magazines also place their articles and latest issues on the Internet. Here's just a sampling of the national newspapers and magazines that have websites.

Atlanta Journal-Constitution—*www.ajc.com*
Boston Globe—*www.bostonglobe.com*
Chicago Sun-Times—*www.suntimes.com*
Denver Post—*www.denverpost.com*
Financial Times (London)—*www.ft.com*
Forbes—*www.forbes.com*
Fortune—*www.pathfinder.com/fortune*
Gannett—*www.gannett.com*
Gannett, Newspapers—*www.gannett.com/web/gan013.htm*
Gannett, Radio Stations—*www.gannett.com/web/gan014.htm*
Inc.—*www.inc.com*
Individual Investor—*www.iionline.com*
Kiplinger—*www.kiplinger.com*
Knight-Ridder newspapers (database of articles)—*newslibrary.infi.net*
Los Angeles Times—*www.latimes.com*
Miami Herald—*www.herald.com*
Money—*www.money.com*
New York Times—*www.nytimes.com*
Philadelphia Enquirer; Philadelphia Daily News—*www.phillynews.com*
San Francisco Chronicle—*www.sfgate.com/chronicle*
The Economist—*www.economist.com*
Tribune Co.—*www.tribune.com*
Wall Street Journal—*www.wsj.com*
Washington Post—*www.washingtonpost.com*
Worth—*www.worth.com*

NEWS SERVICES

An excellent source for financial information is news organizations (such as Bloomberg and Reuters) that place the same articles online that they distribute to hundreds of member newspapers. Where once news organizations jealously guarded the dissemination of their stories, competition has forced most of these organizations to place their stories on the Internet for free. Today, you can access the same stories that will appear in *tomorrow's* newspapers across the country—only 24 hours earlier! Sometimes, having a one-day edge over the general public can make a big difference when buying or selling a stock. Listed below are the sites of major news networks and those of news "aggregators," sites that link to various financial news services.

ABC News—*www.abcnews.com*

Bloomberg news service—*www.bloomberg.com*

BusinessWire—*www.businesswire.com*

CBS Marketwatch—*http://cbs.marketwatch.com*

CNBC—*www.cnbc.com*

CNN Financial—*http://cnnfn.com*

C-Span—*www.c-span.org*

Daily Stocks—*www.dailystocks.com*

Fox network—*www.foxnews.com*

Lycos Stock Find—*www.stockfind.newsalert.com*

Microsoft Investor—*www.investor.msn.com*

NBC News—*www.nbcnews.com*

NewsEdge—*www.newspage.com*

PR Newswire—*www.prnewswire.com*

Reuters MoneyNet—*www.moneynet.com*

Streeteye—*www.streeteye.com*

Yahoo finance—*http://quote.yahoo.com*

STOCK EXCHANGES

The major stock exchanges provide up-to-date, official quotes on individual stocks or contracts. Some of the better sites, such as *www.nasdaq.com,* provide background on each company they list, as well as charts, graphs, portfolio tracking services, and links to company homepages and news services. For a quick link to all world stock markets, click on *www.qualisteam.com.*

American Stock Exchange—*www.amex.com*

Chicago Board of Trade—*www.cbot.com*

Chicago Board Options Exchange—*www.cboe.com*

Chicago Mercantile Exchange—*www.cme.com*

Kansas City Board of Trade—*www.kcbt.com*

London Metal Exchange—*www.lme.co.uk*
London Stock Exchange—*www.londonstockex.co.uk*
NASDAQ stock market—*www.nasdaq.com*
New York Cotton Exchange—*www.nyce.com*
New York Mercantile Exchange—*www.nymex.com*
New York Stock Exchange—*www.nyse.com*
Pacific Stock Exchange—*www.pacificex.com*
Philadelphia Stock Exchange—*www.phlx.com*
Tokyo Stock Exchange—*www.tse.or.jp*
Toronto Stock Exchange—*www.tse.com*
Vancouver Stock Exchange—*www.vse.ca*

TRADE GROUPS

Investors can often find pertinent information about an industry through the websites of trade associations. Nearly all major associations have home pages, some of which contain results of studies and surveys, industry sales and demographic information, and links to companies and suppliers. A few associations place their trade publications online as well. A complete listing of trade associations is impossible to reproduce, but here is a sampling of useful industry websites.

The Aluminum Association—*www.aluminum.org*
American Bankers Association—*www.aba.com*
American Iron & Steel Institute—*www.steel.org*
American Petroleum Institute—*www.api.org*
Auto Industry links—*www.tgx.com/autobodypage*
Automotive Parts & Accessories Assoc.—*www.apaa.org*
Auto magazines, publications—*www.car-stuff.com*
Beverage Industry—*www.beverage-digest.com*
Computers—*www.idc.com*
Copper industry links—*www.copper.org*
Intl. Energy Agency—*www.iea.org*
Manufactured Housing Institute—*www.mfghome.org*
National Association of Realtors—*www.realtor.com*
National Restaurant Association—*www.restaurant.org*
Oil and gas industry links—*www.oillink.com*

Oil industry rig data—*www.bakerhughes.com*
Precious Metals, links—*www.goldsheet.simplenet.com*
Semiconductor Industry Assoc.—*www.sia.org*
Semiconductor industry links—*www.infras.com*
Real Estate Investment Trusts—*http://www.nareit.com*
Retail—Intl. Council of Shopping Centers—*www.icsc.org*
Steel industry links—*www.steel.org/hotlinks*

ACCOUNTING AGENCIES
Accounting is the language of business. The more you know about the rules under which companies operate, the better. The two rule-making bodies for public companies, The Financial Accounting Standards Board (FASB) and the American Institute of Certified Public Accountants (AICPA), maintain their own websites where they provide background and descriptions of the accounting rules they propose and approve. FASB's site can be accessed through Rutgers University at *www.rutgers.edu/Accounting/raw/fasb/*. The AICPA can be found at *www.aicpa.org*. A related trade group, the American Accounting Association, can be found at *www.rutgers.edu/Accounting/raw/aaa/*. To find general information about the industry, plug into *www.cpalinks.com,* which offers links to dozens of related accounting sites. Investors might also wish to search the websites of the accounting firms that audit the books of most public companies. From time to time, these firms issue industry studies or surveys that can help you evaluate a company or its prospects. Some of their sites also include articles and news stories on personal finance and taxes. Among the websites are:

Andersen Consulting—*www.ac.com*
Arthur Andersen—*www.arthurandersen.com*
Deloitte & Touche—*www.dtonline.com*
Ernst & Young—*www.ey.com*
Grant Thornton—*www.gt.com*
KPMG Peat Marwick—*www.kpmg.com*
Price Waterhouse Coopers—*www.pwcglobal.com*

STOCK INFORMATION AND INVESTMENT ADVICE
Briefing Room—*www.briefing.com*
The Financial Center—*www.tfc.com*
Daily Rocket—*www.dailyrocket.com*

Daily Stocks—*www.dailystocks.com*
Data Broadcasting Corp.—*www.dbc.com*
Interquote—*www.interquote.com*
Investools—*www.investools.com*
Investors Edge—*www.stockpoint.com*
Microsoft Investor—*www.msn.com*
Quicken—*www.quicken.com*
Wall Street City—*www.wallstreetcity.com*
The Street—*thestreet.com*
The Syndicate—*www.moneypages.com/syndicate*
Thomson Investor Network—*www.thomsoninvest.net*
Yahoo—*www.quote.yahoo.com*

FINANCIAL INFORMATION AND EDUCATION

American Association of Individual Investors—*www.aaii.org*
Equity Analytics—*www.e-analytics.com*
Ibbotson Associates—*www.ibbotson.com*
Investment newsletters—*www.newsletteraccess.com*
Moody's Investor Services—*www.moodys.com*
Morningstar, Inc.—*www.morningstar.net*
Motley Fool—*www.fool.com*
Natl. Association of Investors Corp. (NAIC)—*www.better-investing.org*
Standard & Poor's—*www.standardpoors.com*

MISCELLANEOUS FINANCIAL TOPICS

Bonds—corporate and Treasuries—*www.bondsonline.com*
Business valuation—*www.nvst.com*
Corporate profiles—*www.hoovers.com*
Earnings estimates—*www.zacks.com*
Economic charts, links—*www.yardeni.com*
                            http://condor.depaul.edu/~dshannon
Executive pay—*www.paywatch.org*
Global investing—*www.global-investor.com*
                            www.ifc.com
                            www.tradershaven.com

Gold and silver—*www.bullion.org*
www.goldsheet.simplenet.com
Historical financial charts—*www.globalfindata.com*
www.pinnacledata.com
Insider trading—*www.fedfil.com*
www.biz.yahoo.com
www.insidertrader.com
www.dailystocks.com
www.cda.com
Merger announcements and statistics—*www.nvst.com/rsrc/mergerstat*
www.securitiesdata.com
Portfolio tracking—*www.investor.msn.com*
www.yahoo.com
www.stockup.com
www.dailystocks.com
www.quicken.com
Quote services—*www.wwquote.com*
Stock buybacks, splits, dividend announcements—
www.dailyrocket.com
Stock charts—*www.bigcharts.com*
Stock options, executive options—*www.cbot.com*
www.biz.yahoo.com
www.nceo.org
www.e-analytics.com
Stock screening services—*www.marketplayer.com*
www.rapidresearch.com
http://www.stockscreener.com
Technology stocks—*www.techstocks.com*

Index

ABOUT THE AUTHOR

Timothy P. Vick is the founder and editor of *Today's Value Investor,* a nationally distributed stock newsletter based in Hammond, Indiana, as well as contributing editor and analyst for *Dow Theory Forecasts,* one of the nation's oldest market newsletters. Prior to his work as an analyst, Mr. Vick was an award-winning business and government journalist in Chicago. He continues to write a stock market column that appears every weekend in the Chicago area. His views on the stock market have been quoted by national and regional media, including *CNN, The Washington Post, Sacramento Bee, Gannett Newspapers, The Associated Press, Louisville Courier-Journal, Lexington Herald-Leader,* and *Ft. Lauderdale Sun-Sentinel,* as well as financial magazines such as *Investor's Business Daily, Kiplinger's, Money, Financial World,* and *Futures.* Mr. Vick is a frequent guest on radio talk shows. He is the author of *Lessons for the Individual Investor,* published in 1997. Mr. Vick graduated with honors from Ball State University with a bachelor of science in history, and received an MBA in management with honors from Purdue University. He resides in Munster, Indiana, a suburb of Chicago, with his wife and two young children.